Sedulius Scottus

On Christian Rulers

and

The Poems

medieval & renaissance texts & studies

VOLUME 17

Sedulius Scottus

On Christian Rulers

and

The Poems

Translated with Introduction

by

Edward Gerard Doyle

medieval & renaissance texts & studies

State University of New York at Binghamton

1983

Library of Congress Cataloging in Publication Data

Sedulius, Scotus, fl. 848–860.
    The De rectoribus Christianis and Poems of Sedulius Scottus.

    (Medieval and Renaissance texts and studies; 17)
    Translation of: De rectoribus Christianis, and Carmina.
    Bibliography: p.
    1. Education of princes. 2. Political Science—Early works to 1700. I. Doyle, Edward,
1949–   . II. Sedulius, Scotus, fl. 848–860. Carmina. English. 1983. III. Title. IV. Series:
Medieval & Renaissance texts & studies; 17.
JC383.A3S4313   1982   321.6   82–14174
ISBN 0–86698–024–5

For my wife, Linda

Contents

Acknowledgements

I owe thanks to a variety of people for substantial assistance in the completion of this book, which grew out of the dissertation I completed at Harvard University in 1978. Professors Morton Bloomfield, Charles Dunn, and John Kelleher at Harvard encouraged me to pursue research on Sedulius Scottus and to undertake the translation of his political tract, *De rectoribus christianis*, and his poems. They were all kind enough to read the manuscript carefully and give me the benefit of their criticism and suggestions. I am also grateful to Professor Steven Marrone of Tufts University, who checked my translation of *De rectoribus christianis* for accuracy and offered many helpful comments, and to Professor Ernst Kitzinger of Harvard for his illuminating remarks on several of Sedulius' poems describing paintings, sculptures, and architectural ornaments. Thanks are also due to the librarians at Widener Library, Harvard University, for their perseverance in tracking down rare texts and monographs among their vast collections, and to the editors and staff of Medieval & Renaissance Texts & Studies, Suzanne Bone in particular, for their smooth and efficient handling of the editorial and production process for this book. Finally, not to be forgotten are the contributions of Ludwig Traube and Siegmund Hellmann, whose pioneering scholarship on Sedulius over three-quarters of a century ago produced the excellent criticism editions on which my translations are based.

Sedulius Scottus

On Christian Rulers

and

The Poems

Introduction

The purpose of this book is to provide a translation with annotations for the more important works of Sedulius Scottus, an Irish poet and scholar who flourished in the middle decades of the ninth century. These works—a "mirror for princes" Sedulius titled *De rectoribus christianis (On Christian Rulers)* and his poems—have an importance for medievalists and Celticists alike. Sedulius' works are strongly rooted in the literary and intellectual tradition of Continental Latin culture, hence providing medievalists with a greater understanding of the Irish contribution to the Carolingian renaissance in the ninth century. For the Celticist, Sedulius' career and accomplishments shed much light on the level of Latin learning and scholarship in medieval Ireland, and attest to the rich and active cultural life of Irish monasticism in the sixth through ninth centuries.

His life and times

Nothing is known except by inference about Sedulius before he arrived in Liège around the middle of the ninth century. Several poems which Sedulius addressed to Bishop Hartgar of Liège and to the Emperor Lothar I's wife, Irmingard, allow us to mark the approximate dates of his arrival between 840, Hartgar's first year as bishop of the city, and 851, the year of Irmingard's death. We do not possess a single line of his in Irish, although Frank O'Connor, on a certain "literary instinct," would name Sedulius the author of the delightful and well-known Old Irish poem, "The Scholar and His Cat."[1] As for Sedulius' Irish name, O'Connor maintains that "clearly it was Síadal, an Old Irish form of the same Latin name (Sedulius)."[2] Ludwig Traube, on the other hand, has convincingly argued that the name Sedulius is not Irish in origin; just as the name Virgilius was popular in Ireland, so also Sedulius was adopted out of admiration for another Roman poet of that name, Caelius Sedulius, the author of the *Carmen Paschale.*[3]

Sedulius himself tells us little about his Irish background. In one of his poems he identifies himself and his companions as "learned grammarians and pious priests of God";[4] but he is silent, unfortunately, when it comes to information about his place of birth in Ireland, his family or tribal ties, his education, and the monastic house or houses he may have been associated with in his native land. James Carney, on the basis of the provenance and the details found in the margins of several manuscripts attributed to Sedulius' scholarly circle, believes that Sedulius and his learned companions probably came from the province of Leinster, perhaps from Kildare.[5]

What did Sedulius look like? He tells a certain Vulfengus:

> Though neither of us is adorned with radiant hair,
> yet we hope for hair as white as the snow.[6]

And because he describes himself as "dark Orpheus," may we surmise that he had black hair and a dark complexion? Sadly, this vague reference to his possibly swarthy features is our only hint to the physical appearance of Sedulius. It is, moreover, impossible to determine the exact age of Sedulius when he reached Liège, since we lack any evidence by which to confirm the date of his birth. Considering the extent of the education and scholarship he had acquired by that time, we may guess that Sedulius was then in his late thirties or early forties.

Why did Sedulius and his companions leave Ireland to seek a new home somewhere in the Frankish kingdom? Sedulius offers no positive clues as to their reasons for setting out towards the Continent. Nora Chadwick has proposed that he may have been a member of a group of emissaries dispatched to the court of Charles the Bald by Maelsechlainn, an Irish king, to announce an Irish victory over the Norsemen in 848.[7] There is no concrete proof, however, to place Sedulius among these emissaries to Charles the Bald.

We could blame the savage attacks of the Vikings in Ireland during the ninth century for forcing such men as Sedulius to abandon their homes and positions for more secure conditions on the Continent. Without a doubt, the Viking onslaught against Ireland had a most devastating effect upon the churches and monasteries, the wealthy centers of artistic, literary, and scholarly activity among the Irish. Iona was burned in 802; in the 820s Bangor, Downpatrick, Moville, and Clonmore were plundered. After 832 the Viking terror grew especially intense: Armagh, Glendalough, and Kildare, the most influential and powerful monastic communities in Ireland, were ravaged by Viking raids. By the 840s the Vikings even began to build fortresses and permanent bases in the Irish countryside for more extensive and sustained warfare.

Besides the physical destruction which the Vikings inflicted upon churches, scriptoria, and monasteries, their continued presence profoundly affected the attitudes and practices of the Irish themselves. Kathleen Hughes has observed that because of the Vikings "Ireland was submerged by confusion and anarchy. . . . Inevitably the changed political situation caused partial disintegration of the old legal stability. The security of the pre-Viking system depended on its balance, for though there was no strong executive authority, each grade of society had been kept in control by those above it. Now the law of status was completely undermined."[8] The increasing civil disturbances in Ireland and the fierce attacks upon the monasteries produced a damaging psychological effect upon scholars and scribes like Sedulius who depended upon peace, stability, and the availability of funds and materials for their livelihood.

The Viking threat inspired an anonymous Irish poet to write:

> The wind is bitter tonight;
> it swirls the ocean's white hair.
> Tonight I do not fear the fierce warriors from Norway
> coursing on the Irish sea.[9]

As a result of Ireland's turmoil, nothing would have been more natural than for Sedulius and his fellow scholars to escape the Viking hordes by seeking refuge on the Continent. They had every reason to expect a warm reception from the Franks. For Charlemagne and his successors, because of the general illiteracy of even the higher Frankish clergy, sought to attract prominent and able scholars from other lands to settle in their realm. Several notable figures accepted their invitation: Peter of Pisa (later bishop of Aquileia), Paul the Deacon from the kingdom of the Lombards, Alcuin from Northumbria, and Theodulfus from Spain. Many talented Irishmen, too, emigrated to Frankish lands and played an active part in the intellectual revival of the Carolingian renaissance: Dicuil, the geographer; Cruindmelus, the grammarian; John Scotus, the philosopher; and a host of others.

Whatever the hopes and expectations, Sedulius paints a vivid picture of the distressing circumstances in which his little party arrived in Liège:

> Wretched sight! Furious Boreas torments us,
> learned grammarians and pious priests of God,
> for that swift tempest spares no dignity,
> as he mangles us with his sharp, cruel beak.[10]

Sedulius then continues to contrast their sorry state with the generous welcome they subsequently received from Bishop Hartgar, who like a loving father took the weary Irish travelers into his care:

> he clothed and enriched us with threefold honor,
> so we became the flock of a most gentle shepherd.[11]

Bishop Hartgar not only bestowed shelter and protection upon these Irish scholars "bringing their precious gifts of learning,"[12] but, recognizing their erudition, chose them as his chief ministers in the revival of learning and arts in Liège, the intellectual capital of Louis the German's kingdom. Henri Pirenne, among others, has speculated that Hartgar appointed Sedulius *scholasticus*, or director of studies, at the Cathedral School of St. Lambert.[13] If so, Sedulius' duties would have included the supervision of students in the school, the borrowing and copying of manuscripts for the library, and the correspondence with other centers of learning. But like so many aspects of Sedulius' life, his professional connections to St. Lambert's School, if any, remain obscure.

In addition to whatever official position he may have held, Sedulius, through his poetic skills, became the chief bard of Liège, or, as he puts it, the "new Orpheus" and "companion of the muses."[14] He sang the praises of Hartgar and Hartgar's successor, Bishop Franco (855–901), and celebrated the arrival in the city of a number of important personages, including Emperor Lothar I, Charles the Bald, and Louis the German.

Sedulius' poetry imparts valuable information about the flourishing cultural revival in Liège under the stewardship of its bishops and the patronage of Frankish royalty. In the words of Alice Stopford Green, "The story of Liège for fifty years, from 809 to 856, would be almost a total blank save for what Sedulius has to tell. His verses throw the single ray of light across that deep obscurity."[15] Sedulius affords us a personal glimpse of the city's central figure, Bishop Hartgar, generous friend of the arts and host to a growing colony of Irish scholars. We learn from Sedulius that Hartgar's intellectual gifts were ideally suited to the task of transforming Liège into a center of education and cultural activity:

> Three languages ornament Hartgar's golden tongue,
> like three witnesses uttering words of truth.
> He exchanges worldly wealth for eternal rewards,
> that he may some day obtain the riches of heaven.
> Hartgar, blooming cedar of paradise, forever flourish,
> as you bear on your head the ripe fruits of learning.[16]

Hartgar's contribution to the arts in Liège went beyond scholarship to the architectural beautification of the city. Under Hartgar's auspices, a lofty and splendid palace was constructed in Liège and decorated with all the artistic resources at his disposal. Sedulius admires Hartgar's accomplishment in these verses:

> Your halls are gleaming with serene light;
> the ceilings glisten, adorned with art's latest style;
> a multitude of colors smile upon your dome,
> and many beauteous forms glitter throughout.
> O garden of Hesperides, you who quickly wither in
> sudden tempests, your flowers endure for but a day;
> but here, however, your violets and beautiful roses
> have clung to cupola and dome in perpetual bloom;
> and purple-red or jacinth never fear the harsh
> blasts from the scorching south wind.[17]

The bishop also enriched the social and religious pageantry of the city. His poet, Sedulius, wrote a song for the Nativity which the choir was to sing on Christmas morning. It describes a pageant for the Church in which Hartgar, the choir, and all the members of the congregation, had a role:

> The Blessed Virgin gave birth to Jesus,
> Ruler of the World and son of the Almighty.
> Thus, in our pageant the church's chorus plays the role

of that radiant virgin bearing God's son.
Joseph, pious and holy, was Mary's sacred spouse
and the husband to the mother of God.
Our fair pastor, betrothed to us in joy, is here;
he appears to us in Joseph's noble likeness.[18]

Hartgar brought prestige and royal favor to Liège through his active role in the
political affairs of his day. Sedulius reports that Emperor Lothar I chose Hartgar as
his ambassador on a mission to the pope in Rome. In three poems, which form a
short cycle, Sedulius provides us an account of Hartgar's journey from beginning to
end. Travel in the winter, Sedulius tells us, promised to be no easy task for the
bishop and his entourage:

Monstrous Winter, shaggy with icy locks,
what catastrophe and crime are you preparing?
Will our tears and prayers not appease you,
a wild beast born from Scythian rocks?
Go, gracious father blessed by good fortune,
through the snowy fields and ice-glazed roads;
let your horses' pounding hooves trample Winter,
and let harsh blows lash its dire countenance.[19]

Once in Rome, Hartgar's audience with the pope was apparently successful:

When serene Hartgar went to Simon Peter's court,
he glowed with splendor among angelic bands.
Approaching Hartgar, Peter said: "Dear friend,
we welcome you, your Lambert's chief care.
All of heaven sings: 'Hail, golden hope of
heaven, for you will always dwell among us.' "[20]

Finally, the bishop returned to Liège, where he received an appropriate welcome
from the community. Sedulius' muse urges him to express the people's gladness:

Hartgar's name is worthy of merits.
He loves your muse, though she is dark—
let your shepherd's pipe greet this pious father![21]

In addition to his duties as a prelate and diplomat, Hartgar was obliged to take up
arms and lead the defence of Liège against the attacks of Viking raiders. In one poem
Sedulius recounts Hartgar's victory over a fierce band of Norsemen in a manner
which attests to the poet's understandable terror at their violent and destructive
assaults:

> You ward off your enemies with the shield
> of faith, a sacred lorica, and Christ's helmet;
> and, flashing with salvation's golden sword,
>   you destroy them.
>
> Your gleaming host, so stout of heart,
> dashes courageously through the enemy;
> charging on the fields, it devastates the ranks,
>   with arms of Hercules.
>
> O youthful band, slaying fierce enemies,
> receive this glittering crown of merit.
> Lo, the rebel Norsemen have perished in
>   bloody plunder.[22]

After Hartgar's death in 855, Sedulius continued to enjoy the good will of Bishop Franco, Hartgar's successor. Franco, like Hartgar, was occasionally called upon to participate in royal affairs and forced, at least once, to take up arms against the Vikings. Unfortunately, Franco was to witness the sudden end to the cultural renewal initiated by Hartgar when a series of Viking assaults overwhelmed Liège in 881.

Sedulius often speaks with pride of his homeland and his countrymen. In his verses Ireland finds an honored place among the great peoples of the world—the Latins and Greeks—who pay homage to Charlemagne; his Irish brethren are extolled as "four-span of the Lord" and "lights of the Irish race."[23] Yet one looks in vain in Sedulius' poetry for any reference to an Irish king or events in Ireland. And he makes no mention of Britain, an important way station for Irishmen on a journey to the Continent. This is not surprising inasmuch as Sedulius, as scholar and poet, completely immersed himself in the Frankish world. Neither his patrons nor his audience would likely have been interested in such foreign history and lore.[24]

The circumstances surrounding the last years of Sedulius' life and career are as mysterious as his sudden appearance in Liège. Much debate has focused on whether Sedulius remained permanently in Liège or, in a manner typical of Irish scholars at the time, moved on to other Frankish centers of learning or perhaps even to Italy. Two early editors of Sedulius' poems, Ernest Dümmler and Henri Pirenne devised substantially different theories to account for the concluding stages of Sedulius' life and career. Dümmler held that Sedulius, after an illustrious sojourn at Liège, crossed the Alps around 860 into Italy, where he re-established himself at the court of Tado, Archbishop of Milan (860–68).[25] To support his theory, Dümmler cited a small group of poems addressed to Tado, which were published among Sedulius' verses, although his authorship of them was in doubt.[26] Pirenne rejected this theory, contending that Sedulius had no compelling reason to leave behind his comfortable and secure position in Liège "pour des contrées ou il était certainement inconnu."[27] Pirenne further indicated that the poems addressed to Tado, if genuine, were most likely composed by Sedulius on the occasion of a temporary visit to Rome in the entourage of Hartgar, the Bishop of Liège.[28]

Franz Brunhölzl, in his recent *Geschichte der Lateinischen Literatur des Mittelalters* (1975), has taken a sceptical view of some of the traditionally accepted biographical details of Sedulius' life. He has expressed doubt, for instance, that Sedulius, as Pirenne thought, took up permanent residence in Liège and probably died there. According to Brunhölzl, certain verses Sedulius addressed to Bishop Gunthar of Cologne (850–63) and to Bishop Adventius of Metz (858–75) suggest that after 850 he spent some time in Cologne and then Metz.[29] Moreover, Brunhölzl concludes, correctly I think, that the poems in praise of Tado do belong to Sedulius and thus support the argument, once made by Dümmler, that Sedulius eventually traveled to Italy and resided for a time during the 860s at Tado's court in Milan.[30] Beyond that, as Brunhölzl concedes, Sedulius' ultimate fate is unknown.

His scholarly circle

Sedulius and his fellow Irishmen formed a scholarly circle whose labors and accomplishments represent a valuable contribution to the intellectual life of the Middle Ages. As J. F. Kenney remarks, "the manuscripts which we owe to Sedulius and his friends are of very great importance both for Irish history and linguistics and for the general history of European culture."[31] A survey of these manuscripts also reveals the interests and pursuits of Irish scholars in Europe during the ninth century. Among the manuscripts attributed to Sedulius' circle are the *Leyden Priscian,* which contains Priscian's interpretation of the *Periegesis* of Dionysius, his *Artis grammaticae libri XVIII,* and his *De nominibus et pronominibus;* the *St. Gall Priscian;* the *Greek Psalter,* generally ascribed to Sedulius himself;[32] the *Basel Psalter; Codex Sangallensis,* with the four gospels in Greek and interlinear Latin translation; *Codex Boernarianus,* with an interpretation of St. Matthew's gospel, and a Greek text of St. Paul's epistles (except Hebrews) with interlinear Latin translation; *Codex Bernensis 363,* which includes a commentary by Servius on the *Bucolics, Georgics,* and *Aeneid,* as well as poems by Horace and extracts from Ovid's *Metamorphoses.*

What is especially noteworthy about these manuscripts is the variety of texts, both Christian and classical, which the Irish scribes have copied. We find the usual medieval texts on biblical, exegetical, and grammatical subjects, which formed the sacred and secular canon, so to speak, of Christian scholars; but we also encounter major and, in fact, at that time somewhat rare classical works by Servius, Horace, and Ovid. This careful preservation of both Christian and classical or pagan authors is characteristic of Irish scholarship in the Middle Ages and indicates that the Irish tended not to share the prejudice, evident in some ecclesiastical and scholarly quarters, against the dangerous snares and pitfalls of pagan authors. One might also comment that the Irish treated pagan Latin literature (there is no evidence that the Irish had access to or read the great authors of classical Greece such as Homer, Sophocles, Plato, or Demosthenes) with the same respect and conservative reverence which they accorded to their own pagan Celtic lore and traditions.

The colony of Irish scholars over which Sedulius presided at Liège was by no means an isolated intellectual community. Sedulius established and maintained contact with a number of important ecclesiastical and scholastic centers throughout the

Continent. Among his contacts, as his poems show, were the bishops of Metz and Cologne, as well as the abbot of Fulda and the abbess of Avenay. Members of Sedulius' circle also traveled widely on the Continent and resided for a time at several important monastic communities. For example, Sedulius composed a poem of welcome to four Irish friends, Fergus, Marcus, Blandus, and Beuchell; of these, Marcus appears later in residence at St. Gall, while Blandus and Beuchell seem to have gone on to Milan.[33] As for Fergus, whose own poetic abilities Sedulus praised in verse, John Contreni has pointed out that he was also known among the Irishmen at Laon, thus establishing contact between Laon's flourishing scholarly community and that of Liège.[34] Moreover, the names and signatures in manuscripts of Irish provenance from the ninth century support the conclusion that a widespread network of communication and interaction existed among Irish scholars and scribes throughout the Frankish kingdoms. Nora Chadwick affirms that "we cannot doubt that many of the most important manuscripts known to have been written at the centres of Irish learning on the Continent contain Irish names which are those of monks recognized as having belonged to the circle of Sedulius."[35]

His Works

Sedulius is the author of a number of works on grammar, theology, and politics. He wrote a commentary on the grammatical tracts of Eutyches and Priscian. According to M. Manitius, Sedulius actually composed his commentary on Eutyches before he left Ireland; and Sedulius says that he wrote it "by his brothers' request."[36] Since the Irish monastic schools stressed the learning of Latin, it is no surprise to find a scholar of Sedulius' talents preparing a useful grammatical text for his Irish brothers and students. So great was the emphasis upon grammar among the Irish that it became one of the chief disciplines in the curriculum of their schools. E. A. Lowe has noted that the monks of Bobbio, in their poverty, even though they "deleted beautifully written texts of Cicero, Seneca, Pliny and Symmachus, in order to make room for church fathers and councils, spared the Latin grammarians."[37]

The theological writings of Sedulius include a commentary on the epistles of St. Paul, and another on Matthew. The commentary on Paul is of particular interest because some of its passages indicate that Sedulius was acquainted with the commentary on St. Paul by Pelagius, a text for which the Irish showed a particular preference in their exegetical writings. Kenney has observed that the Pelagian matter in the text of Sedulius places it among a little group of similar Pauline commentaries, "all but one of which are of direct Irish origin. This makes it probable that he either wrote his *Collectaneum* (commentary) in Ireland, or used books brought from Ireland."[38]

Sedulius also composed a *Collectaneum* which brings together a large number of excerpts drawn primarily from classical authors. As S. Hellmann has shown, Sedulius made extensive use of this work in his "mirror for princes," *De rectoribus christianis*.[39] The *Collectaneum* demonstrates the wide range of classical Latin texts with which Sedulius was familiar and displays the often remarkable attainments of Irish scholars in the Middle Ages. Besides numerous patristic selections, we find extracts from rare treatises on military tactics by Vegetius and Frontinus; extracts from Valerius Maximus, the *Augustan History*, and the *Proverbs of Seneca;* and extracts from Macrobius' commentary on the *Dream of Scipio* (from Cicero's *De republica*). The most interesting aspect of this text is its unusual variety of extracts and fragments from Cicero. Sedulius was evidently acquainted with the following works of Cicero: *In Pisonem, Pro Fonteio, De inventione, Pro flacco, Philippicae, Paradoxa,* and *Tusculanae,,* as well as the spurious *Ad Herennium.* Some of these Ciceronian texts, such as *In Pisonem,* were almost unknown in the Middle Ages, and a few passages are only preserved for us in this *Collectaneum* of Sedulius. Regarding Sedulius' knowledge of Cicero, M. L. W. Laistner concludes: "That Sedulius had access to no less than seven works by Rome's greatest prose writer is a very noteworthy circumstance, when it is remembered that few scholars of the Carolingian Age knew more than two or three. Although the total number of Ciceronian writings then known was considerable, many libraries had only single works and only a few were better stocked."[40]

Also part of this collection is the *Proverbia Graecorum,* a body of sayings supposedly translated from the Greek. This text is now generally regarded as a copy or adaptation made in Ireland from Greek originals as early as the sixth century. For the *Collectaneum* as a whole Sedulius "Obtained the greater part of his notes from Irish, not Continental, sources."[41] The *Collectaneum,* therefore, should be an excellent source for scholars wishing to study the intellectual milieu in Ireland during the early medieval period.

Ludwig Traube has assigned to Sedulius a work entitled *De graeca,* which is said to be a revision of a recension of the *Hermaneumata* of the Pseudo-Dositheus.[42] This was one of the texts preserved by the Irish, and it may have been used as a means of maintaining some knowledge of Greek in the Irish schools.[43] Indeed, Sedulius has been credited with a knowledge of Greek which was uncommon for his time.[44] The Irish, in general, carried on the study of Greek in their schools long after the active learning of Greek had virtually disappeared in Western Europe. The difficulty for scholars, however, has been to determine the degree of Irish competency in Greek as a learned tongue. Some have maintained that the Irish merely dabbled in Greek to show off their wisdom and erudition; others have argued that the Irish achieved a level of fluency in Greek. To my mind the most realistic appraisal is that, while the Irish may have continued the study of Greek in the early Middle Ages, few Irish scholars could evince more than a smattering or imperfect knowledge of Greek in their work. There is some evidence that Sedulius did, in fact, possess a fair knowledge of Greek. Kenney says of the *Greek Psalter* that the scribe, thought to be Sedulius, demonstrates some competency in Greek;[45] and even though Sedulius cannot approach the calibre of a Greek scholar like John Scotus, it seems clear, nevertheless, that his attention to Greek was of a serious scholarly nature.

De rectoribus christianis
and Carolingian political literature

The work of the greatest historical interest by Sedulius is the "mirror for princes," *De rectoribus christianis*. Sedulius composed this tract on the duties of a king sometime between 855 and 859 for Emperor Lothar I's son, Lothar II, who became king of Lotharingia in 855. It is written in Boethian style, with each prose section recapitulated in verse; and the Latin is relatively pure and fluent. Sedulius does not base his instructions to the king on native Irish views of kingship or political practices, but rather on models and precepts from the Bible, as well as Roman historical sources such as the *Scriptores Historiae Augustae* and Cassiodorus' *Tripartite History*. Unless in the passage on the eight pillars which uphold the kingdom of a just prince (which James Carney seems to think is translated from Old Irish),[46] Sedulius makes no reference to Irish literature and tradition. Yet perhaps something of Sedulius' Irish background may be detected in his very act of instructing the king, for in Ireland the chief function of every learned poet was to advise the king of his royal responsibilities. Francis Byrne, for instance, considers the Old Irish "mirror for princes," *The Testament of Morand*—dated around 600 and completely pagan in its description of kingship—to be the oldest such work in medieval Europe.[47]

Although there is no discernible Irish influence in the ideas and content of *De rectoribus christianis*, the Irish did play a role in developing and popularizing the genre of the "mirror for princes" or the *speculum principum* to which Sedulius' tract belongs. Between 630 and 650, an unknown Irishman wrote a short treatise on monarchical rule, which formed part of a larger work on the morals of society entitled *De duodecim abusivis saeculi* (*On the Twelve Abuses of the Age*).[48] It achieved wide popularity in later centuries, and its treatment of the just and unjust king deals with some of what would become the major themes of the *speculum principum* in the Carolingian period.[49] A king must avoid the crime of tyranny, using his power instead to restrain the schemes of the unjust. Yet no king can govern justly unless he first governs himself with virtue and discipline. On the one hand, a just king must also endeavor to protect the Church and to appoint upright men to conduct the affairs of the realm. An unjust king, on the other hand, is subject to divine wrath and suffers wars, natural catastrophies, and the loss of his throne. For, above all, as the author emphasizes, a king receives his power and authority from God and is answerable to Heaven for his stewardship of the people.[50]

It is not until the ninth century that we encounter the *speculum principum*, of which *De duodecim abusivis saeculi* is an important and influential precursor, as a popular form of discourse. Between 812 and 815 Smaragdus of St. Mihiel (possibly of Irish birth) composed his *Via regia* for Louis the Pious.[51] Jonas of Orleans wrote *De institutione regia* in 834,[52] and Sedulius *De rectoribus christianis* more than two decades later. Hincmar of Rheims followed later with *De regis persona et regio ministerio*.[53] Related to this type of political writing are Cathvulf's short address in epistolary form to Charlemagne in 775,[54] some letters of Alcuin to various royal personages between 793 and 804,[55] and three letters of Lupus of Ferrières to Charles the Bald.[56]

Several common features distinguish the "mirrors for princes" of Smaragdus, Jonas, Sedulius, and Hincmar from *De duodecim abusivis saeculi* as well as from the letters on the subject of kingship by Cathvulf, Alcuin, and Lupus of Ferrières. For one thing, their discussions on the duties of the king are much broader in scope and their primary themes receive significantly expanded treatment. In addition, the authors of the *Via regia, De institutione regia, De rectoribus christianis*, and *De regis persona et regio ministerio* develop a more structured and substantial conception of the office and role of the king, and display a wide array of learning to buttress their basic arguments.[57] These characteristics not only denoted the art and style of the Carolingian *speculum principum* but established the format and pattern of the genre which served as the vehicle for much of the political writing of the Middle Ages.

The impetus behind the growing popularity of this genre in the ninth century was provided by historic changes affecting Carolingian government and society. The period witnessed a momentous effort, initiated by Charlemagne and continued by his successors, to effect no less than the spiritual and social regeneration of the Frankish nation. Under Charlemagne's initial guidance and direction and with the vigorous participation of Churchmen and scholars, a unique ideological program came into being whose aim was to transform the Frankish people, their society, and their institutions into a new and regenerated Christian state. The Frankish people were destined to become the "populus Dei," within the context of Augustine's vision of the "civitas Dei," thereby displacing the secular nature and historical foundation of the old Frankish nation.

Walter Ullman has termed this ambitious undertaking of social and political change "ecclesiology." He states that "the Renaissance aimed at by Charlemagne was the transformation of contemporary society in accordance with the doctrinal and dogmatic notions of Christianity, as it was seen in the light of patristic lore. . . . For the first time, at least as far as Western Europe is concerned, we are here confronted by a conscious effort to shape the character of a society in consonance with the axioms of a particular doctrine, here the Christian norms."[58]

The all-encompassing nature of this radical policy, incorporating social, political, and spiritual objectives, by necessity involved the Church and its bureaucracy in every phase of its implementation. Of course, Churchmen in the past had been active in secular affairs and exerted an influence on issues affecting the moral and material welfare of the people. But now the Church and its leaders were needed not only for their ethical and doctrinal leadership, but for their management of the workings of government. In effect, only the Church possessed the resources of learning, technical skills, and organization to enact the wide-ranging social, legal, and educational reforms envisioned by Charlemagne.

As Charlemagne's program evolved, the functions of Church and State became increasingly intertwined. This, in turn, prompted a fresh evaluation by Sedulius and other learned ecclesiastics of the roles to be assigned the spiritual and temporal powers in the transition from a secular society to the "populus Dei." This need to define the responsibilities and authority of Church and king not only provided the intellectual stimulus that turned the minds of Carolingian writers to political theory; it generated a new body of political literature, the "mirrors for princes," which

A. J. Carlyle has called the "writings of men whose tradition of society and govern-ment is that out of which our own has directly and immediately grown."[59]

Sedulius and his contemporaries focused on the office of the king not as it had de-veloped in secular or pagan Germanic tradition but within the context of a society re-established, as it were, upon the Christian principles of the "civitas Dei." They do not address specific political, economic, and social ills or posit original solutions to prob-lems affecting government in general. Rather, their political discussions draw heavily from biblical and patristic authority for models of kingship appropriate to a Christian society. Thus Sedulius explains his method of exposition:

> For these are the glory of kings and garlands for glitter-
>   ing sceptres:
> the tenets of the Lord, the examples of the ancients,
> and the deeds, famous over the world, of renowned
>   princes.[60]

De rectoribus christianis bears a general resemblance, in theme and subject, to the treatment of kingship found in the other "mirrors for princes" of its time. Sedulius organizes his instructions to the king around three major themes. The first is that the king above all others receives his office and authority directly from God; the second, that as a minister of God the king is bound to fulfill the divine law embodied in Christian principles both in his own actions and in his leadership of the "populus Dei"; and the third, that the king and the Church, the source of Christian doctrine as revealed in Holy Scripture, must cooperate in their joint ministry as upholders of Christian norms and beliefs. These themes reflect the ideals of Charlemagne's ec-clesiological program as well as the current concerns of Churchmen and scholars charged with the responsibility of overseeing and administering a sweeping trans-formation of government and society.

According to Sedulius, the king rules by the grace of God. His true authority stems not from his temporal power but from the mandate of his divine appointment by God:

> Therefore, so much as an upright ruler acknowledges that he has been called by God, to the same degree he is vigilant with dutiful care that he regularly de-termines and examines all things before God and men according to the scales of justice. For, what are the rulers of the Christian people unless ministers of the Almighty? Moreover, he is a faithful and proper servant who has done with sincere devotion whatever his lord and master has commanded to him. Accordingly, the most upright and glorious princes rejoice more that they are appointed to be ministers and servants of the Most High than lords or kings of men.[61]

Because the king is answerable to God for his office, like the model kings of the Old Testament, David and Solomon, his authority assumes a sacred character. In addi-tion, Sedulius goes on to describe the king as the "vicar of God," whom the divine order "has granted authority over both orders (of prelates and subjects), that he decide what is just for every person."[62] The direct implication is that the king is not subordinate to the ruler of the Church; and by holding the highest office in the "civitas Dei," the king, it is suggested, may even exert his influence and authority in preventing irregularities in the Church. Thus Sedulius enjoins the "vicar of God" to provide diligently for the holding of frequent synods so that he may apply his consent and authority to the "true and upright" decrees of the bishops:

> Moreover, such a ruler, with diligent care, should wisely plan to convene synodal assemblies two or three times every year, in order that what is known to pertain to the true worship of God, to the reverence of his churches, and to the honor of his priests, or what may have been committed against the Lord's commandments, in such a holy and harmonious assembly may be discussed.[63]

On this important point of royal versus ecclesiastical authority, Sedulius differs markedly from the view expressed by Jonas of Orleans in his earlier treatise, *De institutione regia*. Jonas preached the supremacy of the Church over temporal authority, observing that:

> All the faithful should know that the Church universal is the body of Christ and its head is Christ, and in the Church universal there are principally two distinguished persons, the priestly and the royal. The priestly is the more excellent inasmuch as he must answer to God for kings themselves.[64]

In contrast to Jonas, the power Sedulius accords the king in relation to the Church represents a decided advance in royal authority as it pertains to governing the "civitas Dei." However, while Sedulius assigns first place to the king in a state whose foundation is moral and religious, he does not exempt the ruler from obedience to the law, which is based on Christian teachings and divine revelation as expounded by the Church. For Sedulius, the king retains the sacred authority of his office only so long as he rules justly and in strict compliance with the divine mandates to which the entire "populus Dei" is subject; when he fails in these essential responsibilities, he then incurs the punishments prescribed by God for the crimes of wicked rulers. What are these divine mandates to which the king must adhere in his leadership of a Christian kingdom? Sedulius writes:

> A prudent ruler, therefore, should strive to keep his heart steadfast in the grace of the Most High if he wants the transitory kingdom entrusted to him to maintain some appearance of stability. And, since the Lord is just and merciful, and must be adhered to with a devout heart, a ruler should display manifold works of mercy that he might obtain a great and glorious reward. Let him both cherish and maintain justice, and let him scorn unjust and evil deeds among his subjects and correct them with a zeal which is praiseworthy and in accord with wisdom. So long as a ruler is steadfast in divine precepts, his kingdom becomes more and more stable in this world. . . .[65]

It is stressed that without "piety" and "religion" a king lacks the means to fulfill God's will both as a Christian and a king. These crucial royal attributes reflect the ideal of Carolingian political thinking which holds that a king's spiritual duties and personal moral rectitude constitute the very essence of his office and his right to wield authority. The king, therefore, has authority and divine sanction only when he exhibits piety in the spiritual and religious sense. The upshot of this in *De rectoribus christianis* is that without piety, the visible sign of a just ruler, the king is seen in violation of the divine law from which he derives his authority and so can be deprived of his office. In fact, by spurning piety, that is justice, mercy and love, he actually ceases to be king.

This idea is of paramount significance in the Carolingian conception of kingship. There can be no such person as a bad or evil king; a wicked or impious ruler, by divine judgment, loses his office, and whatever power he might continue to exert is not based on true authority but on the coercion of tyranny. With this in mind, Sedulius emphastically reminds the king that his

> heart and constant devotion in governing his office should not withdraw from that Lord who has conferred upon him such great favor and a glorious ministry. For if the Most High Ruler should see a prince unfaithful, whom He has ordained his faithful servant, He might angrily pluck from that prince the office which He conferred upon him. For if an earthly king can rescind his authority from any unfaithful man and bestow it on another whom he knows to be more faithful, how much more can the divine Ruler of all men, whom the clouds of no man's treachery can deceive, withdraw his favors from false men and bestow them on others known to be proper servants of his will?[66]

Sedulius presents a number of examples from biblical and Roman historical sources to illustrate the harsh fate of rulers who disobey God's will and violate their kingly office: King Saul, Julian the Apostate, and Theodoric, among others. God's punishment of unjust rulers, moreover, can come directly from heaven in the form of natural disasters and calamities, or it can be effected through the power and authority granted to holy bishops and priests to manifest the divine will to the people of God. Sedulius relates the interchange between the Emperor Theodosius II and St. Ambrose to demonstrate the active role to be played by the Church in restraining evil rulers and compelling their obedience to God's law. He recalls that Ambrose vehemently rebuked and condemned Theodosius on account of the emperor's merciless slaughter of Thessalonians. Ambrose not only denied him access to the Church, but also refused to absolve Theodosius of his sin. The resolution of the situation involves an important facet of ninth-century political theory:

> But the priest (St. Ambrose) said: "What sort of penance have you shown after such great crimes? With what medicines have you treated incurable wounds and injuries?" Then the emperor replied: "It is your office to teach and devise remedies, but mine to accept what you have adduced." When St. Ambrose heard the emperor's words, which demonstrated his humility and showed him

ready to submit to the rigors of penance, he applied to the emperor the healing remedy for such wounds. . . . It is clear, therefore, that it behooves just and pious princes to heed the beneficial corrections of priests as spiritual doctors, humbly and willingly.[67]

The basic principle at work in this situation is that the king who sins against God's law, which reigns supreme in the Christian state or "civitas Dei," becomes immediately subject to divine wrath and retribution. Moreover, the agent of God who proclaims his law and administers his judgment against transgressors is the priest or bishop. Sedulius not only patterns his ideal king after Old Testament models like David and Solomon; he also depicts the role of priest or bishop, sharing a responsibility with the king for the "populus Dei," after that of the Old Testament prophets Nathan, Samuel and Jeremiah. In a very real sense, when the king falls away from piety and justice, the priest, like the prophets of old, becomes an adversary of the king. Hence, Sedulius recalls for the king the chastisement of David by the prophet Nathan:

When David was censured by the prophet Nathan after his violation of Bathsheba and the murder of Uriah the Hittite, he was not angry at his accuser, but rather, acknowledging his sin, he immediately became furious at himself.[68]

The Augustinian notion implied in this Old Testament analogy of prophet and king is that the ministries of priest and king, Church and State, are not separate but complementary. On the one hand, priests are seen as mediators between God and his people; they interpret divine law and anoint the king whom God has chosen to shepherd his people. The king, on the other hand, must carry out and enforce the laws and decrees based on the divine dogmas and doctrines of the Church, lest he be called to account by the bishops for transgressing against the moral and spiritual mandates to which all Christians owe obedience. How well this theme was adapted by the Church to the political reality of the ninth century is exemplified in the deposing of Louis the Pious in 833 by an assembly of bishops at Compiegne. A. J. Carlyle describes the action which the bishops brought against the king: "It was at Compiegne in the year 833 that Lewis was compelled to abdicate, and the bishops, there assembled, published a statement in which they set forth the great faults that Lewis had committed—how he had neglected his charge, and done things displeasing to God and man; and they relate how they exhorted him to repentance, inasmuch as he had been deprived of his earthly power in accordance with the counsel of God and ecclesiastical authority."[69]

Where do the people themselves stand in the distribution of political power within the state? In Sedulius' scheme of government, in which all authority and power reside in God, only the king and the Church are legitimate actors in political affairs. Therefore, the people's role in the political process was seen as minimal, while the Church tended to assume a primary role in conferring or rescinding the authority of the king. It is no accident that aggressive bishops in the ninth century introduced into the royal inauguration ceremony the Old Testament ritual of anointing the king. For their capacity to consecrate the king and sanction his appointment by God contained within it the implicit authority to judge an unjust or immoral ruler and remove him, if necessary, from office. Furthermore, as Hincmar once emphatically stated, the bishops' authority to consecrate the king entitled them to assert their superior dignity and institutional autonomy:

> et tanto est dignitas pontificum major quam regum, quia reges in culmen regium sacrantur a pontificibus, pontifices autem a regibus consecrari non possunt (and the dignity of bishops is so much greater than that of kings, because kings are elevated to the royal throne by bishops, whereas bishops cannot be consecrated by kings).[70]

The third principal theme of *De rectoribus christianis* is that king and Church must coordinate their authority and power to promote the spiritual and material welfare of the people. Sedulius urges the king

> to subordinate his personal interests to what will benefit the Church so that insofar as he is mindful of God's blessings which divine favor has bestowed upon him, to such a degree he may honor the giver of such blessings. A just prince is then known to honor the Most High when he shows himself the helper and protector of those who labor in the Lord's field, as it were, the stewards of the Great King. For, it is certain that the Almighty in his kindness will graciously dispose the affairs of an earthly prince to the degree He sees that prince solicitous with regard to His affairs, namely, those of Holy Church.[71]

As previously mentioned, the king is empowered and encouraged to convene Church synods in which

> it is proper that the prefects themselves of the churches be examined as to how they perform their ministries, or how they both instruct the people entrusted to them with divine doctrine as well as inspire them with the example of holy behavior.[72]

Yet, although Sedulius has designated the king the "vicar of God," with the inference that the ruler's authority might extend to assuring the proper administration of the Church, in practice he advocates a marked division of responsibility between the king and Church. He cautions the king not to interfere in the deliberations of synods and not to meddle in ecclesiastical business:

> It is essential, therefore, that a king be prudent, humble, and exceedingly careful lest he presume to judge anything with respect to ecclesiastical affairs. . . . By no means should he pass judgment by himself in such matters, lest, perhaps, by erring he may incur some detestable offense in the sight of the Lord.[73]

The limitations imposed on the king to prevent his encroaching on the ecclesiastical province of spiritual and canonical matters reflect the general tendency in the Carolingian "mirrors for princes" to distinguish recognizable spheres of authority between Church and State. By such distinctions, Sedulius and his fellow theorists hoped to avoid institutional conflicts between King and Church which might disrupt the workings of government, and shatter the unity of purpose and effort so essential to the Christian society they envisioned. Of course, the ideal of Church and State guiding the "populus Dei" by laboring diligently and harmoniously within their respective spheres of authority was easier to postulate than to realize. Given the unsettled conditions of life in the Frankish kingdoms—political rivalry among Charlemagne's successors, a depressed economy, internal rebellion, and external Viking threats—the resources of Church and State were stretched to the limit. Moreover, the pressing ecclesiological agenda for both the king and Church—legal and ecclesiastical reform, development of an educational system, material relief for the poor, and the spiritual improvement of the people—was bound to generate friction between Church and State over basic issues of authority and jurisdiction. As A. J. Carlyle has pointed out, "we cannot doubt that all parties, lay or clerical, would have, in theory, held that the powers were co-ordinate, and in their own spheres, independent of each other. But, as a matter of fact, circumstances were too much for theory (as advanced in the "mirrors for princes"), and not only did the definition and delimitation of the boundaries of the province of each power (temporal and spiritual) prove a task of insuperable difficulty, but each power in turn found itself compelled to trench in some measure upon the province of the other."[74]

From this brief sketch of *De rectoribus christianis* it is evident that Sedulius' discussion of power and authority in the context of Church-State relations within a Christian society bore direct relevance to the political, social, and religious developments affecting Carolingian government. Sedulius, though he draws upon the past for his models of kingship and royal power, grappled with some of the central issues confronting the Franks and their institutions. If he seems hazy at times in defining the roles of King and Church and in proposing a workable relationship between them, he is comparable in this regard to Jonas, Smaragdus and Hincmar. For in Carolingian society, as the influence of ecclesiastics expanded in so many important areas—legislation, education, the administration of justice, and the official bureaucracy—the secular and religious boundaries in government became more ambiguous. Thus Walter Ullman has stated:

It was the ecclesiastics who staffed the royal chancery and thus became instrumental in the formulation of government measures or active in a corporate capacity as diocesans or advisers to their bishops in the numerous Frankish councils of the ninth century, which were to become the chief media of the ecclesiastical legislation upon which the rulers relied. In whatever capacity they were engaged, they were vitally concerned with one of the major instruments by which the Renaissance of Frankish society and government was to be implemented—the law applicable to the whole of Frankish society.[75]

Beyond the substance of his "mirror for princes," Sedulius' importance rests on his contribution to the revival of political writing, which had lapsed during the centuries of turmoil following the demise of the Roman empire in the West. And if his thoughts and methods echo the past of Roman and biblical authorities, they also foreshadow the future political debates on Church-State relations and the very foundation of government that engrossed the best minds of the later Middle Ages. In this sense, the "mirror for princes," from the modest beginnings of Sedulius and his politically-minded colleagues to Erasmus and the changing theories of kingship and government which accompanied the rise of national monarchies in the sixteenth century, forms a continuous tradition.

His poems

Ludwig Traube collected and edited the Latin poems of Sedulius in the *Monumenta Germaniae Historica* (see *Poetae Latini Aevi Carolini, 3* (Berlin: Weidmannsche Verlagsbuchhandlung, 1896), pp. 151-240). Traube ascribed a total of 83 poems to Sedulius, most of which were composed during the episcopate of Bishop Hartgar of Liège (840-855). He also included eight other poems dedicated to Bishop Tado of Milan and others, which bear the style of Sedulius, but which he thought sufficiently distinctive to indicate possible authorship by another poet. Their resemblance to Sedulius' style is striking, however, and there is no certain proof that they do not belong to Sedulius.

In one of his verses, Sedulius refers to himself as the "Virgil of Liège,"[76] but no poet of the Carolingian period can equal the vision, power, and beauty of Virgil's art. This is not to say that the Carolingian poets did not entertain such lofty aspirations. What we possess today of their poetic endeavors fills several massive volumes of the *Monumenta Germaniae Historica*. But a perusal of these, though the range of subjects treated is not small, on the whole brings disappointment. One finds an abundance of narrative and elegiac poems, whose monotonous conformity to their models—the classical poets Horace, Virgil, and Ovid and the early Christian poets Ausonius, Prudentius, and Venantius Fortunatus—generally stifled originality and innovation. Moreover, most of the writers that can be identified were Churchmen or monks, and their literary efforts too often draw upon uninspired religious or didactic themes which are overburdened with pedanticism and carried to inordinate length.

Still, although the Carolingian era produced no one of Virgil's stature, at the courts, schools, and monasteries of the Franks a modest number of literary craftsmen composed verse of a relatively high order. Among this select group are Paul the Deacon, Theodulfus, Sedulius, Walafrid Strabo, and the ill-starred Gottschalk. These learned poets and scholars, unlike their less talented contemporaries, evince in their verses a superior appreciation of their Latin models which did not restrict them to slavish imitation but freed their poetic imagination to fashion a form and style distinctly their own. Particularly admirable are their exceptional metrical skills which permitted experimentation with modes of composition beyond the standard hexameters and elegiac couplets.

In this regard, M. L. W. Laistner has called Sedulius "the most versatile metrical artist since Prudentius."[77] Indeed, Sedulius stands out in his time for his variety of lyric meters, all scanned by quantity. Besides sapphics, elegiacs and hexameters, he was a master at anapestic and iambic, asclepiad, trochaic tetrameter and others. While Sedulius adhered almost exclusively to the classical mode of quantitative verse, he did experiment once with rhythmical composition, an increasingly popular and important verse form whose development in the eighth and ninth centuries, along with the use of rhyme, owes much to Irish influence. His sole attempt at rhythmic verse is an amusing trifle addressed to a friend named Robert to thank him for a gift of wine. It opens with an unusual touch, a grammatical declension of Robert's name in all six Latin cases (a technique of grammatical word play which does not occur with frequency until the twelfth century).

> Bonus vir est Robertus,
> Laudes gliscunt Roberti,
> Christe, fave Roberto,
> Longaevum fac Robertum,
>
> Amen salve, Roberte,
> Christus sit cum Roberto'—
> Sex casibus percurrit
> Vestri praeclarum nomen.[78]

After enumerating his friend's virtues (perhaps with future gifts in mind), Sedulius closes his "swinging song," as Helen Waddell has dubbed it,[79] with unorthodox levity.

> Qui tristibus Falerna
> Largiri gaudes dona,
> Poteris fonte vitae
> Alma sanctorum sorte.
>
> Nec tanta de Siloa
> Grata manant fluenta.
> Haec suxi—non negabo,
> Haec sugam: sicera, abi.[80]

Sedulius not only demonstrated special competence in handling diverse classical meters, but exhibited a wide familiarity with the literary achievements of the great classical poets, mainly Virgil and Ovid, and with the equally cherished Christian poets such as Juvencus, Prudentius, Caelius Sedulius, and Venantius Fortunatus. Gerard Murphy has noted that "of all the Vergilian scholars of that age, however, be they Irish or Continental, none shows a greater appreciation of Vergil's work than Sedulius Scottus."[81] It is certainly true that Sedulius reveals a broad knowledge of Virgil's poetry and on occasion borrows a line or phrase from the *Eclogues, Georgics,* or *Aeneid*. Compare these lines, for instance, from Poem 49 of Sedulius with lines 56–57 of Virgil's third eclogue:

> Nunc viridant segetes, nunc florent germine campi,
> Nunc turgent vites, est nunc pulcherrimus annus. (Poem 49, 1–2)
> Et nunc omnis ager nunc omnis parturit arbos;
> Nunc frondent silvae; nunc formossismus annus. (Ecl. 3, 56–57)

The Latin of Sedulius is of high quality; it is classical in style and diction and achieves an elegance and fluency of expression that make him stand out from many of his literary rivals, both Irish and Continental. In fact, his excellent Latin represents a high point of Carolingian poetry, so that F. J. E. Raby has remarked "after Sedulius Scottus the standard of composition definitely fell; for not until the eleventh century do we meet with poets of a similar order."[82] Sedulius also brings to his verses the extensive reading and interests of a scholar. He fills his poems with learned allusions to the Bible, classical mythology, mystic numbers, astrology, and other types of arcane wisdom. If he could not always resist the temptation to show off his precious Greek, a weakness for which the Irish were notorious, it is understandable considering his background. However, Ludwig Bieler's point is well taken: "the poems of Sedulius Scottus would be all the more enjoyable for the absence of these (Greek) tags."[83]

Sedulius the poet shows us many different sides of himself: scholar, wit, eulogist, and pious priest. Perhaps his least appealing verses are those in which the scholar overwhelmingly predominates. Inasmuch as Carolingian verse was imbued with so much of the academic influence of the schools, it should not surprise us to find Sedulius composing on abstruse subjects only another scholar would appreciate. A few lines from his versification of a philosophical problem on "truth" will suffice as an example.

> If truth is found, it will not be equity;
> yet equity is the source of blessed truth.
> If it is equity, then it will not be justice,
> since truth may not be called by a false name.[84]

This may not be high poetry, but it often passed for cleverness among the scholarly-oriented Carolingian poets.

Even in the sage milieu of the schools, however, a bit of fun sometimes enlivened the dry verses exchanged among scholars. In a verbal duel with a learned colleague, using Latin palindromes as weapons, Sedulius celebrated his apparent triumph with a humorous boast.

> Our triumphant simplicity routs our trilingual brother—
> joyous youth, award us the palm of victory!
> Did not the digger of a pit fall into it with ruin,
> and he who wished to conquer collapse in defeat?

> A horned beast subdued his hornless enemy,
> and a rhinoceros tore his opponent's brow.
> Sage, contend not with the learned—
> if he wants to fight, where are his horns?[85]

Happily, these kinds of "academic" exercises in verse are not typical of Sedulius' work. Despite his erudition, Sedulius' verses are attractive and engaging because they are grounded, for the most part, in real life. They do not pursue exalted themes of philosophical, theological, or allegorical import; rather they focus on people and events from the poet's own experiences, including the feasts and good cheer shared with his Irish brothers, praise of friends and patrons, and the social and political affairs of Liège. Henri Pirenne puts it this way: "La poésie, en effet, n'est pour lui qu'un jeu d'esprit, qu'un délassement agréable, qu'un travail lucratif parfois. Ne lui demandez ni héroisme, ni vigueur, ni grandes émotions; sa muse est trop frêle pour tels efforts, son souffle trop court pour de tels élans."[86] It is precisely Sedulius' "jeu d'esprit" and "délassement agréable" which grace his poems with a lively sense of immediacy and personality so lacking in more ponderous and allegorical literary products of his age.

We see Sedulius' witty side when he employs his muse to obtain from his patrons the food, drink, and shelter required by his group of Irishmen as a reward for their scholarly labors. The need for such domestic comforts actually provided a fruitful source of inspiration for Sedulius. For, like other Irish *peregrini* before him, Sedulius depended upon the support of wealthy patrons, royal or ecclesiastical, in exchange for his scholarly and literary services. He obviously did not belong to the strict ascetic tradition of the Céli Dé, then current in Ireland, which frowned on even the smallest pleasures and sought intellectual and spiritual fulfillment in hard, rigorous discipline of the body and soul. On the contrary, Sedulius is a moderate, congenial personality, who enjoyed the pleasant surroundings of a comfortable dwelling as well as good food, fine wines, and hearty beer.

On one occasion he dared "shame" Bishop Hartgar into procuring a suitable dwelling for himself and his fellow scholars. He begins with a colorful description of Hartgar's dazzling palace but then contrasts it with his own gloomy halls, appropriately designated an "Asylum for the Blind."[87] Only Hartgar, Sedulius assures us, can relieve the Irish of their inhospitable accommodations:

> Adorn our ceilings with panels and lovely paintings,
> and give us a new key and a firm bar for our door;
> then put in sparkling windows made of glass,
> so that the streaming rays of gentle Phoebus
> may illumine, noble bishop, with radiance,
> your scholars who love the light.[88]

No doubt Hartgar got his message, but Sedulius never tells us if his request for more respectable lodgings was successful.

Sedulius' "demands" on his benefactor Hartgar also included provision of various delicacies and meats capable of satisfying the educated palate of a scholar. The poet's favorite comestible seems to have been lamb or mutton. One of his oft quoted poems is a mock-heroic piece about a ram, a gift from Hartgar, which was abducted by a thief and then mangled by a pack of dogs. It combines a remarkable blend of poetic exaggeration, comic license, and display of learning. Sedulius, deprived by fate of his savory meal, laments in epic language the "tragic" death of his ram, about which he says "There might have been a hot bath for you / (but only to please my beloved guest of course!)"[89] In high style he recounts how the thief abandoned the ram to a raging pack of dogs, leaving him to struggle alone against those vicious hounds:

> The deserted ram stood and fought bravely,
> butting with his horns and inflicting many wounds.
> The outmatched dogs were amazed by that horned ram
> and feared they had attacked a lion.
> They barked at the ram with growling words,
> but the noble ram spoke clearly and graciously.
> "What madness seizes your hearts?" he said.
>
> . . . .
>
> yet if your fury and hoarse barking
> stir bloody violence in my tranquil breast,
> I swear by my head, horns, and noble brow,
> to win fitting spoils of battle from you."[90]

To heighten the grandeur of his scenario, Sedulius makes references to mythology (Aries, Luna, Pan, and Cerberus); he does not hesitate to play on biblical passages and sacred scripture to complete his burlesque. He even compares the ram's glorious death in battle against the dogs to that attained by Christ on the cross:

> As the lamb enthroned on high, God's son himself,
> tasted sharp death for man's sins,
> gentle ram, following death's road and
> mangled by vicious dogs, you died for a sinful thief!
> Even as a sacred ram was sacrificed instead of Isaac,
> so you, good ram, are an offering for that thief.[91]

In any case, Sedulius creates this absurd likeness between ram and both Christ and Isaac not for irreverence' sake but to showcase his wit and scholarship and to elicit a laugh (which he probably got) from Hartgar.

To complement fine cuisine, Sedulius cultivated a connoisseur's appreciation for the excellent wines often available at Liège. Like many clerics and monks, he despised the thin beer which served as general refreshment in so many monasteries and schools; and he never missed an opportunity, in poetic complaint to Hartgar, to replenish his ever-dwindling supply of "the sweet gifts of Bacchus" or, at the very least, to obtain for himself a keg of full-bodied beer.

> The parched Meuse does not gladden us with wine,
> and we lack the sweet grace of golden Ceres.
> Thin beer, that cruel monster, vexes us scholars—
> O blessed Christ and Lord, help us in our need!
> Such undrinkable beer is bitter to taste,
> for it is not Cere's sweet child,
> nor the daughter of the Jordan or the Meuse,
> but instead, that wild brook Kedron begat it.
> It numbs all the skills of the scholar's mind,
> as it drives away merriment and brings on gloom.[92]

Sedulius and his fellow sons of Ireland did not stay gloomy for long. At a festive banquet, perhaps in Hartgar's palace, they indulged themselves in a rousing evening of wine and song:

> A noble assembly of brothers takes pious pleasures,
> and you, renowned Lyaeus, dispense us fresh delights.
> You offer kisses of peace with your draughts of cheer;
> mighty Bacchus, you captivate all these learned men.
>
> ·
>
> Let all the brothers consume a measure of wine,
> since "modius" is a glorious six-letter word;
> let each one drink two-sixths of a measure,
> and every drinker sing iambic verses.[93]

Bernard Bischoff thinks these verses are a parody of the Carolingian *caritas-lieder*, or songs of brotherly love, associated with the tradition of the communal drink held in monasteries on certain feast days.[94] Parody or not, the apparent zest of Irishmen like Sedulius for such wine-induced gaiety frequently shocked the sensibilities of more reserved and sombre scholars and clerics. The poet Theodulfus, whose life, learning, and poetry observed a solemn decorum, disliked the "rowdy" and ebullient Irishmen and satirized them with his well-known barb linking "Scottus" with "sottus."[95]

Despite the disapproval of more sober-minded poets, Sedulius is most entertaining when he speaks to us personally and directly about the simpler enjoyments of life—a feast, warm hospitality, and genial fellowship—his muse unencumbered by artificial sentiments. According to an article by Boris Jarcho, in these kinds of verses Sedulius can be seen as the precursor of the Goliards, scholar-poets of the twelfth century scandalously devoted to the pursuit of wine, women, and song.[96] In earnest fashion, Jarcho argues that Sedulius the poet has much in common with that "ordo vagorum," citing textual and thematic similarities between Sedulius' verses of "weltliche freuden" ("worldly delight") and the risqué songs of the Goliards.[97] The

salient motifs of those "disreputable rhymers"[98] characterize the poet as a vaga-
bond, impecunious and in dire need of patronage; an ardent servant of Bacchus,
Gluttony, and Eros; a plaintive victim of the unstable wheel of Fortune; an irreverent
mocker of conventional morality; and a ribald jester and punster. These lines from
the Archpoet, high priest of the Goliards, are a sample of their "licentious" songs.

> To me heaviness of heart
> is a bitter thing;
> jests I love and find
> sweeter than honey.
> Whatever Venus commands
> is a pleasant task,
> for she never dwells
> in a listless heart.
>
> . . . .
>
> It is my aim to
> die in a tavern,
> with the taste of wine
> on my dying lips;
> then let the chorus
> of angels joyously sing:
> May God be merciful
> to this drunkard![99]

Jarcho's argument that Sedulius, in his verses requesting largesse in the form of
mutton or wine, shows himself a member of the "gens Goliae" is unconvincing. The
poems in question, taken in context, represent the witty trifles of a scholar-poet
composed in moments of respite from his intellectual labors and literary studies, not
the carnal and brazenly profane airs characteristic of the Goliards. Conspicuously
missing in his verses, as Jarcho acknowledges, is the Goliards' preoccupation with
sex, which consisted of an almost pagan addiction to wenching in their favorite
haunts, the taverns, or seducing their "ladies" in the "sacred" rituals of nature's
rebirth in the springtime. Sedulius makes no mention of the arts of Venus nor of
yearning to sport with Amaryllis in the shade. What's more, neither in personality,
style, nor poetic persona does he fit the Goliard mold as "a reckless wanderer, beg-
ging favors with a clever rhyme" or as a rebel "against authority and decency."[100]
He portrays himself not as a rhyming beggar but as a professional court poet and
"Sophus," deserving of the support of royal patrons, and the respect of his learned
colleagues. Sedulius' self-assurance and pride in his office as poet is perceived by
Franz Brunhölzl as having "no parallel in the Continental Latin literature of the early
medieval period."[101] Even in his poems to Hartgar seeking food, drink, or better
quarters, Sedulius conveys a sense of the dignity he accords to his office as poet;
and, as alluded to earlier, his sometimes "demanding" tone with the bishop reveals
no trace of the obsequiousness of the beggar or vagabond. When Sedulius

reproaches Hartgar for not ensuring his poet the trappings and accommodations befitting his rank and station as Liège's own Virgil, Orpheus and Homer, Sedulius' manner, as Brunhölzl reasonably interprets it, is reminiscent of the superior social standing and status enjoyed by poets and scholars in his native Ireland. "Sedulius characterized himself as a *fili*, as one of these learned high poets, who clearly did not belong to the Old Irish learned caste of the *filid*, but yet like them formed, on the basis of their education, a respected profession and, ranked above the bards in the social scale, enjoyed a higher status. As a *fili* Sedulius thus can rightly feel slighted when he compares his shabby lodgings with the luxurious house of the bishop."[102]

As for Sedulius' attitude toward conventional morality and authority, he was anything but a rebel. In addition to his "public standing" as a poet and scholar, Sedulius was undeniably a man of the establishment, able to move comfortably in the refined circles of bishops, lords, and kings. Political or social satire has no place in his poetic canon, and his numerous eulogies of ecclesiastics and nobles confirm his admiration and acceptance of the political and social mores of the Carolingians. In his role as court poet especially, Sedulius belongs to a tradition which does not look forward so much to the Goliards and the burst of literary innovation, both in Latin and the vernacular, of the twelfth century, as back to the literary styles and conventions of the Latin classics and the early Christian poets.

If Sedulius has a kindred spirit in medieval literature, it would be Venantius Fortunatus, not the Archpoet. Like Sedulius departed from Ireland, Venantius left his native Italy to seek patronage and fame among the Franks of Gaul in the sixth century. In the course of a flourishing career as courtier and man of learning, Venantius composed a variety of poems—epitaphs, epigrams, panegyrics, metrical epistles, religious pieces, and humorous trifles. His charm, like that of Sedulius, stems from his warm and easygoing personality; and his muse, too, seems happiest at celebrating the pleasures and conviviality of the feast. But unlike Sedulius, Venantius appears to have had little difficulty in satisfying his needs. In "To Gogo, that he can eat no more," he was moved to "protest" the lavishness of his host:

> Nectar and wine, apparel, learning, and wit—
> you overwhelm me, Gogo, with generous gifts.
> Our Cicero you are, and Apicius too;
> as full of words as with food content!
> One favor I ask you, no more of the juicy beef:
> for my stomach revolts, embroiled by too much meat!
> Where the ox lies, dare the chickens approach?
> No equal warfare do horn and wing maintain.
> My eyelids are drooping, as I drift into slumber;
> slower and slower my songs drop off to sleep.[103]

Venantius was read as a classic by the Carolingians. His refinement of manner and literary gifts were more than enough to perpetuate his fame and guarantee himself an admiring audience among the well-read and equally sophisticated poets at the courts of Charlemagne and his successors. Sedulius was no exception. Poems 63 and

85 of Sedulius, which celebrate the reawakening of nature in the springtime as it displays its manifold gifts of beauty in honor of Easter Sunday, borrow profitably in tone and imagery from Venantius' "De resurrectione Domini." In smooth elegiacs Venantius begins by announcing the triumphant arrival of Easter, whose message of joy and life renewed is manifested in the resurrection of nature, which is the glorious symbol of Christ's own resurrection:

> Salve festa dies toto venerabilis aevo,
> Qua Deus infernum vicit, et astra tenet.
> Ecce renascentis testatur gratia mundi,
> Omnia cum Domino dona redisse suo.
> Tempora florigero rutilant distincta sereno,
> Et majore poli lumine porta patet.[104]

What follows is a beautiful description of the spring of the year, when the days lengthen, the earth is bathed in light, and the flowers adorn the meadows and fields:

> Mollia purpureum pingunt violaria campum,
> Prata virent herbis, et micat herba comis.
> Paulatim subeunt stellantia lumina florum
> Arridentque oculis gramina tincta suis.[105]

One by one the signs of spring appear: the leaves start to bud, the bees leave their hives and buzz among the flowers, and the birds, roused from winter, join the nightingale in song.

> Tempore sub hyemis foliorum crine revulso,
> Jam reparat viridans frondea tecta nemus.
> Myrta, salix, abies, corylus, siler, ulmus, acernus,
> Plaudit quaeque suis arbor amoena comis.
> Constructura favos apis hinc alvearia linquens,
> Floribus increpitans poplite mella rapit.
> Ad cantum revocatur avis, quae carmine clauso,
> Pigrior hyberno frigore muta fuit.
> Hinc Philomena suis attemperat organa cannis,
> Fitque repercusso dulcior aura melo.[106]

Poem 63 by Sedulius captures much of the spirit and feeling of his model, conveying at once a feeling for both the spiritual exaltation of Christ's victory over death and the wondrous revival of nature from the decay of winter. Like Venantius, Sedulius opens by proclaiming Easter the most sacred of holy days and spring the splendid witness to Christ's act of salvation:

> Haec est alma dies, sanctarum sancta dierum,
>   Veris pulcher honos signiferique decus;
> Hic est namque dies, dominus quem fecit Iesus,
>   In quo laetatur cosmicus orbis ovans.[107]

Along with the sun, the moon and the stars, the earth rejoices in the light of longer spring days, a myriad of blossoming buds, and its verdant robe of flowers:

> Victorem celebrat Christum rota fulgida Solis,
>   Dum fit nocte nitens maior in orbe dies.—
> Tellus florigeras turgescit germine bulbas,
>   Floribus et pictum gaudet habere peplum.[108]

Then the gentle voices of the birds, with the sweetest sounds of spring, join with the elements in honoring man's redeemer.

> Nunc variae volucres permulcent aethera cantu,
>   Produnt organulis celsa trophea novis.[109]

In poem 85, another piece on Easter, Sedulius develops a similar motif. Here too Venantius is his model; but though Sedulius borrows a few lines directly from "De resurrectione Domini," his muse is on her own. The result is a successful fusion of the spiritual theme of Easter with one reflecting the poet's obvious delight in describing the physical loveliness of nature's springtime array.

> Salve, festa dies, festarum sancta dierum,
>   Qua deus infernum vicit et astra tenet.
> Tellus en vario pandit sua munera partu
>   Spondens agricolae vincere posse famen.
> Surrexit Christus sol verus vespere noctis,
>   Surgit et hinc domini mystica messis agri.
> Nunc vaga puniceis apium plebs laeta labore
>   Floribus instrepitans poblite mella legit.
> Nunc variae volucres permulcent aethera cantu,
>   Temperat et pernox nunc philomena melos.[110]

Nature's power and splendor are consistent elements in the poems of Sedulius. He does not impart to us the intense personal experience of nature that we find in Irish hermit poetry, but he does take pleasure in nature description to evoke a feeling of celebration, plenty, and on occasion, fear and dread. In a poem from *De rectoribus christianis* Sedulius depicts the terrifying events of *dies irae*, as nature with all its tumultuous force strikes at man with the wrath of God:

> When the swirling tempest of the east wind rages,
> resounding with a great commotion
> and thundering from the mountains
> on high with a darkening storm,
>
> and the forests come crashing to the ground,
> and the motion of the sea becomes turbulent,
> and the wind casts forth threats against
> the heavens with a clapping thunderbolt,
>
> it is then that fear grips
> the hearts of trembling mortals,
> lest the wrath of heaven overthrow
> the race of men on earth.[111]

On the theme of nature, Sedulius' most charming poem is the "Contest of the rose and the lily," which represents a spirited debate between a rose and a lily amidst the rich and lovely setting of the earth in bloom:

> The four seasons had completed their cycle,
> and the earth, robed in splendor, burst into bloom.
> Milk-white lilies contended with rose garlands,
> when the rose's golden mouth spoke these words:
>   Rose:
> "Purple bestows rule and reflects kingship's glory,
> but whites, offensive in hue, are vile for kings.
> Feeble whites grow pale with wretched guise,
> yet the whole world venerates purple."
>   Lily:
> "Fair Apollo deems me the earth's golden beauty
> and has adorned my face with elegant grace.
> Why do you prate, O rose stained with shameful red?
> Are you conscious of guilt? Are you blushing?"[112]

The debate continues until Spring, bedecked in a lush robe of flowers, finally reconciles his two daughters. This poem not only exhibits Sedulius' talent for a lively and animated treatment of a nature theme, but also his taste and imagination. In structure, spirit, and style, it is similar to Alcuin's pleasing poem in the bucolic tradition, "The Strife between Winter and Spring." In his little eclogue Alcuin's speakers are Winter and Spring, who debate their respective merits in the presence of a young and an old shepherd. The latter concludes the contest by siding with Spring and praising the coming of spring, whose herald is the cuckoo:

> Desist, Winter, wasteful and foul,
> and let the cuckoo, the shepherd's friend, come!

> May the happy buds break on our hills,
> the pastures be green and the ploughed fields peaceful.
> Green branches offer shade to weary men,
> and the goats, udders full, come to the milking;
> all the birds salute the sun in song—
> O cuckoo, quickly come![113]

Both these poems have a special interest for students of literature because they represent early specimens of a type of dialogue which was greatly influential in the development of the theatre in the Middle Ages and as debate formed the structure of many poems, some of high achievement.

Sedulius' love for nature was genuine, and his muse soared highest in describing its power, from the daunting wind and thunder of a winter storm to the soft and fragrant breezes of a warm summer day. But overall his handling of nature themes falls short of the simple and unaffected charm of Walafrid's "The Little Garden," with its vivid description of the poet's luxuriant garden overflowing with beautiful herbs and flowers.

One aspect of Sedulius' verses which has drawn the least attention from scholars is his formal panegyrics. The tradition of panegyric poetry was well established in medieval literature as a result of the rhetorical genre of eulogy inherited from the Greeks and Romans. Moreover, as Ernst Curtius writes, "throughout the entire Middle Ages, there was a strong demand for poems eulogizing or glorifying secular and spiritual magnates."[114] Two centuries before the Carolingians, Venantius Fortunatus made a name for himself composing formal verses of praise for Frankish royalty at the Merovingian courts and for the bishops who gave him their support; and his reputation as the court poet *par excellence* made him a favorite model for the poets attracted to the courts of Charlemagne and Charlemagne's successors. It was by their skills as eulogists that the Carolingian poets, Sedulius included, were able to win the respect and patronage of royal and ecclesiastical personages.

We may suppose that because of Hartgar, Sedulius was introduced to the world of the Carolingian nobility and the values and conventions, both social and literary, of the Frankish courts. There he made the acquaintance of Emperor Lothar I, Charles the Bald, Louis the German and other powerful individuals whose generosity could be very helpful to a scholar in need of support or to a poet seeking fame and position. Sedulius seems to have made the most of these contacts, considering the number of panegyrics he composed, perhaps "on commission," for Emperor Lothar I and his royal family. In one he utilizes the rather standard rhetorical technique of describing Lothar's virtues and qualities as surpassing all things of worth:

> I bear a hundred thanks to our emperor:
> may God's right hand exalt him!
> But I have erred, for I will praise his myriad
> victories not a hundred but a thousand times.
>
> . . . .

> O Zion, behold Solomon, your august king!
> God's grace has sent us from heaven this
> glittering star and illustrious leader,
> more glorious than purple, more precious than topaz,
> more pleasing than amber, and more delightful than mead![115]

Sedulius' praise of Lothar did not go unrewarded. He hints, at one point, that Lothar, in addition to a gift of fine apparel, may have shown him official favor as his court poet:

> He adorned me, his poet, in splendid attire,
> that the Franks might admire his gleaming sage.[116]

If his praises of Lothar express his admiration for the emperor, his formal eulogies of Irmingard and Berta, Lothar's queen and daughter, reveal something of Sedulius' personal esteem for them. Amidst the flattery befitting a queen, Irmingard is also addressed as a "gentle flower" and "lovely rose."[117] Sedulius particularly honored Berta, who elected the religious life after her husband's death, for her wisdom, faith and spiritual devotion:

> Heaven's court has received your earthly husband;
> but now God, your divine spouse, is ever with you.
> ·
> Your spouse Jesus arrayed you in a snow-white gown,
> and adorned your face with roses of chastity.
> He graced your breast with gems of virtue,
> and chose his bride with goodly hope.
> Preserve, O Christ, the emperor's fair daughter,
> and cherish, Blessed Mary, this lovely pearl.[118]

A court poet had to be able to eulogize for all occasions: coronations; the welcoming of visiting dignitaries; the celebration of military victories, births and marriages; and the mourning of friends and patrons who had died. Sedulius' efforts in the way of formal eulogies bore mixed results. He merits our attention most when his verses are infused with his personal regard for the person praised or the drama of a spectacular event. For this reason, his eulogies of Hartgar, which reflect the warm and cordial relationship between the bishop and himself, are generally judged his best. Besides his interesting and entertaining little cycle on Hartgar's trip to Rome, quoted earlier, Sedulius composed a short but spirited welcome for Hartgar returning from one of his numerous journeys on Church or royal business. He first sets a mood of sadness, as Hartgar's forlorn poet has been forced to retire to the lonely life of the forest while the bishop, his sole inspiration, has been away:

> I, Tityrus, mournful at heart, remain in the forests,
> for the shepherd is away and there is no peace.

Shepherd, has anyone stolen you? Zephyrus or the horned Rhine?
Father, has some four-footed glory carried you off?
Perchance, has Aurora's brilliant team on reddish wings,
and flying Cupid, borne you far from home?
Aurora chose you, earth's most radiant star,
and for love of you spurned her Tithonus.
Or is it that God's gracious right hand and the angels
at the same time bear you away and return you?[119]

After duly flattering his patron, Sedulius proclaims his return to Liège with a real sense of joy:

May your splendid presence bless the Franks with grace,
and your sparkling glory illumine your churches,
even as Apollo wandering across shining Olympus lightens
the world with his glittering and wondrous lamp.
O golden light of the earth, you have come at last,
as the Lord brings hope and repose to your people.[120]

Through all the hyperbole, Sedulius succeeds in conveying Hartgar's popularity in Liège and the happy greeting he received from his flock. Naturally Sedulius is relieved as well and assures his patron of his renewed poetic powers and his continued service as Hartgar's official poet:

People of every age are filled with jubilation,
as they break into song to celebrate your arrival;
and my muse has not withdrawn with silent lips
but with clear voice chants harmonious melodies.[121]

In a poem announcing the Emperor Lothar I's courageous and decisive defeat of Viking raiders, Sedulius' skills as a eulogist and his undisguised fear and hatred for the Norsemen combine for a rousing and dramatic account of the Frankish army's heroic deeds on the field of battle:

O Lothar, did not the Norsemen fear you?
For, when they saw your gleaming hosts,
that hostile horde rushed to their ships
    in headlong flight.

The splendor of arms and the sole appearance of
a valorous leader vanquished the enemy,
as fear gave wings to their soles and
    naked feet.

No hope was left them but a single ship,
so they sought out cavernous pits.
They quake with terror at the arms of
        a bounteous prince![122]

Sedulius, who so cherished life and its little pleasures, moves us most when mourning the death of a friend. His sapphic ode on the death of Bishop Hartgar is at once a formal lament in its tone and choice of images and metaphors, and an expression of Sedulius' personal sorrow at the passing of his beloved friend and patron. The eulogy begins with the public anguish over Hartgar's death:

All the Franks cry out in lament,
and the Irish land, and Rome in Italy,
sigh and mourn the death of our
        Bishop Hartgar.

You rich and poor, high and humble,
ordained ministers of the Lord of Hosts,
and fair nobles of every age and sex,
        shed your tears!

Since you have fallen, good bishop,
star and radiant light, the stars
flicker and grow dim, and the sun hides
        its gleaming face.[123]

If the praise seems extravagant and formal, it is intended to be so and what Hartgar would have expected given both the social and poetic conventions of his day. The value and function of this kind of eulogy lay not in its sincerity or focus on the personal grief of the poet, but on the public importance accorded to Hartgar's death by the poet as spokesmen for the community. Still, Sedulius cannot suppress his deep sense of loss:

Resplendent lily, visage of the rose,
flourishing palm, and stout cedar,
see how sudden ruin has withered you—
        alas, good father!

Woe to me, your wretched poet,
for my words can barely express,
O Christ, the anguish that has seized
        my miserable heart.[124]

For the most part, Sedulius' eulogies fall within a genre valued among the Carolingians but alien to the literary taste of the modern reader. They also demonstrate, in their conventional nature, none of the originality and animation of his informal verses. This short encomium to Charles the Bald is representative of many of his poems of praise:

> Bear him cinnamon and precious gifts of myrrh,
> and bring him sweet spices and Irish flowers!
> For God, the All-Creating, has poured
> forth oil from heaven and anointed him king.
> O noble ruler, you are the third branch
> and royal scion of two mighty emperors.
> O peoples, spread Panchean flowers for your king;
> strew lilies, I pray, in his most royal path![125]

The theme, metaphors and phrases in these lines occur over and over again in the panegyrics of Sedulius. In fact, Sedulius repeats himself more than any other poet of the ninth century in this type of poetry, prompting Pirenne to complain of "les fréquentes répétitions, les phrases stéréotypeés qui frappent même à une premierè lecture."[126] In one poem after another Sedulius draws upon a set repertoire of royal epithets, images and expressions which are organized and presented in an almost identical fashion (see Poems 12, 14, 23, etc.). The general formula is as follows: the poet gives hail to the king, prince, or lord; praises the king's noble ancestry and recounts his valiant deeds; and extolls his generosity, proclaims his justice, and sometimes points out the worthiness of his wife and heirs. Though the order and number of these components may vary, they form the basic structure of most of Sedulius' professional eulogies and panegyrics.

In technique and content, Sedulius' praise poems resemble the bulk of Carolingian panegyrics. They also incorporate the standard rhetorical topoi which Carolingian poets utilized to ornament their verses. Following are some of those most commonly used: all peoples and lands pay homage to the king; the king's authority extends to the far corners of the earth, even to Thule (Iceland?) and India; every age and sex celebrates the king's arrival or his triumphs; his name deserves to be praised across the earth; both rich and poor exalt the king's fame; the seas, earth, and skies acknowledge his power.

Sedulius was especially fond of flattering his royal patrons with elaborate comparisons of their deeds and accomplishments to those of the most revered kings of the Old Testament, David and Solomon. In this piece Sedulius informs Charles the Bald that he surpasses even Solomon in virtue, piety, power and wisdom:

> The world reveres Solomon for but one temple,
> but Charles is famed for a thousand temples.
> Solomon was Jerusalem's glorious king,
> yet Charles rules a hundred Jerusalems.
> Mount Zion and the Mount of Olives loved Solomon,

> however the Alps wait upon Charles, our radiant king.
> The Jordan's sparkling waters praised Solomon,
> but the horned Rhine exalts and honors Charles.
> Ancient wisdom enlightened Solomon's mind,
> while Charles drinks waters fresh and ancient.[127]

Although the repetition of the language and motifs, and the predictability of theme, leave little room for the personality of the poet or diversity of theme, it would be a mistake to ignore the panegyrics' place and significance among his verses. In them we behold Sedulius in his social role as court poet, composing in a traditional mode of Continental Latin poetry highly regarded at the time. James Carney sees in them a sign of Sedulius' Irishness and his bardic style acquired in Ireland.[128] It is a principal trait of Irish bards or professional poets that their panegyrics were prized not for their originality or diversity of theme but for their almost rigid adherence to traditional formulas of praise and accepted modes of poetic structure and expression. While it would be tempting to attribute Sedulius' peculiarly heavy reliance on repetition and formulaic construction to his familiarity with the conventions of Irish bardic poetry, it is impossible, however, to isolate what is distinctly Irish or Carolingian about his panegyrics within the broad characteristics of the genre as a whole.

With so much of his time and energy devoted to formal praise of patrons, informal verses of humor and wit, and the rigors of scholarship, it is not surprising that Sedulius found little opportunity for poems of a religious nature. He did, as we have seen, compose occasional pieces in celebration of Easter and Christmas, and raised his thoughts to heaven in a number of his poems; but unlike the early Christian poets whom he knew well and many of his contemporaries, Sedulius, based on the poems we have, never attempted the sustained treatment of a religious theme. The hymns of Prudentius and Caelius Sedulius, which inspired much of the religious poetry of the early medieval period, exerted little influence on him. As a courtier and informal poet, Venantius was something of a mentor for the Carolingians and particularly for Sedulius. But nothing exists among Sedulius' verses to compare with Venantius' execution of spiritual themes in *Vexilla regis* and *Pange, lingua* nor with the Christian elegies of Paulinus of Nola. Among the Carolingians, it was Theodulfus of Orleans whose *Gloria laus et honor* and other devotional poems made him one of the finest religious poets of the eighth and ninth centuries. For the development of Carolingian religious and liturgical verse, therefore, we must look to Theodulfus, Raban Maur, Walafrid Strabo, and others. Sedulius' paucity of religious verses is not only unusual within the context of Carolingian poetry, but of Irish poetry as well. In the eighth and ninth centuries Ireland experienced a flowering of religious verse both in Latin and Old Irish: the hermit poems, the loricas, and the hymns.

If we get a glimpse of Sedulius the pious priest, it is in a few rather short prayers and invocations. In these four lines, the Celt comes out in his metaphors as he asks Christ to defend his friend Dermot with his shield:

> O Christ, we pray, protect Dermot with your shield
> and lead him and his friends safely to our city.

> Gracious Lord, skillfully pilot their ships,
> for without you, Father, all hope is vain.[129]

Sedulius also sought God's protection from the droughts that so often inflicted suffering upon the people:

> O God, eternal font, pity the poor Moselle;
> replenish her cloud-borne waters with plentiful rain.
> Who else, Lord, can rain clear waters with bounteous will,
> for no one is, has been, or ever will be your equal?[130]

Natural disasters were not the only threat to the people's lives and welfare. After an unsuccessful attack by the Vikings, Sedulius offered thanksgiving on behalf of the Christian people for the intercession of God in warding off the danger:

> Let the heavens rejoice, the sea, and all the lands;
> let Christ's happy peoples exult and marvel at
> the mighty deeds of the Lord, the Father,
>   thundering Godhead.
> . . . .
> Give glory to God, for our Almighty Father's
> strong arm has inflicted sudden ruin
> upon rebellious Norsemen, the wicked
>   foes of piety.[131]

While Sedulius does not exhibit the intensity of spiritual and religious devotion of other Christian poets, his faith, as expressed in these prayers, was not lacking. Although more worldly than some, his weakness for material pleasures and the praise of his patrons was balanced by an unaffected humility. Thus in his *Confession*, he summed up his life and career rich in achievement with the modesty of a man able to see himself in perspective before God:

> I read or write, and I teach or search for truth;
> I call on heaven's throne by night and by day.
> I eat, drink freely, and with rhymes invoke the muses;
> and snoring I sleep, or keep vigil and pray to God.
> My heart, full of shame, laments the sins of life—
> O Christ and Mary, pity your wretched man![132]

Whether Sedulius lies buried in Liège or Milan, his legacy of accomplishments is indisputable. Under his direction, a scholarly and cultural circle prospered in Liège until the destruction wrought by the Vikings plunged the city into darkness. His circle of scholars has left us manuscripts important to our understanding of intellectual history and medieval tradition. Sedulius himself excelled in the disciplines most esteemed by his contemporaries, grammar and theology; yet his own works also reveal an uncommonly wide acquaintance with classical literature. His *De rectoribus christianis* has brought Sedulius recognition as one of the founders of the political literature of the Middle Ages; and his polished Latin verses give us insight into the sophisticated world of the early medieval courtier, as well as into the personal world of an Irish scholar on the Continent. Above all, Sedulius' attainments reflect the spirited and vigorous role of the Irish in the Carolingian renaissance and the development of medieval culture.

Translator's notes

I have based my translation of *De rectoribus christianis* on the excellent Latin text edited and published by S. Hellmann in *Sedulius Scottus* (Munich: C. H. Beck'sche Verlagsbuchhandlung, 1906). I have also consulted Ludwig Traube's edition of the verses extracted from *De rectoribus christianis* published in *Poetae Latini Aevi Carolini*, 3 (Berlin: Weidmannsche Verlagsbuchhandlung, 1896), pp. 154–166. For the poems of Sedulius I have primarily used the Latin edition published by Traube in *Poetae Latini Aevi Carolini*, although I have frequently compared his manuscript readings with the selected poems edited by Henri Pirenne in "Sedulius of Liège," *Mémoires couronnés de l'Académie Royale de Belgique*, 33 (Brussels, 1882), pp. 51–72; and by Ernest Dümmler in *Sedulii Scotti Carmina Quadraginta* (Halle: n.p., 1869). In my textual notes I have cited any instance where I followed the MS instead of Traube's emendations or deviated from his reading of the text.

In my translations I have tried to achieve a clear and fluent English style while trying to convey, at the same time, a sense of the rhythms and diction of the Latin. In the prose of *De rectoribus christianis* I have endeavored to preserve as much as possible the rhetorical and formal language and structure of the original. On occasion, I have had to be somewhat free in my translation of Sedulius' long and complex sentences in order to avoid a stilted rendering of his language. Although I have translated Sedulius' verses into prose, a line by line arrangement is presented to simulate poetry. At times translation required the deletion of a word or phrase here and there, but I have been careful not to allow such changes to alter significantly the meaning or sense of a line. As in his prose, Sedulius often seeks rhetorical effects in his poetry which cannot be literally translated except in distorted English. A particular problem arose with Sedulius' device of "echoing distichs" in which the first half of one line is exactly repeated in the second half of the line which follows it:

> Tempest adest niveum sincera luce coruscum,
> Quo dominus natus; tempest adest niveum.

To render a literal translation of these echoing distichs would likely prove tedious for the reader, and so I have avoided strictly translating them. The poems are translated in the order in which they appear in Traube's edition. Where Traube seems to have incorporated two separate pieces under one title, I have distinguished them as Poem

25A and 25B. The notes are arranged according to the number of the line to which they refer. All translations in the introduction and notes, unless otherwise indicated, are my own.

Notes

1. Frank O'Connor, *A Short History of Irish Literature* (New York: Capricorn Books, 1968), p. 52.

2. Ibid., p. 51.

3. Ludwig Traube, *O Roma Nobilis* (Munich: Verlag der k. Akademie, 1891), p. 43.

4. Sedulius Scottus, *Poetae Latini Aevi Carolini*, ed. Ludwig Traube (Berlin: Weidmannsche Verlagsbuchhandlung, 1896), vol. 3, Poem 3, line 14 (all translations are my own).

5. James Carney, "Sedulius Scottus," in *Old Ireland*, ed. R. McNally (New York: Fordham University Press, 1965), p. 235.

6. Sedulius Scottus, Poem 16, lines 13–14.

7. Nora Chadwick and Myles Dillon, *The Celtic Realms* (London: Weidenfeld and Nicolson, 1967), p. 191.

8. Kathleen Hughes, *The Church in Early Irish Society* (Ithaca: Cornell University Press, 1966), pp. 205–6.

9. Whitley Stokes and John Strachan, eds., *Thesaurus Palaeohibernicus* (Cambridge: Cambridge University Press, 1903), 2:290 (my translation from the Old Irish).

10. Sedulius Scottus, Poem 3, lines 13–16.

11. Ibid., lines 25–26.

12. Ibid., Poem 11, line 32.

13. Henri Pirenne, "Sedulius of Liège," in *Mémoires couronnés de l'Académie Royale de Belgique* 33 (1882): 23.

14. Sedulius Scottus, Poem 6, line 76 and Poem 7, line 20.

15. Alice Stopford Green, "Sedulius of Liège," *Journal of the Ivernian Society* 6 (1914): 231.

16. Sedulius Scottus, Poem 1, lines 27–32.

17. Ibid., Poem 4, lines 1–10.

18. Ibid., Poem 11, lines 5–12.

19. Ibid., Poem 5, lines 13–20.

20. Ibid., Poem 7, lines 101–6.

21. Ibid., lines 156–58.

22. Ibid., Poem 8, lines 13–24.

23. Ibid., Poem 34, line 25.

24. Not all scholars are agreed that Sedulius entirely ignores events in Ireland and Britain in his poetry. Ludwig Traube (*O Roma Nobilis*, p. 46) has argued that Poems 45–47 were actually composed by Sedulius before he reached the Continent. He interpreted Poem 45 as celebrating an Irish victory over the Vikings; and he saw Poem 46 "Sedulius against a plague" as inspired by the Viking raids in Ireland. Both Traube and Nora Chadwick (*The Early British Church* [Cambridge: Cambridge University Press, 1958], p. 103) have suggested that Poem 47, "On a certain altar," is addressed to King Rhodri Mawr of Wales (844–77). Their judgment, however, is based on the doubtful reading of the name "Roricus" in the poem.

25. Ernest Dümmler, "Die handschriftliche Ueberlieferung der lateinischen Dichtungen aus der Zeit der Karolinger, II," *Neues Archiv der Gesellschaft für ältere deutsche Geschichtskunde* 4 (1879): 319.

26. Ibid.

27. Pirenne, p. 29.

28. Ibid.

29. Franz Brunhölzl, *Geschichte der lateinischen Literatur des Mittelalters* (Munich: Wilhelm Fink Verlag München, 1975), 1:449–50.

30. Ibid.

31. J. F. Kenney, *The Sources for the Early History of Ireland: Ecclesiastical* (New York: Octagon Books, 1966), p. 554.

32. On fol. 53 at the end of the psalter is the subscription "CHΔTΛIOC CKOTTOC EΓΩ EΓPAΨ'A" ("I Sedulius Scottus wrote it"). See Kenney, p. 557, and Traube (*O Roma Nobilis*) pp. 48–49 for a discussion of this manuscript.

33. Nora Chadwick, *The Early British Church*, p. 105.

34. John Contreni, *The Cathedral School of Laon from 850 to 930: Its Manuscripts and Masters* (Munich: Arbeo-Gesellschaft, 1978), pp. 88–89.

35. Ibid.

36. M. Manitius, *Geschichte der lateinischen Literatur des Mittelalters* (Munich: Beck, 1965), 2:318.

37. E. A. Lowe, ed., *Codices Latini Antiquiores* (Oxford: Clarendon Press, 1947), pt. 4, p. xxiii.

38. Kenney, p. 565.

39. S. Hellmann, *Sedulius Scottus* (Munich: C. H. Beck'sche Verlagsbuchhandlung, 1906), pp. 121–22.

40. M. L. W. Laistner, *Thought and Letters in Western Europe* (London: Methuen and Co. Ltd., 1931), p. 251.

41. Kenney, p. 566.

42. Traube, *O Roma Nobilis*, p. 48.

43. For the study of Greek in Ireland see Bernard Bischoff, "Das griechische Element in der abendländischen Bildung des Mittelalters," *Byzantinische Zeitschrift* 44 (1951): 27–55.

44. P. Boyle, "Sedulius Scottus of Liège," *The Irish Ecclesiastical Record* vol. 5, ser. 7 (1916), p. 549.

45. Kenney, p. 557.

46. Carney, pp. 247–48.

47. Francis Byrne, *Irish Kings and High Kings* (London: B. T. Batsford Ltd., 1973), p. 24.

48. Pseudo-Cyprianus, *De duodecim abusivis saeculi*, ed. S. Hellmann, in *Texte und Untersuchungen zur Geschichte der altchristlichen Literatur*, 34, (1909).

49. *De duodecim abusivis saeculi* was known by and influenced other authors of instructions for princes in the eighth and ninth centuries: Cathvulf, Jonas of Orleans, Sedulius Scottus, and Hincmar of Rheims. It was also quoted in the records of Church councils and synods of the ninth century, e.g., the Paris synod of 829 and the council at Metz of 859.

50. Pseudo-Cyprianus, chapter 9.

51. Smaragdus of St. Mihiel, *Via regia*, ed. Migne, in *Patrologia Latina* (Paris), 102:935–70.

52. Jonas of Orleans, *De institutione regia*, ed. J. Reviron, in *Les idées politico-religieuses d'un évêque du IXe siècle Jonas d'Orleans et son "De institutione regia"* (Paris: J. Vrin, 1930).

53. Hincmar of Rheims, *De regis persona et regio ministerio*, ed. Migne, in *Patrologia Latina* (Paris), 125:833–56.

54. Cathvulf, *Epistolae*, in *Monumenta Germaniae Historica* (Berlin: Weidmannsche Verlagsbuchhandlung), 4:502–5.

55. Alcuin, *Monumenta Alcuiniana*, ed. W. Wattenbach and E. Dümmler (Berlin: Weidmannsche Verlagsbuchhandlung, 1873).

56. Lupus of Ferrières, *The Letters of Lupus of Ferrières*, trans. Graydon Regenos (The Hague: Martinus Nijhoff, 1966); see nos. 31, 37, and 46.

57. For an excellent survey and discussion of the Carolingian "mirrors for princes" see Hans

Anton, *Fürstenspiegel und Herrscherethos in der Karolingerzeit* (Bonn: Ludwig Röhrscheid Verlag, 1968).

58. Walter Ullmann, *Carolingian Renaissance* (London: Methuen and Company Ltd., 1969), p. 7.

59. A. J. Carlyle, *A History of Mediaeval Political Theory in the West*, 2nd. ed. (Edinburgh: William Blackwood and Sons Ltd., 1927), 1:197.

60. Sedulius Scottus, *De rectoribus christianis*, preface, lines 19–21.

61. Ibid., chapter 1.

62. Ibid., chapter 19.

63. Ibid., chapter 11.

64. Jonas of Orleans, chapter 1.

65. Sedulius Scottus, *De rectoribus christianis*, chapter 3.

66. Ibid.

67. Ibid., chapter 12.

68. Ibid.

69. Carlyle, p. 250.

70. Hincmar of Rheims, *Hincmari Rhemensis Epistolae* (Moguntiae: Typis Joannis Albini, 1602), p. 44.

71. Sedulius Scottus, *De rectoribus christianis*, chapter 11.

72. Ibid.

73. Ibid.

74. Carlyle, p. 261.

75. Ullmann, p. 11.

76. Sedulius Scottus, Poem 7, lines 19–20.

77. Laistner, p. 335.

78. Sedulius Scottus, Poem 58, lines 1–8.

79. Helen Waddell, *Mediaeval Latin Lyrics* (Middlesex: Penguin Books, 1929), p. 325.

80. Sedulius Scottus, Poem 58, lines 49–56.

81. Gerard Murphy, "Vergilian Influence Upon the Vernacular Literature of Medieval Ireland," *Studi medievali* NS 5 (1932): 374.

82. F. J. E. Raby, *A History of Secular Latin Poetry* (London: Oxford University Press, 1957), vol. 1, p. 247.

83. Ludwig Bieler, "The Island of Scholars," in *Revue Du Moyen Age Latin* 8 (1952): 229.

84. Sedulius Scottus, Poem 64, lines 1–4.

85. Ibid., Poem 80, lines 1–8.

86. Pirenne, p. 35.

87. Sedulius Scottus, Poem 4, line 35.

88. Ibid., lines 40–45.

89. Ibid., Poem 41, lines 135–36.

90. Ibid., lines 59–66; 71–74.

91. Ibid., lines 117–22.

92. Ibid., Poem 9, lines 7–16.

93. Ibid., Poem 32, lines 23–26; 36–39.

94. Bernard Bischoff, "Caritas Lieder," *Mittelalterliche Studien*, 2 (Stuttgart: Anton Hiersemann, 1967), p. 166.

95. Theodulfus, *Poetae Latini Aevi Carolini*, 1, p. 487, lines 155–74, in *Monumenta Germaniae Historica* (Berlin: Weidmannsche Verlagsbuchhandlung, 1881).

96. Boris Jarcho, "Die Vorlaufer des Golias," *Speculum* 3 (1928): 523.

97. Ibid., p. 531.

98. George Whicher, *The Goliard Poets* (Cambridge, MA: n.p., 1949), p. 2.

99. Archpoet, "The Poet's Confession," lines 25–32; 89–96 in *Die Gedichte des Archipoeta*, ed. M. Manitius (Munich: Georg D. W. Callwey, 1913).

100. Whicher, p. 4.

101. Brunhölzl, p. 460.

102. Ibid., p. 461.

103. Venantius Fortunatus, *Opera* (Cameraci: A. F. Hurez, 1822), Book 6, Poem 2, lines 1–10.

104. Ibid., Book 3, Poem 7, lines 1–6.

105. Ibid., lines 15–18.

106. Ibid., lines 25–34.

107. Sedulius Scottus, *Poetae Latini Aevi Carolini*, Poem 63, lines 1–4; see my translation.

108. Ibid., lines 19–22.

109. Ibid., lines 23–24.

110. Sedulius Scottus, *Poetae Latini Aevi Carolini*, 3, Poem 2 (it corresponds to my Poem 85).

111. Sedulius Scottus, *De rectoribus christianis*, chapter 15.

112. Sedulius Scottus, Poem 81, lines 1–12.

113. Alcuin, *Carmina*, ed. Ernest Dümmler, *Poetae Latini Aevi Carolini*, 1 (Berlin: Weidmannsche Verlagsbuchhandlung, 1881), pp. 270–72.

114. Ernst Curtius, *European Literature and the Latin Middle Ages*, trans. Willard Trask (Princeton, New Jersey: Princeton University Press, 1953), p. 55.

115. Sedulius Scottus, Poem 26, lines 1–4; 12–16.

116. Ibid., lines 9–10.

117. Ibid., Poem 24, lines 11 and 12.

118. Ibid., Poem 78, lines 27–28; 31–36.

119. Ibid., Poem 2, lines 1–10.

120. Ibid., lines 11–16.

121. Ibid., lines 24–27.

122. Ibid., Poem 60, lines 29–40.

123. Ibid., Poem 17, lines 5–16.

124. Ibid., lines 21–28.

125. Ibid., Poem 44, lines 1–8.

126. Pirenne, p. 38.

127. Sedulius Scottus, Poem 28, lines 33–42.

128. Carney, p. 248.

129. Sedulius Scottus, Poem 27, lines 1–4.

130. Ibid., Poem 83, lines 1–4.

131. Ibid., Poem 45, lines 1–4; 21–24.

132. Ibid., Poem 74, lines 1–6.

On Christian Rulers

The Preface to *De rectoribus christianis*

(*On Christian Rulers*)

Every profession that is prominent in the triple world[1]
should be guided by art, for art's gifts are many.
With art the Creator of all made the lands, seas, stars, and heavens
and with art he rules the entire beautiful universe.
The wisdom of the heavenly Thunderer has set man through
lofty arts over all the creatures of the earth.
Art controls the war-chariot and steers ships on course
and is necessary for a triumphant military campaign.
And so, the state needs art's assistance so that
it may prosper with a just ruler and a happy people.   10
On this account, I, traversing the flowery meadows of divine
books, have gathered garlands for you, illustrious king,[2]
to adorn the diadem of your supreme mind and
to glorify sceptres ruling in accord with Christ's will.
With my thumb fragrant with balsam I have gathered
baskets of the healing herbs of divine dogma.
Drink the waters of Israel's clear fountains to
satisfy the thirsty palate with a most sweet liquid!
For these are the glory of kings and garlands for glittering sceptres:
the tenets of the Lord, the examples of the ancients,   20
and the deeds, famous over the world, of renowned princes.
By these arts may your kingdom thrive and triumph,
and be prosperously governed for a great many years
until you ascend to the heavenly court,
where the perpetual glory of just rulers prevails.

The End of the Preface

With you the beginning and the end, O Christ the King;
may you, O God, be the alpha and omega of your servant's work.

Here begins the book of Sedulius
On Christian Rulers
and suitable rules by which
the state ought to be properly governed

Chapter I.
Why it is necessary for the pious ruler,
endowed with royal power, to dedicate above all else
worthy honors to God and to his holy churches.

As soon as a Christian ruler has received the royal sceptre and the government of the kingdom, it is fitting that he first return acts of thanksgiving and suitable honors to God and to Holy Church. In fact, from the very beginning the state is most gloriously consecrated when royal solicitude and sacred devotion are aroused with both holy fear and love of the Heavenly King and when care is taken for the glorious benefit of the Church by prudent counsel, so that he whom royal purple and other symbols of royal authority adorn externally will also be adorned internally by praiseworthy vows to God and to his Holy Church. For indeed, a king is notably raised to the summit of temporal rule when he devotes himself with pious zeal to the Almighty King's glory and honor. And so, let the pious ruler fervently strive to obey the will and holy commands of the Supreme Master of all things by whose divine will and ordination he does not doubt himself to have risen to the summit of authority. This is affirmed by the apostle who says: "There is no authority unless it be from God; moreover, all the authorities which exist have been established by God" (Rom. 13:1). Therefore, so much as an upright ruler acknowledges that he has been called by God, to the same degree he is vigilant with dutiful care that he regularly determines and examines all things before God and men according to the scales of justice. For, what are the rulers of the Christian people unless ministers of the Almighty? Moreover, he is a faithful and proper servant who has done with sincere devotion whatever his lord and master has commanded to him. Accordingly, the most upright and glorious princes rejoice more that they are appointed to be ministers and servants of the Most High than lords or kings of men. For this reason blessed David, an illustrious king and prophet, often called himself the servant of the Lord. Also, renowned Solomon, David's son, calling upon the Almighty, said, among other things: "Consider your servant's prayer and his entreaties, O Lord, my God; hear the hymn and prayer which your servant utters before you this day, so that your eyes both day and night may watch over this temple about which you said: 'There will be my name!' " (1 Kings 8:28-29). The emperor Constantine the Great of celebrated memory,[3] who believed and fulfilled the mystery of the saving cross and the Catholic faith, did not claim credit for himself when by his joyous rule religion vigorously flourished. Rather, he gave thanks that Almighty God had deigned to make him the useful servant of his will. Lo, that most distinguished emperor rejoiced more to have been a servant of God than to have possessed an earthly empire. Thus

Constantine, because he had been the servant of divine will, extended a peaceful reign from the sea of Britain to the lands of the East. And because Constantine had subjected himself to the Almighty, with power and faith he won all the hostile wars which were waged under him. He constructed and enriched Christ's churches with splendid treasures. As a result, divine favor granted him triumphant victories, for, without doubt, the more pious rulers subject themselves humbly to the King of Kings, the more they ascend on high to the summit of glorious distinction.

Who, moreover, may not marvel at how many honors Solomon returned to the Lord after he had received the sceptre of kingship with God's backing; how with the most prudent devotion he constructed and marvellously adorned the Lord's temple; and finally, how many conciliatory sacrifices he offered to God? In the end, Solomon received the fruits of his devotion and prayer, just as the Lord, appearing to him said: "I have heard the prayer and entreaty which you offered before me. I have consecrated the temple you built so that I may confer my name there forever, and my eyes and my heart will remain there always. As for you, if you walk before me just as your father walked in simplicity of heart and in justice and if you do everything I have commanded to you and preserve my laws and judgments, I will establish the throne of your sovereignty over Israel forever just as I promised your father, David, saying: 'No one of your line will be removed from the throne of Israel!'" (2 Chron. 7:12; 17-19). And so, if King Solomon deserved to attain such a glorious reward in return for sacred devotion and for constructing the Lord's earthly temple, how precious a mark of glory will a ruler possess if beloved by God he constantly adorns Holy Church, which is the spiritual tabernacle of the living God? Let us now conclude with the delightfulness of verse what we have briefly related in prose.

> He who bears a flourishing kingdom's noble sceptre should
> first offer vows and prayers to the Heavenly Throne.
> All kingdoms, peace, and the life and prosperity
> of distinguished leaders depend upon God's sacred will.
> For royal honor and kingship's radiant diadem consist of
> sacred fear of the Heavenly Throne and love of God.
> Just as milk-white lilies adorn a flowery field,
> and as the rose blushes in its scarlet countenance,
> so a just ruler blooms with a flowering of virtues
> and begets sacred fruits in the summit of his mind.   10
> Both glorious purple and the glittering sceptre of
> his father David adorned King Solomon;
> but prudent zeal of heart inwardly adorned
> that youthful king more in glorifying God.
> Let your state glow like the morning star,
> and in newly rising accomplish illustrious vows.

Chapter II.
How an orthodox ruler should first govern himself.

He who has ascended to the summit of royal dignity by the grace of God should remember that he whom divine will has ordained to rule others should first rule himself. *Rex* is from the verb *regere*, to rule.[4] A man may know that he is rightly addressed by the title of king if he does not fail to rule himself with reason. Hence, let an orthodox king strive with utmost effort so that he who desires to command his subjects well and determines to correct others' errors may not himself commit the evils he strictly reproves in others and may endeavor to practice before all the virtues which he enjoins upon them. Moreover, a just ruler commendably rules himself in six ways: first of all, when he restrains with severity the illicit designs of the will; second, when he considers useful counsels pertaining both to his own benefit and to that of his people; third, when he avoids issuing idle, useless or noxious trifles of inane speech; fourth, when he savors with his mind's palate, more than honey and the honeycomb, both the prudence and words of glorious princes as well as the words of divine scripture; fifth, when he is fearful of committing any dishonor of a pernicious deed; and sixth, when he notably performs lofty deeds whether praiseworthy or of glorious spirit so that he who shines inwardly before the Lord with a devout will may also shine publicly before the people in word and action.

It is fitting for a ruler to observe a threefold rule, namely fear, order, and love. Unless he is equally feared and loved, his rule will in no way stand firm. A ruler, therefore, should attend to good offices and kindness that he may be loved, and should seek to be feared by justly avenging, not offenses against himself, but offenses against the law of God. It behooves such a ruler to be humble in his own eyes, just as it is written: "They have appointed you ruler. Do not permit yourself to be elevated, but, rather, be among them like one of themselves" (Ecclus. 32:1). To be rightly called ruler, he must rule justly not only over men, but also over the passions of his body and mind, just as a certain wise man once said: "Whoever acts properly will be king; whoever acts improperly will not."[5] Let the ruler be most prudent in counsel, at one time in conversation, as reason demands, awesome, but more frequently affable by the grace of sweetness. Let him be a conqueror of sensuality, a victor over pride and savage ferocity, a friend of good men, an enemy of tyrants, and an enemy of criminals and their crimes. Let him be most prudent in war, most steadfast in peace, and most trustworthy in faithful promises. Let him place the divine ahead of the human, deterring his subjects from evil and urging them to good; rewarding with abundance and absolving with compassion; and making good men out of evil ones and excellent men out of good ones.

A ruler should be holy and of benefit to the state; praiseworthy in kindness; notable for every goodness and distinguished in piety, fortitude, morality, and justice; and a man most honorable and worthy of an imperial throne, always keeping the fear of God before his eyes and weighing his judgments according to the just decrees of the Almighty who grants salvation to kings and performs whatever he wishes in heaven and on earth and towards every creature. For, He is the lord of all things, and before him everything in heaven, on earth, and in the infernal regions bends its knee. And in his hand rests all power in heaven and on earth, since he is the King of Kings and the hope for glory of all who rule justly and piously.

> He who rules the passions of his will and subdues the
> dissolute lures of the flesh is rightly called a king.
> Although a king holds a glorious place in marks of honor,
> who by his strength overcomes a tawny lion,
> yet it is more praiseworthy to subdue insolent pride,
> and to tame anger as if it were a ferocious beast.
> That ruler is called great who has crushed fierce enemies
> and as a victor, crowned in laurel, brings back gleaming trophies;
> but there is greater glory for a ruler decked with heavenly
> arms who is able to conquer invisible enemies.   10
> The power to bridle the mind through art is greater
> than possessing the might of the triple world;
> for a just king's heart shines like the temple of the Lord,
> and it is the throne of God, the heavenly judge.
> That abode gleams more precious than yellow gold
> and delights in possessing its beacon of justice.

Chapter III.
The art and diligence by which
a transitory kingdom can remain stable.

Wise men have judged the transitory kingdom of this world to be like the turning of a revolving wheel. For just as the turning of a wheel that at one moment presses down what it holds at the top and at another raises up what it holds at the bottom, so the glory of an earthly kingdom sustains sudden rises and sudden falls and, therefore, contains not real but imaginary and fleeting honors. Only that kingdom is real which endures forever. Now the earthly kingdom, because it is transitory and fleeting, never reveals the truth but only some slight semblance of the truth and of the eternal kingdom. In fact, just as a rainbow, which adorns the vault of heaven with dazzling colors, quickly disappears, so, to be sure, the honor of worldly fame, howevermuch adorned for the moment, is sooner fleeing away.

With what art, therefore, with what action, and with how much vigilance can this transitory kingdom be held to some form of stability? Can an earthly kingdom be kept stable, perhaps, either by violent force of arms or by the tranquil harmony of peace? On the contrary, in the arms and rumblings of war there is great instability. What is more uncertain and more unstable than military campaigns, where there is no sure outcome to the wearisome combat and no victory assured, where often more illustrious men are overthrown by lesser ones, and where equal misfortunes sometimes befall both sides, who both expect victory but in the end enjoy nothing but calamitous miseries? Who can explain how many evils occur under the false name of peace, when even that peace believed constant and firm among good men is sometimes transformed by the perverse counsels of the wicked into destructive tumults of discord, and whence great instability appears in a transitory peace!

What else remains, therefore, except that a king's heart and complete confidence should be fixed not in the force of arms and men nor in the deception of transitory peace, but, rather, in the mercy of the Almighty who knows how to uphold the kingdom he granted in both adversity and prosperity? And so, the prince's heart and constant devotion in governing his office should not withdraw from that Lord who has conferred upon him such great favor and a glorious ministry. For if the Most High Ruler should see a prince unfaithful, whom He has ordained his faithful servant, He might angrily pluck from that prince the office which He conferred upon him. For if an earthly king can rescind his authority from any unfaithful man and bestow it on another whom he knows to be more faithful, how much more can the divine Ruler of all men, whom the clouds of no man's treachery can deceive, withdraw his favors from false men and bestow them on others known to be proper servants of his will? Thus the impious King Saul of Israel was deprived of his kingdom and his life because he did not stand before the Lord as a faithful minister; however, the Almighty found David a man truly chosen after his own heart, and so He raised David to the summit of royal power because He chose him in the foreknowledge that he would be a faithful minister. A prudent ruler, therefore, should strive to keep his heart steadfast in the grace of the Most High if he wants the transitory kingdom entrusted to him to maintain some appearance of stability. And, since the Lord is just and merciful, and must be adhered to with a devout heart, a ruler should display manifold works of mercy that he might obtain a great and glorious reward. Let him both cherish and maintain justice, and let him scorn unjust and evil deeds among his subjects and correct them with a zeal which is praiseworthy and in accord with wisdom. So long as a ruler is steadfast in divine precepts, his kingdom becomes more and more stable in this world and is led with divine help to the eternal joys of stability.

> As a turning wheel swiftly revolves and
> presses in cycle its highest points downward,
> which it rotates in fickleness on
>   its axle,
>
> so the powers of the earth, throughout the triple world,
> are unable to maintain the lofty summit of glory
> when it has fallen away, though they have come to
>   cherish golden sceptres.
>
> The splendid glory of the kingdom of Israel's
> illustrious people had been raised on high   10
> so long as it preserved the sacred and mystical
>   powers of the law;
>
> whence it prevailed in the triumphs of the
> Lord and overcame fierce enemies,

while the Thunderer's kindness glorified
his people.

Alas! The sacred holy land of father Abraham was
laid low by innumerable catastrophes whenever
its people scorned to bend their necks to
the Creator.   20

But the sole remedy of such a people was at once
to entreat the Most High with prayers,
for he alone has the power to uphold kingdoms
with perpetual will.

Princes of this world, joyfully offer the incense
of prayer to our Almighty Lord and magnify him
before whom the supernal princes of
heaven tremble.

Chapter IV.
Royal authority should not be embellished so much with power and bold strength as with wisdom and pious discipline.

All royal power, which has been divinely established for the benefit of the state, should be embellished not so much with vain powers and earthly might as with wisdom and the veneration of God. For, if the eminence of the king is adorned by religion and wisdom, then, without a doubt, the people will be governed by the art of prudent counsel, enemies will be cast down by a merciful Lord and both the provinces and the kingdom will be preserved. Indeed, God intended this to be the nature of man, that he should desire and seek after two things, namely religion and wisdom. Moreover, devout wisdom is the most salutary virtue, the light of pious souls, a heavenly gift and a joy which will last forever. Whoever, therefore, wants to rule gloriously, to govern the people wisely, and to be mighty in counsels should seek wisdom from the Lord who gives abundantly and ungrudgingly to all. And let him strive for such wisdom with zealous effort and love so that this saying: "Blessed the man who finds wisdom, and who abounds in understanding" (Prov. 3:13), as well as other things which are enumerated among the praises of wisdom may distinguish him. For that blessed ruler truly merits praise who is illumined with the splendor of wisdom which is the source of counsels, the font of sacred religion, the crown of princes and the mother of virtues, and compared to it all the glitter of precious gems is deemed worthless. Wisdom is most prudent in counsels, remarkable in eloquence, manificent in deeds, strong in adversity, moderate in prosperity, and perspicacious in judgments. It adorns those who love it with heavenly grace and makes them shine like the heavenly firmament, as it is written: "Just men will shine like the stars, and wise men like the heavenly firmament" (Wisd. 3:7; Dan. 12:3).

Wisdom exalted Solomon above all the kings of the earth, for he cherished it from his youth and became a lover of its beauty. Hence, as it is written in the Book of Kings, the Lord appeared to Solomon in a dream one night and said: "Ask something of me and I will give it to you" (1 Kings 3:5). When Solomon, though just a boy, requested a discerning heart that he might judge the Lord's people and distinguish between good and evil, he received this response from God: "Since you have asked for the word, and since you have not asked for a long life for yourself or riches or the lives of your enemies but for the wisdom for a discerning judgment, here and now I have done what you asked. I have given you a heart so wise and shrewd that there has never been anyone like you up till now, and after you there will come no one to equal you. I have also granted you what you did not ask for, namely wealth and glory, so that not one of all the kings of former days can compare with you. And I will give you long life, if you follow my ways and keep my laws and commandments, just as your father, David, followed them" (1 Kings 3:10–14). O how ineffable is the bountifulness of divine grace! For, if divine grace is sought with a just heart and a pious intention, it gives more than what is asked. Lo, King Solomon asked for neither gold, nor silver, nor any other earthly treasures but rather for the riches of wisdom; moreover, he who had rightly requested a single gift received double, for he was not only enriched with wisdom, but was exalted by the illustrious glory of kingship. Hence, an excellent example is given to the kings of the earth: if they wish to reign long and prosperously in this world, let them ask with a pious heart for spiritual rather than carnal gifts. It befits a prince worthy of God's love, therefore, to have the will to learn and the desire of heavenly things; thus, he truly sets his heart in God's hand and will peacefully rule his kingdom by God's grace throughout a multitude of years.

> A ruler who wishes to be an upright judge,
> who rejoices in the scale and balance of justice,
> and who is eager to pierce falsehoods with a spear
>   of glorious truth,
>
> should call upon the Father of Light, who created the
> fiery sun and moon, and the glittering cosmos,
> that he might shine in thoughts radiant with
>   wisdom's light.
>
> Let him study the prayers of impartial Solomon,
> which flew suddenly through the heavens and   10
> penetrated the golden palace of the
>   Lord of Hosts.
>
> Did not Solomon, enlightened with understanding,
> acquire a skillful judgment, whereby he wisely
> governed upon the royal summit of the
>   Hebrew people?

Of what worth is all the glitter of yellow gold,
and of what value are the purples of
crimson adornment, honors and Scythian gems and
    a diadem,   20

if sharpness of mind, neglected, becomes dull
so that it cannot perceive the true light by
which it may discriminate between good, evil, justice,
    right and wrong?

Hence, the glory of a ruler is to love you,
O Christ, the Word of the Father and Sage Light,
for you reign supreme over the earth and the
    heavenly kingdoms.

In your right hand abides blessed peace
and in your left abundant treasures.   30
You are the Prince of Glory who crowns the humble
    and overthrows the rich.

Chapter V.
The duty of pious guidance which a ruler ought to fulfill with regard to his wife, his children, and his household.

A pious and wise king performs the office of ruling in three ways: as we have shown above, he should first rule himself with reasonable and meritorious discipline; second, his wife, his children, and his household; and third, the people entrusted to him. Hence, a just prince must not only rule himself, while he rejects evils and chooses and firmly upholds what is good, but he must also direct others more closely related to him, namely, his wife, his children, and his household with prudent care and familial affection. And by accomplishing this, a prince attains a double palm of glory in that when he himself is just and holy, he makes others related to him just and holy too, in accordance with the psalmist who said: "You will be pure with the pure and blameless with the man who is blameless" (Ps. 18:26). For it does not suffice to possess personal honor, unless it is embellished with the propriety of a chaste and modest wife, and with the propriety of children, friends, and servants, as David said: "He who walks in immaculate ways served me" (Ps. 101:6). Just as a lily of the field is enhanced in beauty by the manifold beauty of other plants and of violets and just as the moon shines more pleasingly in the glow of the surrounding stars, so, truly, a just and wise king is greatly adorned by the fellowship of other good men.

A ruler, therefore, should perspicaciously endeavor to have a wife who is not only noble, beautiful and wealthy, but also chaste, prudent, and compliant in holy virtues. For, so much as a wife is closer (to a man) in law, to that extent she becomes either noxious with the poison of wickedness or pleasing with the sweetness of morals. To be sure, a foolish wife is the ruin of a household, the exhaustion of wealth, the fullness of crimes, and the abode of all evils and vices, who ornaments her exterior mien with diverse observances, but knows not how to adorn the interior beauty of her soul. Whomever she loves today, she hates tomorrow, just as a certain man once said: "A wife unfaithful to her husband is the shipwreck of all things."[6] However, a chaste and prudent wife, diligently attending to useful matters with a humble demeanor and cheerful speech, peacefully manages her children and family; and, on behalf of her husband's welfare, if necessary, she sets her life against death and defends his wealth with an honorable reputation. Whoever was her friend yesterday is her friend today. In effect, she becomes the increase of wealth, the support of the household, the delight of her husband, the glory of the family, and the union of all virtues. Indeed, it is proper for such a one not only to be bound and subservient to her husband with a chaste bond, but also to reflect always an image of holiness and pious behavior, and to be an inventress of prudent counsels. Just as by the persuasion of an evil wife pernicious dangers are begotten, so by the counsel of a prudent wife many benefits are produced that are pleasing to the Almighty, whence the apostle said: "The unbelieving husband will be saved by a believing wife" (1 Cor. 7:14).

Not only unbelieving but also pious and orthodox princes often ponder and give heed to the marvelous prudence in their wives, not reflecting on their fragile sex, but, rather, plucking the fruit of their good counsels. Hence, it is said about Placilla, the venerable wife of the glorious emperor Theodosius, that through her the prince, though he himself was upright, just and wise, enjoyed another useful opportunity by which he might triumph from good works. His wife, having instructed herself completely beforehand, often admonished the prince concerning divine laws. She was not puffed up by the dignities of royal power but was inflamed by divine love. In fact, the abundance of blessings she received increased her love for her benefactor; and indeed, she came unexpectedly to high station. She took the greatest care of the crippled and lame, but not by using slaves or other servants; rather, she acted through herself, coming to their dwellings and offering to each what he needed. In this way visiting the hospitals of the churches, she ministered to the sick with her own hands, cleaning their pots, tasting broth, offering spoonfuls, breaking bread, serving food, washing cups, and doing all the other things which are customarily performed by slaves and servants. To those who tried to restrain her from such things she would say: "It is the office of our emperor to distribute gold; but I offer this service on behalf of that Emperor who has conferred upon me so many blessings." Moreover, to her husband she would often say: "You should always remember, my husband, what you once were and what you are now. If you always remember these things, you will never be ungrateful to your benefactor, but will lawfully rule the empire you have received and will appease the author of all these things."[7] And, with such words, she presented to her husband some useful profit and abundant virtue.

> A pious and wise king rules himself, his family, and
> his subjects with threefold direction.
> A wife virtuous in morals stands forth as the glory of the king

like a fruitful vine.
Nobility in threefold virtue should beautify her with the
    roses of a chaste heart;
for if milk-white necks glisten with lovely elegance,
    chastity should glisten even more.
As Christ united the Church to him with a chaste love,
    so a wife should cleave to her husband;   10
in her heart gentle simplicity like the beauty of a dove
    should always abound.
Piety, prudence, and sacred authority should adorn her,
    just as gracious Esther shone.[8]
A king and queen should cherish the bonds of peace;
    in both there should be agreement and concord.
Hateful discord must not separate the pair whom the divine
    law of peace has joined together.
Discipline should rule their glorious offshoots
    so that seemly branches may flourish.   20
A withered young branch never thrives on a vigorous tree.
    A good cultivator provides for this:
if a ruler and his queen are to rule the people justly,
    let them first rule their own family.
Let them decorate the heavens with descendants created as if from
    the noble stock of Abraham.

Chapter VI.
Counselors and friends that are suitable for a just prince.

In human affairs no art, as they say, is more difficult than to rule well amidst the stormy tempests of this turbulent world and to govern the state wisely. And this art attains its highest degree of perfection when the state itself has prudent and superlative counselors. Three rules, however, ought to be observed in deliberations. The first is that divine counsels should be preferred over human ones, since it is more important to heed God than men. If anyone, therefore, intends and desires to guide the ship of state successfully as a just ruler, let him not fail to observe the excellent counsels of the Lord which have been set forth in Holy Scriptures. The second rule is that a wise ruler should rely not so much on his own counsel as upon that of his most prudent counselors. Whence, the eminent maxim of the emperor Antoninus in deliberations was always: "It is better that I follow the counsel of so many excellent friends than that so many such friends should follow my will alone."[9] Solomon also confirms this, saying "Plans come to naught where there is no counsel; where there are many counselors they succeed" (Prov. 15:22), and "There will be security where there are many counsels" (Prov. 11:14). For a prudent man summons other prudent men into counsel and does nothing without their advice; but a foolish man deliberates by himself and does whatever he hastily desires without the counsel of others. Finally, the third rule in counsels to be observed is that a just ruler should not have deceitful and pernicious counselors. Who, indeed, should trust in the counsels of the wicked? For, just as holes in the midst of fields, and pitfalls in open thoroughfares, and unexpected snares impede the feet of travelers, so do the counsels of the wicked mixed with villainous poisons evilly hinder the just and holy in their paths. And just as good counselors raise the state upwards, so evil ones press it downwards in ruinous calamity. Such wicked counselors, therefore, should be in every way repudiated and detested, since those who scorn God's commandments by living evilly will never be devoted to an earthly prince. Indeed, for whom can those who are evil to themselves be of any benefit?

However, just as the most salubrious counsels and precepts of Almighty God should be made known, it is also true that sometimes the plans of prudent rulers should be kept secret from their enemies. For there are no better counsels in the state than those of which an adversary is ignorant. And, without doubt, a journey is safe if the enemy hasn't any idea that it is being undertaken. Two things, however, are especially contrary to counsel, namely, haste and anger; for anger blinds the judgment so that it may not discern useful counsel. And, as lengthy counsels do not lead to repentance, so do hasty counsels usually lead to ruin. Counsel, on the other hand, is especially brought to a successful outcome, when a king's trust is fixed in the support of the Almighty. After God, whence come good counsels if not from faithful and excellent friends who merit being enlightened with supernal grace lest they err in counsel, and by whose prudent deliberation inspired by divine mercy the grape of good counsel is often plucked? It is improper for a just ruler to keep friends who are cruel tyrants like dangerous serpents, which the example of the panther demonstrates. For the panther belongs to the class of quadrupeds and, as naturalists assert, is the friend of all animals except the serpent. And so, let all rulers maintain the friendship of those whom they know to be virtuous. Who, moreover, are good friends unless they are holy and venerable, not malicious, thievish, seditious, or crafty, or conspiring to evil, or enemies of good men, or lustful, or cruel, or deceivers of their prince—but, rather, pious, continent, and religious men who love their prince, who neither mock him themselves nor wish him to be mocked by others, who neither cheat nor deceive, and who never beguile, being always truthful, sober, prudent and faithful to their prince in all things? Through such worthy men, therefore, the state prospers, and the fame and glory of a pious ruler increase.

> Just as a ship without a rudder flounders in the deep,
>   and is buffeted about by swollen winds and waves,
> so, without counsel, alas, glorious sovereignty and
>   splendid dominions collapse and fall to ruin.
> For there are some whose words are charming and, yet,
>   beneath lie hidden the hideous poisons of an asp.
> They urge all things with soothing speech,
>   and their words are murmured like a deceitful snare.
> By their counsel the state seems firmly supported,
>   whereas it may collapse in ruin, O woeful misery!   10

Hence, it behooves him who holds supreme power
   to pluck now the sweet grape of counsel.
Like gazelles on a mountaintop who are ever watchful and
   quickly flee when they catch sight of any dangers,
so a just ruler with sound judgment and wise counsels
   is vigilant and discerning in foreseeing adversity.
As an excellent pearl is obtained from thirsty oysters
   and honey is gathered from sweetly flowing honeycombs,
so useful counsel, which is fitting and beneficial, should be
   drawn from the pure font of faithful friends.   20
The true guardian of friendship proves to be without gall,
   and what is good pleases him but what is evil does not.
He truly knows how to say "it· is so, it is so" or "no, no,"
   and in him a secret heart and pious mouth are in one accord.
To him steadfast faith is dearer than life itself;
   he cannot weave cunning tricks in his mind.
The blare of trumpets does not make him waver,
   for a steady anchor abides in a faithful heart.
Neither riches nor weights of gold can deceive him,
   lest his precious trust be violated.   30

Chapter VII.
Why princes become evil.

Now order demands that we touch briefly upon evil princes, since we have already related useful matters about just princes and what is needed to govern the state. Hence, it is first asked, what cause transforms good princes into evil ones? In this regard, it may be said: first, royal licence; second, abundance of wealth, since great wealth becomes the root of evils; third, wicked companions, detestable attendants, greedy eunuchs, and foolish and despicable courtiers through all of whom there springs up, even in that ruler who seemed just, forgetfulness of God's commands; and finally, it can not be denied, ignorance of public affairs. Thus, four or five men gather together, and they form one plan to deceive the emperor or king. They tell him what ought to be approved; the emperor, shut up in his dwelling, is unaware of the truth and is forced to know only what those men tell him. He appoints unfit judges and removes those from the state who ought to be retained. Whence, even a just, cautious, and glorious emperor is betrayed, and is made miserable because around him truths are concealed. For often by tumultuous disorder both piety and truth, the handmaidens of God, are oppressed, since slander greatly prevails when detractors are believed worthy of trust whom a twofold and cruel disease corrupts, namely, love of falsehood and hatred of truth.

   Like a turbulent storm, an excessive abundance of
   riches has the effect of subverting rulers.

For rulers who at first are illustrious in governing
often become evil with wicked intentions.
Men who in character were precious gold
soon appear base and horrid like lead;
and those rich with the fruitfulness of the grape arbor
grow wild like the scorned wild vine.
Moreover, greedy companions with evil
dispositions deceive a reckless lord,   10
whence that once honorable lord by many deceptions
becomes ambivalent, wavering like a reed.
And wretched, he is ignorant of falsehood's tricks,
nor do the lights of truth illumine such a lord;
for honors, gold, wealth, subterfuges, lies,
the seductive charms of a woman's face,
lying loved ones, pomp, and power
are ever blinding the eyes of the king.

Chapter VIII.

Greedy and impious kings,
and how many punishments on their account
divine vengeance inflicts upon the people or themselves.

Now it seems appropriate that we examine some things relating to impious rulers, so that having recognized their maliciousness as well as their most wretched end in this world and perpetual damnation, a prudent ruler, by abstaining from evil deeds, may become more careful and good, and may also strive earnestly to please the Most High Benefactor. What, moreover, are impious kings if not the greatest thieves of the earth, ferocious like lions and fierce like bears? Of such men it is written: "Like a roaring lion and a hungry bear is the wicked prince over an impoverished people" (Prov. 28:15). For an impious king, like a lion, sharply answers every petition with good-for-nothing and malicious words unsupported by the advice of prudent men, abusing the just and exalting the evil; his days are shortened, and his memory will pass away like a sound; and, indeed, he has been more sinful than capable. Accordingly, such men are friends of the evil, enemies of the just, slaves of lust and avarice, slaves of every wickedness, and ministers of the devil, always laboring and yet producing nothing; raging abysses, afflictions of the human race, fodder of everlasting hell, like a cedar, suddenly exalted, but soon cast down into the depths of Tartarus. Thus, the psalmist says: "I saw an impious man exalted above others and raised up like a cedar of Lebanon, and as I passed by, lo! he was no more. I sought him, but his location was not to be found" (Ps. 37:35–36). Indeed, impious princes prosper like the green things and the plants of the field which spring forth in beauty and tomorrow wither and are not seen again. Hence, it is said through the prophet: "Those men ruled, but not by my authority; princes came forth, but I disregarded them" (Hos. 8:4). They neither know nor wish to walk along the right and royal way but rather prefer to turn off to the right or left. What the Lord spoke through Isaiah fits them: "They have forsaken the Lord of Hosts, and they have walked in twisted paths" (Isa. 1:4 and Prov. 2:13). Such men are deceitful in counsels, fierce and deceptive in speech, and evil in deeds; moreover, their end will be in accordance with their deeds. Again, the prophet Isaiah says of them: "The Lord of Hosts has planned to this end in order that he may disgrace the pride of majesty and lead all the illustrious men of the world to shame" (Isa. 23:9). Blessed Job also says: "The fame of the impious is short and the glory of the hypocrite lasts for but an instant" (Job 20:5). And so, this temporal life compared to eternity is likened to the shortest moment. Woe, furthermore, to those who exchange the glory of eternal felicity for the short moment of present happiness!

How many evils on their account divine vengeance inflicts upon the people or the rulers themselves, we are unable to expound, but it is appropriate to divulge a few examples out of many. The impiety of King Pharaoh, which had grown from the hardness of his heart, brought on ten plagues to himself and to the Egyptian people and submerged both Pharaoh and his men under the Red Sea and to the lowest depth of infernal Acheron. Who does not know how great the vengeance of a severe judge that overthrew Antiochus,[10] Herod, and Pontius Pilate? What may I say about Nero,[11] Egea,[12] and the most impious Julian,[13] and others so alike in their wickedness? Has not the mouth of hell devoured them all with their followers after a most horrible death? In order, however, that I may pass over countless examples, I will treat of the miserable departure from this world of the most cruel King Theodoric.[14]

Because Theodoric was an adherent of the Arian heresy and a persecutor of good Christians, in the latter end, just as it had been revealed to a certain holy man, he was led unclothed, barefoot, and with bound hands before Pope John[15] and noble Symmachus[16] and was cast into the Vulcanian cauldron. For since he had killed Pope John by torture in prison and had also slain noble Symmachus by sword, Theodoric was cast into the fire by those whom he had unjustly condemned in this life. O how severe and just are the judgments of the Almighty whose fitting vengeance has pursued the savage tyrant with relentless determination! For he who unjustly inflicted a transitory death upon the Lord's servants justly perished with the twofold death of the body and the soul; and he who had despoiled others of this present life had himself been deprived of temporal as well as eternal life. And so, he has accomplished a twofold service: for himself he has won the torment of hell, where he will be tortured for an eternity of ages, and for the holy he has won the palm of divine glory. The unjustly condemned become suddenly crowned and judges too, sent by God against the cruel tyrant; however, he who has given a false judgment becomes suddenly condemned and delivered over to the flames of eternal damnation. In this case, therefore, a terrifying example is set forth so that the powers of the earth may not persecute the Lord's servants whom Almighty God avenges with the mighty arm of his power. More may be said on the subject of wicked rulers; but now, in my following remarks, let us pass to more important matters.

Are not kings of the earth
disgraced by evil deeds compared
to wild boars, bears, and tigers?
Are they not the greatest thieves
on earth, or savage lions, or
rapacious hawks with sharp claws?
It befell Antiochus, Pharaoh, Herod
and miserable Pilate to lose their
transitory kingdoms and to sink
with their companions to hell: 10
hence, severe punishments always afflict such
wicked men both here and in eternity.
Why do you wreath your brow with flowers
and adorn yourself with glittering purple?
For the fiery furnace awaits you below
which even showery rain will not abate.
Inasmuch as you do not love the Lord of Light
you will pass away into the outer darkness.
There your parched glory
will forever wither away;   20
but a heavenly crown and blessed
light will glorify the just.

Chapter IX.
The peaceable and compassionate king
or those to whom favors should be given.

There are seven things more beautiful than God's other creations, as wise men
say: the cloudless sky, when it marvelously resembles the color of silver; the sun in
its brilliance, when in its orbit it illumines the world's inhabitants with its glorious
splendor; the moon in its fullness with its face uncovered by the retreating clouds,
when in its proper course it follows in the tracks of the sun; the fruitful field, when it
is painted with a multitude of flowers and curling buds; the perpetual motion of the
sea, when the serenity of the heavens and the clouds is beautifully reflected in the
waves as they softly touch the shores; the multitudes of just men dwelling together
in one faith; and a peace-loving king in the glory of his reign, when in the royal hall
he bestows many kindnesses with rewards displayed and gifts distributed.[17] For a
just and peaceable king distributes gifts with a joyous countenance and diligently
considers anyone's cause, despising neither the sick nor the indigent among the
people. Moreover, being veracious, he pronounces verdicts with counsel and judg-
ment of mature and prudent men, abasing evil men and exalting the good. His days
will be lengthened with glory, and his memory will last forever. A peaceable prince is
like a flowery and fertile paradise near at hand and like a noble vine overflowing with
abundant fruit, confounding every discord by the splendor of his presence. For, when

he cherishes peace in the royal hall of his heart, without doubt he prepares a mansion for Christ, since Christ is peace and desires to dwell in peace. Furthermore, where there is peace, there is found truth in debates and justice in actions. Hence, just as a prudent pilot strives to evade the dangers of a turbulent sea with the favorable calm of the weather, so does a peaceable ruler with careful deliberation strive to restrain violent discords by serene tranquillity of mind and peaceful harmony. And so, it behooves a prince to preserve the threefold rule of peace, that is to say, above himself, in himself and near himself, for he should be peaceable toward God, within himself, and toward those around him.

The goodness of peace is so great, indeed, that even in earthly and mortal affairs nothing is wont to be heard with more pleasure, nothing more desirable can be sought, and, finally, nothing more beneficial can be found. The fruit of the peaceable heart, however, is to display benevolent compassion and mercy towards subjects and friends, by which virtues both a pious ruler and his kingdom may be gloriously preserved, as is attested by Solomon, who says: "Compassion and truth preserve the king, and his throne will be strengthened by mercy" (Prov. 20:28). Truly, there is nothing that better commends a just ruler to the people as favorable and worthy of love than mercy and peaceful concord. Such mercy, although I will omit other examples for brevity's sake, made Augustus Caesar renowned; and it eminently blessed the Antonines, Constantine the Great, Theodosius I and Theodosius II, and other distinguished princes. It also, among other marks of virtue, consecrated Charles the Great, the most venerated emperor before all the princes of the earth; and adorned the most pious emperor Louis. Why need I give further examples? Certainly the serene mercy of piety has both glorified illustrious princes on earth and established them in fellowship with the saints in heaven; for they have dedicated not only their possessions, but also their very persons entirely to Almighty God.

Nothing, however, ought to be granted by a just and pious king unless it be a kindness. But a kindness, if one looks for some repayment in this world, perishes and comes to naught. For we are not able to keep the merit of a kindness intact when we are repaid for it, since such largesse is not rightly called a kindness so much as, rather, a business transaction. Favors should be granted which afterwards do not impair the reputation, piety, and justice of a good prince. They should be given according to each person's merits and the utility of things and not in accordance with the greediness of the takers who do not easily deny themselves, since whatever is difficult or impossible, they wickedly and cruelly demand. Thus the emperor Nerva used to say: "Friends presume to merit all things for themselves, and, if they have not extorted something, they become even more atrocious."[18] Hence, in every dispensing of gifts let a moderate proportion and just intention be observed in the giver so that on behalf of the state's prosperity, the Church's benefit, and the attainment of heavenly glory all things may be distributed through the munificence of a serene prince to good men, better men, and the best men.

> The divine founder of the world, the Emperor of all things,
> and the sole Creator made everything he created beautiful.
> Among these creations there are seven which are more beautiful:

the painted sphere of heaven in the dazzling beauty of its light,
the bounteous and radiant glory of the sun among the stars,
the moon filled with light beneath a twin-horned garland,
the fruitful and flourishing garden with its flowers in bloom,
the serenity of the sea soothing the images of all things,
the multitude of the pious worshipping you, O God,
and the ruler glorious and illustrious in all things.   10
Generous and serene and endowed with holiness,
such a ruler stands pre-eminent in justice and purity of heart.
Before him those blinded by arrogance and falsehoods tremble.
He graciously honors the just with royal generosity,
and, peaceful and blessed, he becomes a noble vine;
he is the image of the Trinity, worthy of the state of Heaven.

Chapter X.
The many pillars which support the kingdom of a just prince.

In considering these things it should also be understood, as wise men hold, that there are eight pillars which strongly support the kingdom of a just king. The first pillar is truth in all royal affairs; the second pillar is patience in every matter; the third, generosity in gifts; the fourth, persuasiveness or affability in speech; the fifth, the correction or suppression of evil men; the sixth, the friendship and exaltation of good men; the seventh, the lightness of tribute imposed upon the people; and the eighth, the equality of justice between the rich and the poor. And so, there are eight pillars which both uphold the kingdom of a just king in this world and guide him to the immutability of eternal glory.

No building keeps stable through the ages
    if it cannot depend upon its supports.
These pillars can sustain temples gleaming with light,
    but without them the palace of kings cannot stand firm.
Hence, to stand firm upon the sound pillars of a just ruler,
    the state calls upon the favor of God.
The first pillar shines bright with the beauty of truth,
    while patient rule rightly holds second place.
The third, with a generous right hand, gives gifts to the deserving,
    and the fourth, eloquence, utters pleasing words.   10
The fifth restrains evil men and gleams with wondrous zeal,
    and the sixth, mighty, joyously glorifies the just.
The seventh mercifully lightens the people's tribute,
    and the eighth weighs the scale of justice.
The state, supported, rests on these sturdy pillars,
    and, like Mount Zion, remains stable upon them.

Chapter XI
Why a just prince should support ecclesiastical causes
with benevolent and vigorous solicitude,
and concerning synodal assemblies.

Since the summit of royal power is sustained by these eight pillars, it behooves a ruler worthy of God's love to subordinate his personal interests to what will benefit the Church so that in so far as he is mindful of God's blessings which divine favor has bestowed upon him, to such a degree he may honor the giver of such blessings. A just prince is then known to honor the Most High when he shows himself the helper and protector of those who labor in the Lord's field, as it were, the stewards of the Great King. For, it is certain that the Almighty in his kindness will graciously dispose the affairs of an earthly prince to the degree He sees that prince solicitous with regard to His affairs, namely, those of Holy Church. Hence, a prudent ruler should strive to accomplish those things which are pleasing to God, if he desires that God may bring about those things which are prosperous and glorious to him. Moreover, such a ruler, with diligent care, should wisely plan to convene synodal assemblies two or three times every year, in order that what is known to pertain to the true worship of God, to the reverence of his churches, and to the honor of his priests, or what may have been committed against the Lord's commandments, in such a holy and harmonious assembly may be discussed. As a result, what has been done well may be corroborated, and, if wicked deeds have been committed, they may be corrected for the better. And, in that assembly, it is proper that the prefects themselves of the churches be examined as to how they perform their ministries, or how they both instruct the people entrusted to them with divine doctrine as well as inspire them with the example of holy behavior. If all these matters are subtly handled with harmonious peace and canonical justice, there arises a fruitful benefit to Holy Church, and for the venerable ruler, by whose benevolent deliberation and authority such matters are resolved, a garden of great merit is generated.

Indeed, a sacred council of bishops is the precious crown of a religious prince. In such a council the most famous emperor Constantine the Great, exulting in the Lord, gloried, for he assembled the holiest men from nearly all the nations under heaven and in which Christ's gospel is proclaimed, that is, more than three hundred bishops, radiant both in doctrine and miracles, to discuss the Catholic faith in one body, the Council of Nicaea. And so, the Christian practice has grown to such an extent that among all orthodox princes of the churches synods are convened to discuss the necessary services of Holy Church which should only be examined by synodal councils and determined by canonical decrees. It is essential, therefore, that a king be prudent, humble, and exceedingly careful lest he presume to judge anything with respect to ecclesiastical affairs before he examines synodal decrees. For ecclesiastical judgments are especially perilous before God unless they are administered with utmost justice, and particularly so, if the innocent are tried in their absence by false accusers and lying witnesses, since that is inconsistent with Christianity. Wherefore, we read in the Gospel: "Since when does our law judge a man without first hearing from him and knowing what he is about?" (John 7:51). Above all, therefore, a pious ruler, like a luminous eye, should perspicaciously attend to what is just and lawful according to the canonical decrees of holy bishops, and should apply to those which are true and upright the consent and support of authority. By no means should he pass judgment by himself in such matters, lest, perhaps, by erring he may incur some detestable offense in the sight of the Lord.

For this reason, the emperor Valentinian of blessed memory, when asked by the holy bishops to what extent he deigned to participate in the emendation of sacred dogma, said, "Since I am the least of the people, it is not right for me to examine such matters, but rather, priests, to whom this responsibility belongs, should be assembled among themselves in a place that they have chosen."[19] Moreover, the emperor, both endowed with the virtue of humility and fortified with the fear of God, said these things, lest he might, perhaps, offend the Most High by preferring his own judgments to better ones. As I mentioned earlier, the magnificent and most wise emperor Constantine[20] did this very thing by not trusting in himself, but rather in the prudence and wisdom of holy bishops. The blessed Jovianus,[21] a prince worthy of God's love, observed this with resolute faith; for, when he was an enemy of the Arian heresy and a follower of the decrees of the Nicaean Council, he procured for himself from the momentary height of an earthly kingdom the glory of an eternal one. What can I report about the two most blessed emperors, Theodosius I and Theodosius II,[22] and the manifestation of divine favor? They pleased God so much that with the Lord's inspiration, they subjected royal dignities, their authority, and the summit of imperial honor to divine precepts and canonical regulations and always maintained pious zeal towards the churches of God with indefatigable charity. Thus, the Lord of the universe exalted them in this world, and after the glory of their earthly happiness, blesses them forever in heaven as his beloved ministers. If anyone, however, would emulate the fame of such princes, if any Christian ruler wishes to reign prosperously and gloriously in this world and to attain the palm of eternal happiness, let him imitate the always faithful devotion of those emperors towards the worship of God; and let him show himself to be benevolent, merciful, strict in judgments, gentle in humility of heart, compassionate with heart-felt mercy, bounteous in liberality, and sparkling with a zeal for God's church in accord with His will, if he looks to reign perpetually with holy and just rulers among the citizens of heaven.

> A magnificent prince, whom God has exalted that he
> might preside over the people as a glorious sceptre-bearer,
> should duly pay homage to the Heavenly Throne, that is,
> the Creator who brought forth the cedars of Lebanon,
>
> who raises aloft the highest mountains,
> and who causes the fields to bud with flowers,
> and the Father who decorated the heavens with stars,
> the King of Heaven who stands above the Cherubim—
>
> he in his greatness ordains the kings of the earth.
> Hence, let a ruler distinguished with honors   10

which the God of heaven has conferred upon him
prudently strive to please Him who rules all things.

The mighty Judge who bestows the gift of kingship
glorifies the one who worships him in word,
with a pious heart, with guidance, and with morals,
and who willingly favors the Church of Christ.

The preserver of canons and the finest ruler
shines forth radiant in a garland of justice.
He is rightly king who, being holy, preserves the
sacred dogmas and decrees of the fathers in all things.   20

A multitude of bishops renders him illustrious
just as jewels glitter in a diadem,
milk-white lilies beautify a field,
and shining stars illuminate the heavens.

Chapter XII.
Why it is glorious for a pious ruler
to submit to the most beneficial
admonitions and reproofs of priests.

A virtuous ruler must become endowed with the weight of humility and with the virtue of obedience that he might perceive in himself the virtues, namely, humility and obedience, which he esteems in his subjects. And, thus, if it happens that he is censured by prudent men, let him bitterly lament that he, himself, is reprehensible and make haste to fly immediately to the remedies of penance; besides, he who has willingly sinned should freely and gladly accept the rod of correction, and before the Creator stirs his hand to strike, he should be extremely diligent in correcting the crime committed lest, afterwards, the severe judge strike that much more sharply in proportion to how much longer and mercifully he waits. If any ruler of a kingdom has sinned in private or in public, let him hasten to go before the face of the Lord in confession (Ps. 94:2) even as it is read concerning the holy king and prophet David. When David was censured by the prophet Nathan after his violation of Bathsheba and the murder of Uriah the Hittite, he was not angry at his accuser, but rather, acknowledging his sin, he immediately became furious at himself. And, he who grew merry after the crime was committed now bewailed himself with bitter penance. After that, by his tears, he who had perpetrated such grave crimes before the Lord obtained mercy and from the fountain of tears attained to abundant joy, just as he says elsewhere: "Those who sow in tears reap in exultation" (Ps. 125:5).

Still it does not seem proper to omit what is said about the wonderful humility and penance of the glorious prince Theodosius. For, when he had arrived in Milan after the ruthless slaughter of many thousands of people and had, as usual, wished to enter into the holy temple, blessed Ambrose, hearing about a disaster so full of anguish, confronted him outside at the doors and with these words prohibited the approaching emperor from entering the sacred threshold: "Do you not know, Emperor, how great is the magnitude of the slaughter you have made? And does your mind not perceive, after the occasion of such fury, its excessive presumption? But perhaps your imperial authority forbids the recognition of sin. With what eyes, therefore, will you behold the temple of our universal Lord? With what feet will you tread its sacred pavement? How will you lift up your hands from which innocent blood trickles even now? How will you receive the Lord's sacred body in such hands? How will you presume to raise the chalice of the precious blood to your mouth, when from the madness of your words so much blood has unjustly been shed? Withdraw, therefore, withdraw, lest you dare to augment prior wickedness with a second sin. Accept the bond which the Lord of all things has just now bound; it is, indeed, the greatest remedy for health."[23] The emperor yielded to these words—for he had been brought up with divine instructions and clearly recognized which are the prerogatives of priests and which of kings; and he returned, weeping and lamenting, to his palace.

And, when eight months had passed in succession, the celebration of our Savior's birth approached. The emperor, however, remaining at the palace in perpetual grief, shed an unceasing flood of tears. Moreover, Rufinus, then a controller who held a singular trust with the prince, upon entering and seeing the prince prostrated in sorrow, approached in order to inquire about the reasons for his tears. But the prince, most bitterly weeping and more vehemently shedding tears, said: "You, Rufinus, make sport and do not feel my sorrows. But I bewail and lament my misfortune, since the churches of God are opened to slaves and beggars who, readily entering, pray to their Lord, while I cannot even approach him. Moreover, even the heavens above have been closed to me." As the emperor spoke, he interrupted each word with sobs. When Rufinus tried to reconcile St. Ambrose with the emperor, he was, nevertheless, unable to do so. The emperor, receiving this news now in the middle of the street, said: "I am going on and acknowledge the just contumelies directly." And when he had reached the sacred lintels, Theodosius did not even presume to enter the holy basilica, but coming to the priest and finding him sitting in an audience chamber, he begged him to unbind his fetters. Ambrose, however, said that his presence was tyrannical and accused Theodosius of raving against God and scorning his laws. Then the emperor replied: "I do not rave against ecclesiastical decrees, nor do I seek to enter the sacred lintels improperly. On the contrary, I earnestly beseech you to release my fetters and to entreat for me the mercy of our common Lord, and not to keep closed against me the door which our Lord opened to all those repenting." But the priest said: "What sort of penance have you shown after such great crimes? With what medicines have you treated incurable wounds and injuries?" Then the emperor replied: "It is your office to teach and devise remedies, but mine to accept what you have adduced." When St. Ambrose heard the emperor's words, which demonstrated his humility and showed him ready to submit to the rigors of penance, he applied to the emperor the healing remedy for such wounds. When the emperor had received it, he returned many thanks to St. Ambrose. Hence, both the bishop and the emperor, both of whose deeds were admirable, shone forth with excellent and manifold virtue, particularly in the boldness and fervent zeal of the former and the obedience and pure faith of the latter. Furthermore, the emperor preserved the rules of piety he had received from that great priest even after returning to the city of Constantinople. For, when he had proceeded to the church at the time of a feast, having presented his gifts upon the altar, he immediately went outside. And when Nectareus, the bishop of the church, had sent to inquire why he had not wished to remain inside, the prince responded: "With difficulty I have been able to learn the difference between an emperor and a priest, and with difficulty I have found the master of truth; for I have recognized Ambrose alone to be rightly called bishop." Hence, so profitable is a rebuke uttered by a man abounding in virtues.

It is clear, therefore, that it behooves just and pious princes to heed the beneficial corrections of priests as spiritual doctors, humbly and willingly. This is declared by Solomon who says: "Like a golden earring or shining pearl is the man who censures the wise and obedient ear" (Prov. 25:12). It is better, moreover, to be reproached by a wise man than to be deceived by the flattery of fools. For, if we ardently desire that our bodily wounds be healed by doctors and in their presence we are not ashamed to reveal them, and in the pain of treatment we are comforted by the hope of cure, how much more ought we to have greater care for the wounds and injuries of our souls, until a spiritual physician can fully apply a remedy, however painful, through which we may have certain hope of our healing! In fact, just as a surgeon's scalpel is not evil simply because it cuts out the wounds and removes the putrid flesh, so, in the same way, correction is to our benefit.

> As the dawning light in the
> reddish sky from Phoebus' shining
> crown becomes pleasing to earth's
> inhabitants after night's gloomy clouds,
>
> as rain to the thirsty fields
> after summer's torrid heat,
> and flowery, serene spring
> after Boreas' fierce chills,
>
> so a preventative medicine effects
> a precious cure for the soul.   10
> As to those who now relieve panting
> afflictions with healing herbs,
>
> whereby they will have driven away
> the body's pains with keen, watchful care;
> if they dispense such potent medicines
> to weak flesh, the servant,

why does stronger medicine not
cure its honorable mistress,
by imitating the powers of making a
spirit able to rejoice in God?   20

Can anyone remove the wounds of
guilt without a skilled physician?
Let rulers beware, therefore, if they
have yielded in their heart to vices;

and let them consult skillful physicians
to whom they may learn to subject themselves,
and who as ministers of Christ's love
are able to drive away diseases.

They destroy harsh poisons with
oil and with salubrious wine   30
and also with celestial herbs gathered
from the garden of Paradise.

They even recall spirits from the underworld
with the word and a powerful staff
and lead them back with heaven's sacred
art to the pastures of life.

Chapter XIII.
The rational zeal, tempered with piety, of a just ruler.

It is not easy for men to avoid the manifold snares of the Enemy. For, insofar as
one has avoided the passion of lust, he runs into avarice. Avarice having been
shunned, the pitfall of envy is set. If he has crossed over this pit, he confronts the
vice of wrath; moreover, the Enemy sets many other traps by which he can ensnare
the foolhardy. And, to be sure, the Enemy easily manipulates the bodily passions as
ready servants in order that he might destroy the soul; but with divine help a vigilant
mind pulls apart the plots of his machinations. As I have said above, the emperor
Theodosius, having a common share in human nature, also possessed a mutual
share of man's passions, and by confusing cruelty with justifiable wrath, he became
a slave to excessive passion. For the reader's benefit, I shall recount the incident. The
city of Thessalonica is large and populous, and when civil discord had arisen in the
city, certain magistrates were stoned and dragged off. Angry at this, Theodosius did
not restrain the infirmity of his wrath, but rather ordered cruel swords to be drawn
against everyone and the innocent to be slain together with the guilty. In fact, it is
reported that seven thousand men were killed. There was no trial beforehand, but
they were all cut down at once like a harvest. As a result of this affair, St. Ambrose,

inflamed with holy zeal, gravely rebuked the emperor and condemned his irrational furor and nefarious crime with harsh reproofs.

It is appropriate, therefore, that a just and prudent ruler of the state always be on guard lest, by determining to avenge immoderately an injury to himself or to his followers, he may incur the guilt of irrational fury. Let him, rather, take great care to restrain his anger; and let him temper the incitements of just wrath with pious compassion lest he, perchance, take on the fury of a ferocious lion by raging against his subjects in excess of what is right. Thus it is written: "Do not be like a lion at home, overturning your household and oppressing your subjects" (Ecclus. 4:30). For it is just as necessary for a just and merciful ruler to spare his subjects as it is to vanquish those who are arrogant. In this regard the emperor Antoninus[24] asserted that he preferred to spare one citizen than to kill a thousand enemies. In punishing crimes, therefore, lenience should be blended with severity, and out of both a blend should arise so that subjects are neither exasperated by excessive harshness nor made lax by too much leniency.

No crime should bear the measure of correction or punishment unless proper judgment precedes it. Nor is it seemly for a tranquil ruler, if he desires to make a just judgment, to be confused by violent anger which is like poisonous gall, since judgments of the excessively wrathful are blind. For, whoever is clouded by the darkness of wrath cannot discern the clear light of justice and truth. Accordingly, the strong shield of forebearance should be opposed to the assult of irrational rage. As it is written, "a patient man is greater than a powerful one, and he who rules his temper, than he who is a conqueror of cities" (Prov. 16:32). He is definitely stronger who overcomes violence and rage, the beast confined within him, than he who kills a lion.

Who can recount the many evils which occur on account of sudden furor and the vice of intolerance? King Saul by not restraining his violent wrath slaughtered the priests of the Lord with savage cruelty.[25] Solomon, howevermuch he had been enlightened with the splendor of wisdom, nevertheless, became filled with the passion of rage and ordered his own brother killed, thus putting tyranny before piety.[26] What can I say about the wicked Jews? While they did have zeal, it was not in accordance with wisdom, and they came forth as murderers against the Son of God and his holy disciples. Blessed David, however, endowed with the virtue of patient compassion, often even spared his enemies with tender mercy, while sometimes, inflamed with the zeal of God, he drove the Lord's enemies to the destruction of death. It is appropriate, thus, for a prince beloved by God frequently to direct fiery zeal against the enemies and blasphemers of the Christian name. For, if King Nebuchadnezzar, a pagan, was so furious lest the God of Israel be reviled that he declared the following decree: "Those who have spoken blasphemy against the God of Shadrach, Meshach, and Abednego will be put to death and their homes brought to ruin" (Dan. 3:24), how much more ought orthodox princes to strive zealously against enemies of the Christian faith, doctrine, and religion? Thus they may all the more please the Almighty whose favor ordained them ministers by how much they more fervently endeavor to administer Christ's affairs with praiseworthy zeal!

After glorious labors
and laurel trophies,
when good fortune
auspiciously adorns a ruler

in a glistening toga of peace
and with a royal crown
gleaming with precious gems
and embellished with gold,

and when the decorous ranks
of the palace glitter in purple,   10
how often it happens that violent anger
disturbs the inner palace of his mind!

And within blazes a zeal
born of hidden furor;
a bronze pot does not boil,
raging at the heavens,

like the harsh mind of a
prince infected with poison.
The heart, unwilling to keep
moderation, rages like a lioness.   20

Hence, a ruler in his mind should mingle
incense burning with perfume of peace;
and let him remain tranquil by glowing
with a pleasing countenance.

There should be no judgment
before the truth is known;
for, when knowledge has been gained,
like a lamp the heart shines brightly.

Chapter XIV.
The Christian leader should trust neither in his own strength nor in that of his followers, but in the Lord.

When just rulers, however, strive to vanquish the arrogance of insolent tyranny in their adversaries, they should rely neither upon themselves nor upon their followers' strength, but rather, should fix their complete trust in the virtue and grace of the Most High, for He is the sole and powerful protector of all who faithfully confide in him. Thus, the prophet says: "It is better to trust in the Lord than to trust in men; it is better to confide in the Lord than to confide in princes" (Ps. 118:8–9). Elsewhere he says: "Do not trust in princes or in the sons of men in whom there is no salvation. Man's spirit will depart, and he will return to the earth from which he came" (Ps. 146:2–4). Jeremiah, too, is in accord with this, saying: "Lord, all those who abandon you will be confounded; those who turn from you in the land will be put to shame, since they have abandoned the Lord, the source of living waters" (Jer. 17:13) (and) "cursed is the man who trusts in man and seeks his strength in flesh and whose heart turns away from the Lord" (Jer. 17:5).

Let no one, therefore, trust in man or assume on account of power that no one is capable of resisting him. The Silurus[27] fish, for example, presumed that no one would throw a hook to him, and no one would extend nets, and that, if it happened, he would burst all things asunder. Nevertheless, he did not escape the spear. If, however, anyone marked with singular fortitude is unafraid on account of individual men, it is necessary, at the same time, that he fear many men. For, he who cannot be conquered by one man, is meanwhile conquered by many. The elephant is huge and he is slain; the lion is powerful and he is killed; the tiger is strong and he is slain. It is the part of a prudent ruler to fear and watch out for his inferiors, since superior and more powerful men are often overcome by their inferiors. How fierce is the crocodile and unbearable with his teeth and sharp nails! But he is slain in his belly by a small animal, the water snake. The unicorn stabs the elephant with its horn; the formidable elephant fears the mouse; the lion, king of beasts, is destroyed by the tiny sting of the scorpion. Hence, no man should rashly rely upon his own powers or, indeed, trust in the strength and numbers of his followers. Xerxes, the king of the Persians, prepared for a war against Greece, originally begun by his father, for five years. Xerxes is said to have had seven hundred thousand armed men from his kingdom and three hundred thousand from his auxiliaries, and also twelve hundred beaked ships; furthermore, he had transports numbering three thousand so that for the unexpected army and immense fleet it is rightly recounted that streams for drinking, lands for invasion, and seas for crossing were barely sufficient. However, Leonidas, the king of the Spartans, advanced to war with four thousand men against the innumerable thousands of Xerxes' troops; and, after wiping out the Persians' forces, Leonidas, a victor most illustrious in war, died with his few companions to save their country. After the disastrous outcome of the war in Greece, Xerxes, now contemptible to his followers, was surrounded in his palace and killed. For disgrace is the attendant of earthly glory and intractable pride. Accordingly, it is said by the prophet: "The Lord of Hosts has planned it so that he may remove the pride of all majesty and lead all the great ones of the earth to degradation" (Isa. 23:9). Let the strong man, therefore, not glory in his strength nor the rich man in his riches. For, if the cankerworm and the little grub worm are more powerful than man, wherefore do earth and ashes boast, and why, though man is born of the earth, does he disdain those things which are common to humanity? And so, whoever boasts, let him boast in the Lord who enfeebles the bow of the powerful and arms the weak with strength, and whose plans are that the proud may fall and the humble may rise and to whom the Father has given full authority in heaven and on earth and all things have been set under his feet. If anyone has faithfully fixed in him the anchor of his hope, he will be encompassed with mercy, just as it is written: "He who trusts in the Lord will be sustained" (Prov. 29:25). The hope of the just brings them joy, as witnessed by the psalmist who says: "Grace, however, will enfold the man who trusts in the Lord" (Ps. 32:10), and again: "Happy is the man whose trust is in the name of the Lord" (Ps. 40:5). Who, indeed, has ever trusted in the Lord and been confounded? Who has ever abided in his commands and been abandoned? Who has ever called upon the Lord and been shunned? Truly, the Lord is compassionate and merciful.

> Any mighty warrior who relies upon fierce weapons,
>   confident and vainly trusting in himself or his followers,
> that man will tremble like a quivering leaf
>   which the storm shakes off and the wind blows away.
> The mesh of his breastplate of rigid metal gives
>   way like a spider's fragile web.
> His sharp sword is pliant like a dagger of lead,
>   nor does his trusted shield protect its lord.
> His headpiece covers him like a helmet of wool,
>   and his powerful spear is no more than a reed.   10
> Did not terrible Goliath boast with such things, he whom
>   a rock thrown from an enemy's sling overthrew?
> A shield did not save him, nor were frightening weapons or
>   threatening words of any avail to that barbarian.
> If the lion, the tiger, and the crocodile are slain, and if
>   the huge and savage elephant fears a mouse, thus
> it is in vain for any warrior to rely on his own
>   powers, although he may have limbs of bronze.
> All hope, rather, should be fixed in the Lord of Life,
>   the God of heaven who rules all kingoms by his will,   20
> and the Almighty who allows rulers to trust in the superior
>   strength by which they may conquer with mighty hand.

Chapter XV.
Why divine assistance should be implored against the menacing rumbles of hostile wars.

Now, if at any time the rumors of war grow strong, let the outcome not be trusted so much to physical arms and strength as, rather, pressed vigorously upon the Lord with assiduous prayers; let the assistance of God be sought, for in his hand rest deliverance, peace, and victory. For, if God is called upon with pious devotion, he never deserts his supplicants, but, rather, as an ally mercifully assists them with favorable opportunities. Lo, when the hands and voices of his chosen people are raised toward the Father of Mercy, the ferocity of the enemy is annihilated; and, sometimes, sudden disgrace and the pitfall of death are set for their enemies, while to the pious comes an unexpected victory. And, while pious men enter upon the road to safety of which they had despaired, the impious, on the other hand, enter the pitfall of unforeseen death. Let us prove what we are saying, however, with clear examples.

When Moses, the lawmaker, raised his hands in prayer to the Lord, Israel was victorious, but when he lowered his hands a little, Amalec was victorious.[28] And likewise, because King Hezekiah[29] fought not with physical arms, but rather implored with tears, the Angel of the Lord in one night destroyed one hundred and eighty-five thousand Assyrians. King Josephat[30] sounded praises to the Lord, and in return for that praise the Lord overcame Josephat's enemies in such a way that He turned the snares of the enemy upon themselves and they fell with mutually inflicted wounds. The Israelites, however, making away with the enormous booty from the spoils of the dead, were so overburdened that they were unable to carry everything away; moreover, because of the magnitude of the plunder, they could not bear off all the booty for three days. What can I say concerning the Maccabees who, supported by divine assistance, were often triumphant? Hence, when his fearful people asked, "How can we, so few, engage so great and so strong a multitude, since we are exhausted today with hunger?" Judas, himself, most renowned and undefeated in the wars of the Lord, responded: "It is easy for many to be restrained in the hands of a few, and there is no difference in the sight of the God of Heaven between deliverance by many or by few, for victory in war depends not upon the army's size, but upon strength from heaven. Those men are coming against us in an arrogant and insolent multitude so that they may destroy us, our wives and our children and so that they may despoil us; let us fight, therefore, for our lives and our laws, and the Lord, himself, will crush them before your eyes. Do not, moreover, be afraid of them" (1 Macc. 3:17–22). And so, rushing upon the enemy, he destroyed them and obtained the victory from his adversaries. Not only did these things happen in the Old Testament, but, moreover, similar things have occurred in the New Testament as well. Thus histories relate that the emperor Constantine overcame all his enemies by using the cross of Christ for his standard. And, likewise, the emperor Theodosius, more by praying than by fighting, overthrew certain tyrants and their armies, for to him the Lord sent a tempest with lightning and thunder in aid against his enemies and with Heaven's vengeance he defeated them. Concerning Theodosius (I) a poet elegantly wrote:

> "O thou much beloved by God, for you the sky joins battle,
> and the winds, united, come at the call of the trumpet."[31]

What wonder, therefore, if through powerful elements, the mighty Lord achieves great works, since he is known to perform stupendous miracles even in the case of small flying creatures! For indeed, ecclesiastical history tells us that in the time of the emperor Constantine, the king of the Persians named Sapor[32] besieged the city of Nisibis (which some men called Mesopotamian Antioch) with many thousands. The bishop of Nisibis, as well as its ruler and leader, was St. James,[33] a man illuminated with the radiance of apostolic grace. During the siege, moreover, Effrem,[34] an admirable man and distinguished writer among the Syrians, besought St. James to come to the wall so that upon seeing the barbarians he might cast darts of malediction against them. Having been persuaded, venerable St. James ascended into a tower. And, when he saw the innumerable multitudes of the army, he directed no curse upon them other than stinging flies and gnats so that, through these tiny creatures, the army might recognize Heaven's power. Soon clouds of flies and gnats followed upon his prayer; moreover, they filled up the trunks of the elephants which are hollow and both the ears and nostrils of the horses and other beasts of burden. Those animals, unable to bear the force of the tiny creatures, threw down their riders and their masters and cast them from their backs. They confounded the broken ranks of warriors and, abandoning the army, fled with utmost haste. The emperor was terrified and acknowledged the slight and gentle punishment brought against him by God, who protects the lives of those who devoutly worship him; furthermore, the emperor withdrew his army from the city, for he saw shameful defeat, not victory, in that siege.

We also read about other holy men whom it befell at one time or another to be with Christian people in a military campaign and to have fought against the enemy more by prayer than physical arms, even as St. Germanus,[35] the bishop of Auxerre, is reported to have done. For he was sent into Britain with St. Lupus, the bishop of Troyes, in order to extirpate the Pelagian heresy, at a time when the necessity of war by the Britons against the Picts and Saxons was imminent. The Picts and Saxons, trusting in their army's great size, were planning to overcome the Britons, whom necessity, meanwhile, had drawn together into a military camp. And, because the anxious Britons judged their side to be weaker, they sought the holy bishops' aid. Under these apostolic leaders, therefore, Christ himself commanded in the camp. The holy days of Lent were also approaching, which the presence of the bishops made even more religious, so that the people, instructed with daily preachings, eagerly flocked to the grace of Baptism; indeed, most of the army sought the water of the fount of salvation. A church, constructed of interlaced branches, was built for the feast of our Lord's resurrection, and in the arrangement of the armed camp the likeness of a city was adapted.

After the feast of Easter, the army, anointed with Baptism, advanced; faith was fervent in the people, and since the protection of physical arms was deemed of little value, the help of God was hoped for. Then Germanus himself promised to be the leader of the battle. He picked out swiftly marching soldiers, and he noticed a valley with hills on both sides in the direction from which the enemy's approach was expected. Here he stationed a previously untried body of men with himself as the leader of the force. Presently the enemy's fierce host approached, while those set in ambush observed it drawing near. Suddenly Germanus, raising the standard, urged and instructed them all to join their voices with his in a mighty shout. To the confident enemies who expected to present themselves unexpectedly, the bishops shouted "alleluia" three times. The united shout of all the men followed, and the enclosed hills increased the shout raised with an echo. The enemy force was overthrown with terror, and they feared not only the surrounding rocks but even the frame of the sky above them, and they deemed the swiftness of their feet barely sufficient in their ensuing state of panic. They fled in every direction and threw down their arms, being well content to escape even with naked bodies to safety. Many also, rushing headlong in fear, were drowned in a river they were crossing. The innocent British army, meanwhile, observed its vengeance and became an inactive spectator of the victory granted to it. The spoils cast about were collected, and the God-fearing army embraced the joys of a heavenly victory. The bishops triumphed over enemies vanquished without bloodshed, and they triumphed in a victory obtained by faith, not violence.

And so, by these and other such examples, it is plainly seen that men are shielded from the dangers of death by holy prayers and by divine help rather than by physical arms. Whence consolation in this present life, protection against all dangers, and victory over enemies are above all to be sought, the Lord himself tells us in the Old Testament. Instructing the Hebrew people, he says, "If you live in accordance with my laws and if you keep my commandments and put them into practice, I will give you rain in its proper seasons, and the earth will produce its fruits, and the trees will be filled with fruit. The threshing of the harvest will last until vintage time, and the vintage will reach till the time for sowing. You will consume your food in abundance and will dwell in your land without fear. I will establish peace in your land, that you may lie down to rest without anxiety. I will drive away ravenous beasts, and the sword will not penetrate your borders. You will persecute your enemies, and they will be laid low before you. Five of you will rout a hundred of your enemies, and a hundred of you will pursue ten thousand of them, and before your eyes your enemies will fall by the sword. I will look upon you with favor and will cause you to increase; you will multiply, and I will keep my covenant with you. I will set up my tabernacle among you, and my spirit will not disdain you. I will dwell in your midst, and I will be your God and you my people. I am the Lord, your God. However, if you do not obey me and carry out all my commandments, if you reject my laws and despise my decrees by not practicing what I have ordained and by debasing my covenant, then, in turn, I will do these things to you: I will quickly punish you with want and fever which will dim your eyes and consume your lives; you will sow your seed in vain, for your enemies will devour it; I will turn my face against you, and you will be destroyed by your enemies and subjected to those who hate you; and you will flee though no one pursues you. If, even after this, you are not willing to accept my instruction but continue to live in opposition to me, I will come against you as an adversary. I will strike you seven times on account of your sins, and over you I will sweep the sword, the avenger of my covenant. And, when you have taken refuge in cities, I will send pestilence among you, and you will be delivered into the hands of your enemies," and so forth (Lev. 26:3–17, 23–25). Although these things, to be sure, were spoken by the lawgiver to the first people who strove for earthly goods, they can, nevertheless, now be justly applied to the Christian people, whom their Lord looks out for in their present need and to whom, in addition, are promised the riches to come in heaven. Hence, it is most fitting for such a people to preserve the Lord's commandments and to place all their hope in him who has the power to deliver those who trust in him from all adversity, as well as to lead his chosen people to the enjoyment of prosperity both here and in the life to come.

When the swirling tempest of the east wind rages,
resounding with a great commotion
and thundering from the mountains
on high with a darkening storm,

and the forests come crashing to the ground,
and the motion of the sea becomes turbulent,
and the wind casts forth threats against
the heavens with a clapping thunderbolt,

it is then that fear grips
the hearts of trembling mortals,   10
lest the wrath of heaven overthrow
the race of men on the earth.

Whoever is wise enough to avoid
such perils with a prudent heart,
flees out of fear for such
things to reach a haven of safety.

And so, when a fierce and mighty
whirlwind of adversity strikes,
let the Heavenly Thunderer's right hand
be entreated with all one's powers.   20

That blessed man excels all others,
who, without delay, penetrates the
lofty frame of the heavens
with a swift-flying prayer.

This winged prayer, bright with the
beak of a bird, has golden wings.
Fasting rules the left wing,
and bounty governs the right.

Heaven's inhabitants recognize it;
joyously the company welcomes the   30
newcomer and presents it before the
judgment seat of the Prince of Glory.

Then that milk-white creature
receives precious spiritual favors,
and returns to earthly regions,
laden with gifts of peace.

Chapter XVI.
Concerning adversities that may occur.

If any adversities in this world beset rulers governing properly and observing God's commandments, those afflicted should not suddenly flee from God or despair of his help, but, rather, should act with confidence and trust completely in His benevolence. For this transitory life is a complete trial for the just, in which prosperity sometimes does more harm than adversity, because prosperity casts down God's chosen people, while adversity instructs them. Hence, as wise men assert, the earthly kingdom consists of five periods of vicissitude. The first is a period of struggle, when the kingdom is assaulted by wars and the rumblings of its enemies; the second period is when the kingdom, itself, by its increments, waxes to fullness like the moon; the third, when in its fullness the kingdom, free on all sides from its enemies' attacks, becomes renowned in the fullness of its glory like the splendor of a full moon; the fourth, when the loftiness of that kingdom, like the moon, begins to wane; and finally, the fifth, when by struggles and conflicts the summit of the state topples like the tower of Siloam, and no one is willing to do anything beneficial to sustain the state.[36]

Let it be noted, then, how unsteady and changeable is the glory of an earthly kingdom, which never continues in the same state, but like the moon, increases for a time in prosperity and then decreases in adversity. Immutable glory, moreover, can by no means be acquired in an earthly kingdom, but rather in the kingdom of heaven. For in this world's momentary dominion and in the confused inconstancy of transitory events, just as serenity is often restored after storms of adversity, so, also, serene skies are transformed again into storms. And so, if any adversities occur, the prudent ruler of the state should not be instantly shaken by such turbulent whirlwinds, but, rather, should be strengthened in the Lord with powerful firmness of mind. Also, he should give thanks to the Almighty amidst adversities just as he gave thanks for his Lord's kindness in past times of prosperity. It is not enough that we give thanks to God when we are enjoying the blessings which have come to us, for even the gentile, the Jew, the publican, and the pagan do so. Rather, it is the proper virtue of Christians to render thanks to the Creator even in times of what are considered adversities, so that a joyous heart may burst forth in praise of God and we may cry: "I came forth naked from my mother's womb, and naked I will return. As it pleased the Lord, thus it has been done; blessed be the name of the Lord" (Job 1:21). No matter how often any tribulation confronts us in this world, those good people who are, as it were, holy vessels, offer thanks to God, who deigns to chastise them; but those who are proud, extravagant, or greedy blaspheme against God and cry out, "O God, what great evil have we committed that we should endure such things?" With respect to just men who suffer afflictions, on the other hand, we read the following passage in Job: "Happy is the man who is reproved by the Lord. Do not, therefore, reject the chastisement of the Lord, for he wounds, but he heals; he will strike, but his hands will cure" (Job 5:17–18). Indeed, to the soothing ointments with which God often cures us he frequently adds even the most bitter medicine of tribulation. And, like a most merciful physician who desires to remove putrid flesh and to singe rotten wounds with a cautery, he does not now spare so that he may spare us later, and does not now show compassion so that he may show great compassion afterwards.

As a matter of fact, occasionally wars and other adversities are more beneficial to us than peace and tranquility, since peace makes men soft, negligent, and timid, while war, on the other hand, both sharpens the mind and persuades it to place little value on present affairs as being transitory. And war, by the determination of divine grace, often begets the most sweet fruits of greater peace and concord. Thus, the emperor Constantine concludes: "Friendships are more pleasant which have been restored to concord after occasions of hostilities."[37] Indeed, any good and just leader who desires either to escape from or triumphantly overcome spiritual and carnal enemies, as well as any adversities whatsoever, should be protected and equipped with spiritual arms. He should stand forth like the apostle, armed with the breastplate of justice, protected by the helmet of hope and the shield of faith, and flashing with the sword of God's word. For, we read very often in numerous passages of Scripture that the holy and most noble kings of the earth were protected with such illustrious arms; that they conquered their adversaries and brought back abundant trophies from their enemies; and that they ruled renowned kingdoms both long and prosperously. While I omit others for brevity's sake, the blessed David, endowed with spiritual arms because he feared and loved the true God with all his heart, avoided many perils, and he often struck down the Lord's enemies with a just vengeance.

> As the globe of the moon now waxes bright,
> forming a sphere gleaming with beams of light,
> and then later that horned disk wanes
> > in variation,
>
> so the kingdoms of the earth, in variable course,
> now increase with prosperous renown
> but afterwards royal dominion is diminished
> > by rising misfortunes.
>
> Wherefore do we lament the fleeting nature of human events?
> Like smoke and a swift flowing river,   10
> do not these principles cause the world's
> > cycle to vary?
>
> Darkness follows after a clear day,
> and after serene and tranquil breezes
> a fierce tempest suddenly arises with its
> > darkening clouds.

And likewise a whirlpool of strife and
unexpected catastrophes succeeds a delightful peace,
whence the children of men wither like flowers
    of the field.   20

But a pious prince, after suffering
fresh misfortunes, offers thanks
thus to Almighty God with a contrite heart
    and cheerful mien:

"O Blessed Son of the Heavenly Father,
you who create and renew the whole universe,
to you now we offer thanksgiving for your
    salubrious medicine.

Do you not chastise us with a healing rod,
desiring us to be safe and sleek like lambs   30
in the sacred sheepfold of your flock,
    O most illustrious Shepherd?

And so, from the cup of liquid mixed with myrrh,
which your right hand graciously extends to us
so that we may be saved, we freely drink
    the gifts of salvation.

We pray, moreover, to be armed with the shining
breastplate of justice and the sure and flashing
helmet of hope, with the sword of God's word and
    the shield of faith.   40

With the radiant standard of your powerful cross,
O mighty Lord, grant to the prayers of a
suppliant people, to conquer all the arrogance
    of their enemies."

Chapter XVII.
Do not be insolent when peace has been offered even by enemies or when enemies have been overthrown.

A just prince is adorned with many commendable virtues, especially with mercy, gentleness and tranquility of mind, never accepting discord but rather the concord of peace. And, as much as he is able, he is always loving not only towards his friends, but even towards those of his enemies whom it is proper for a pious and magnanimous ruler to overcome by an example of patience and mercy. This is affirmed by the psalmist who said: "To these, who hated peace, I was peaceable" (Ps. 120:7). Accordingly, a prudent ruler always strives to extend, rule, and govern his kingdom through the bond of peace, since the peace of all things is the tranquility of order and the unification and augmentation of royal power. Even as the greatest affairs collapse amidst discord, so, on the other hand, the least affairs prosper in peaceful concord. Hence, when Publius Scipio[38] asked why the Numantine state had previously remained unconquered and afterwards been overthrown, Tyrseus, a Numantine, responded: "With harmony Numantia was unconquerable, with disharmony it was destroyed."[39] The city of Numantia not only held off forty thousand Romans for fourteen years with only four thousand soldiers of its own but was even victorious.

Now harmony restrains dissensions; it restores harsh things to mildness, adversity to prosperity, and hostilities to the tranquility of friendships, and it is cherished among friends, unconquerable by enemies, and even desirable from one's adversaries. Such harmony is tranquil at home and a victor at war, although it refuses to be implicated in wars except when a most necessary and just cause demands. There are some, however, who become so haughty by the success of earthly felicity and swollen pride that they are not afraid to reject the peace offered to them by their enemies and to undertake unjust wars. Even worse, if they have become entangled in two wars, with the fury of Spartans they do not refuse a third. Often, however, such men are justly destroyed by the rod of divine vengeance, since they are unwilling to accept the gift of peace when it is extended to them. We read that such a thing happened to King Amaziah of Judah[40] who sent messengers to Jehoash,[41] son of Jehoahaz, son of Jehu, King of Israel, saying: "Come, and let us meet with each other" (2 Kings 14:8). Then, King Jehoash of Israel replied to Amaziah, the king of Judah, saying: "The thistle of Lebanon sent to the cedar in Lebanon, saying, 'Give your daughter in marriage to my son.' And the beasts of the forests which are in Lebanon passed by and trampled upon the thistle. Striking forth, you have prevailed over Edom, and your heart is inflated with pride. Be content with your glory, and stay at home! Why, therefore, do you provoke misfortune and ruin yourself and Judah along with you?" (2 Kings 14:9–10). Amaziah, nevertheless, was not satisfied, and Jehoash, the King of Israel, rose up. Both he and Amaziah, the King of Judah, met at Beth-shemesh, a town of Judah, and Judah was cast down before Israel.

Here we may even recall what is said concerning the impious prince Julian in ecclesiastical history. Julian, who held many towns and fortresses, was then capturing even the cities of the Persians. When he had reached the city of Ctesiphon, Julian besieged its king so fiercely that the king tried sending numerous delegations to Julian, offering to yield to him a section of his country if he could freely depart from the battle. Julian, however, did not desire this. He felt no compassion for the supplicants, nor did he perceive in his mind that while, indeed, it is a good thing to conquer, it is, on the other hand, an invidious thing to conquer excessively with a foolhardy belief in magic arts and by anticipating victory with a false hope. While Julian was on his horse and strengthening his army, wearing no arms and expecting certain victory, an unexpectedly thrown javelin passed through his arm and plunged into his side. From this blow he suffered the end of his life. Moreover, it is not to this day known who caused that most just wound, but some say that a certain one of the invisible beings inflicted it, others say one of the Ishmaelite shepherds, and still others say a soldier worn out with hunger and marching. But whether or not he was a man or an angel, it is plainly evident that he acted by divine commands. They even say that, when he had been wounded, Julian suddenly filled his hand with his own blood and cast it into the air, crying, "Galilean, you have conquered," thus acknowledging the victory with blasphemy.[42]

No one, therefore, should with thoughtless arrogance spurn the gift of peace, or after one's enemies have been overthrown, lord it over them with a proud heart as Amaziah and Julian did. Hence it has been written: "Do not gloat over your enemy's death lest, perhaps, similar things happen to you" (Ecclus. 7:8), and again: "Do not rejoice when your enemy has fallen, and let not your heart exult in his downfall; for, indeed, whoever exalts himself in the misfortunes of another is displeasing to God" (Prov. 24:17–18). On this account, not only was blessed David not joyous over his enemies' destruction, but he was, in fact, extremely sorrowful, lamenting with compassionate sympathy the courageous men of Israel destroyed by the Philistines and saying: "Alas, the glorious men of Israel have been slain on their heights! How did the heroes fall? Do not announce it in Gath, nor proclaim it in the crossroads of Ascelon, lest the sons of the Philistines rejoice and lest the daughters of the uncircumcised exult" (2 Sam. 1:19–20). It is clearly demonstrated by such things how great a sense of compassion blessed David felt even towards his enemies.

> O how Almighty God loves peace-loving men!
> To them he promises the kingdom of everlasting Jerusalem,
> and, adorning them with the grace of angelic form,
> he makes them shine in heart and countenance.
>
> With innocence sown in their hearts,
> as with birds that lack gall,
> the heavenly-throned Father delights in this race,
> and God elects them to be his heirs.
>
> He who desires peace shines forth in splendor,
> and is redolent in speech like Attic honey.
> But he who rejects peace dwells in darkness
> and, walking blindly, falls into a pit.
>
> For, a discordant and turbulent emotion of the spirit,
> devoid of counsel, often occasions the perils
> of shipwreck for reckless rulers;
> and indeed, soon after follows the violence of death.
>
> Healing peace, on the other hand, joins together discordant things;
> peace, restraining quarrels, begets rejoicings;

10

peace unites people in a perpetual bond,
and in peace a glorious ruler governs his kingdom.   20

Those to whom the gift of peace is pleasing are
redolent with the spice of virtues like the rich
olive-bearing mount of the Lord, from which milk and honey
with the richness of nectar flow abundantly to Christians.

Chapter XVIII.
Acts of thanksgiving and benevolent prayers
should be returned to God after peace or victory.

Glorious princes, kings, and rulers, having the fear of the Most High before their eyes, did not claim credit for themselves respecting either the tranquility of peace or the triumphs of victory. Rather, attributing everything to the grace of Almighty God, they rendered fitting thanks and sacred offerings to the Lord either for a state of peace or for a settled victory. For it is the Lord who gives prosperity and glory to kings that fix in him the hope of their salvation, who will grant the wish of those who fear him, and who will hear their prayers and deliver them. Moreover, it is the Lord who preserves all those who love him, and, at the same time, will destroy all sinners. Indeed, the Book of Wisdom confirms this very thing, thus: "You who fear the Lord hope in him, and in delight mercy will come to you" (Ecclus. 2:9). Hence it is said also by the prophet Joel: "The Lord is the hope of his people, and the strength of the sons of Israel" (Joel 4:16).

It is fitting to marvel at the Lord and to exalt and honor him with songs of praise and with bounteous devotions on account of the multitude of his mercies, the abundance of his consolations, and the liberality of his kindnesses by which he looks after the human race with ineffable goodness. To this end, the prophet exhorts us, saying: "Let them thank the Lord for his mercy and for his wonderful deeds on behalf of the sons of men" (Ps. 107:21). Furthermore, what is read in Deuteronomy agrees with this: "It is he you must praise, he is your God: for you he has done these great and terrible things which your own eyes have witnessed" (Deut. 10:21). Hence, when the people of Israel had passed through the Red Sea with Moses leading, and the Egyptians had been drowned by the waters, they echoed a song of exultation to the Lord, since they clearly acknowledged his magnificent kindnesses towards them.

What can I say about the famous and blessed rulers and kings of that same people, for, as often as they had been liberated from the hands of their enemies or been victorious over their foes, they gave thanks to their liberator and protector with hymns of praise as well as peace-offerings and other sacrifices acceptable to the Lord? Among these, that pious and hymn-singing David, rejoicing in spirit on account of the favors conferred on him by the Lord, cried: "I will sing to the Lord who granted such goodness to me, and I will sing a psalm to the name of the Most High Lord" (Ps. 13:6). On this account, that people were admonished by the prophet Nahum, who cried: "Judah, celebrate your feasts, and carry out your vows" (Nah. 2:1). Indeed, how many blessings the Lord's people received through such vows is briefly described by the prophet Joel: "Filling yourself with food, you will eat and be satisfied, and you will praise the name of your God who has performed wondrous things with you. And my people will nevermore be put to shame" (Joel 2:26).

Even in the time of the New Testament many of the most pious rulers were not forgetful of the favors of the Most High, but rather, so much as they stood out more powerfully and gloriously than others by the bounty of divine grace, to the same degree they returned fitting honors to Almighty God. Such was true of the great and renowned emperor, Constantine, who was distinguished by extraordinary piety and became, by the will of divine providence, the master of all Europe and Africa. In addition to these, moreover, controlling the greater part of Asia, he everywhere possessed faithful subjects. In fact, some of the barbarians were subject to him of their own accord, others after they had been conquered. Triumphs were everywhere observed, and the emperor was proclaimed the conqueror in all things. The emperor, however, acknowledging and admiring the power of his divine Lord and enumerating the many favors conferred upon him and the human race through God's grace, wrote a letter filled with divine praise and glorious thanksgiving, saying thus: "Defending the most sacred faith, I have shared in the light of truth; guided by the truth of the light, I perceive the sacred faith. Finally, through these things, just as the events themselves confirm, I recognize that this religion is worthy of veneration and that it offers to all men instruction towards the acknowledgment of the most holy God. I publicly profess myself to adhere to such veneration, since with the power of this God supporting me, starting from the boundaries of the ocean, I have taken hold of the entire world with the most firm hope of its deliverance. I worship this God whose standard my army, dedicated to God, carries on its shoulders, and from whom, when anything is asked for with just words, it is granted. From those standards, moreover, I suddenly receive the favors of victory. And, therefore, I profess myself to honor this God with everlasting remembrance, and I believe him to be above all things with a most excellent and perfect judgment. I shall call upon this God on bended knees, for he requires only a pure mind and immaculate soul from everyone, and expects acts of virtue and piety. He is pleased by works of clemency and mercy; he loves peaceful men and regards the factious with aversion. He loves faithfulness, punishes faithlessness, and looks down upon all power with contempt. He avenges the cruelty of the arrogant and destroys those raised up in haughtiness; nevertheless, he returns fitting honors to the humble and forebearing. Hence, for all that has been considered, I return many thanks to God, since, by perfect providence, the entire human race observing divine law properly rejoices in the peace restored to it."[43] And so, the most pious and most Christian emperor spoke these words in giving praise to God for his immense favors.

What ruler, however, will not continually offer sacrifices of thanksgiving to Almighty God seeing that he has been blessed with a Christian name, nurtured from infancy under the care of Mother Church with breast, milk, and protection and raised up to the foremost height of dignity by the grace of divine favor? What ruler will not strive to obey the Lord's will humbly and eagerly or ardently to please his holy servants if even the impious King Nebuchadnezzar honored the God of Israel and if Alexander the Great, though pagan, entered God's holy temple and bowed his head to his majesty, knelt upon bended knees and earnestly asked for his support and offered sacrifices to him, and, moreover, elevated Iaddus, the high-priest of the holy temple, with a great many honors? Theodosius (II), the most sacred light of imperial authority, returned the most abundant thanks for the favors bestowed upon him by God, fulfilling his vows to Christ with a multitude of honors. And, to Jerusalem he sent his wife Eudoxia, who was filled with love for Christ and greatly honored those churches established in Jerusalem as well as those situated in other cities both when she came to Jerusalem and when she left again.

> If peace comes to pass or glorious trophies provoke admiration,
>> let no heedless ruler arrogate such things to himself.
> For God, the all-creating, everywhere despises in his heart rulers
>> who are ungrateful and arrogant.
> On the other hand, he cherishes mild rulers and those offering thanks
>> to the Lord whose manifold riches are granted as favors.
> For indeed, neither wealth nor dominions make men prosperous
>> if there be not praise and honor to the Father on His Heavenly Throne.
> Hence, a prince blessed by divine favor should
>> offer hymn-singing praises and prayers to God whenever   10
> peace smiles upon him, whenever an arrogant enemy is overthrown,
>> whenever riches, abounding in prosperous lands, prevail,
> and whenever God exalts the king and the people
>> by magnificently glorifying them with triumphs.
> Let there be no murmuring among the people, when the manna
>> of tranquil peace and of manifold prosperity redounds.
> Rather, joyful songs should be raised to the heavens,
>> for it is fitting to join in song for such great gifts,
> when the Almighty Spirit fills the lands of the earth and
>> when the celestial kingdoms, too, stand open to the sons of the earth.

Chapter XIX.
The privileges of Holy Mother Church
which a pious ruler should preserve,
and the worthy stewards and ministers of the churches.

A prudent and holy ruler of the Christian people is always mindful of God's favors and, therefore, glorifies the bestower of such kindness with honors, thereby acknowledging that he has been exalted by Him. And he exhibits praiseworthy concern with pious devotion for preserving and augmenting the privileges and rights of Holy Mother Church, the spouse of the living God, and for the honor and reverence due to priests. A ruler then shows that he is a faithful worshipper of God, when in

Christian piety he regularly strives to arrange with sincere fervor whatever pertains to the honor and glory of Christ and his holy church; moreover, if necessary, he opposes himself like a shield against all adversity in defense of God's people inasmuch as he greatly desires himself and his kingdom to be defended with divine protection. He who wishes his kingdom to be increased and extended never fails to enrich God's church with honors, and he who wishes to enjoy peace and security, both temporal and eternal, acts with pious sagacity to promote ecclesiastical peace and security.

Let him, therefore, be a vigorous imitator of those princes who came before him and ruled justly and piously according to God's will, and who ruled the Christian people well and supported Christ's churches with suitable assistance. For they always had the fear of God before their eyes and the hope of heavenly reward and hastened to carry out according to His will whatever they administered or dispensed, not consenting to the iniquities of the wicked, but with utmost zeal making the crooked straight in accord with the scales of justice. For they knew that whoever is empowered to chastise and fails to do so surely makes himself an accomplice to a crime. Such a case involving Eli the priest is related in the Book of Kings.[44] Eli neglectfully spared his sons, who were transgressing the Lord's worship, using force against people offering their sacrifices to God, and sleeping with the women who served at the entrance to the meeting tent; and he failed to reproach them sharply with paternal authority. How great was the vengeance which fell upon them and upon all the people! For those sons of Eli, together with the ark of the Lord, and all the people together, were delivered into the hands of the Philistines, and Israel was vanquished with an exceedingly large slaughter so that thirty thousand foot-soldiers fell in battle and the ark of God was captured. Meanwhile, Eli's two sons, Hophni and Phinehas, were killed, and Eli himself, upon hearing the ark of God had been captured and his sons killed, fell backwards from his chair and died from a broken neck. And so, the priestly office, withdrawn from his family, was transferred to another one, nor did anyone else from Eli's lineage ever again minister in the Lord's temple.

By this example, therefore, and similar ones drawn from Sacred Scripture, it is clear that the most holy princes and rulers did not retain flatterers mixing the honey of sweet words with the poison of wicked persuasion, nor did they consent to the deceptions of unjust and wickedly obsequious men. For, if consent is given to those committing such villainies, not only those transgressing, but also those who consent to them likewise will perish. Just and prudent kings, however, because they themselves live rightly, with pious zeal refute and reform transgressors in an instructive manner. Hence, they acquire for themselves a double token of reward from the Lord inasmuch as they strive to refute evils in their subjects and to incite them to good by words and examples. Indeed, it behooves a ruler beloved by God, whom the divine order has appointed God's vicar in the government of his church and to whom it has granted authority over both orders (of prelates and subjects), that he decide what is just for every person; that under his direction the first order (of prelates) should preside over teaching and ministering properly; and that the order of subjects be faithfully and devoutly obedient. Thus, there should be a praiseworthy intention on a just ruler's part to see to it with appropriate zeal that the stewards of God's churches may lawfully maintain their office. Moreover, royal generosity should impart assistance to them in order that they may fully carry out their office according to God's commandments and the regulations of sacred canons. The secular authorities should not become a hindrance to the stewards of God, but rather, should promote the preservation of God's faith and the cultivation of justice. Thus, as we have said previously, it is necessary that each year synodal assemblies be convened in which ecclesiastical laws and affairs may be justly and lawfully discussed. Therefore, let the just and pious ruler diligently see that the sanctity of the Lord's name, which abides in places consecrated to God, is maintained, insofar as it is possible, with no fault whatsoever. Let him provide that such rectors and stewards are appointed in them who conduct divine affairs without insatiable greed and luxury, who grant sufficient food and clothing to God's servants and handmaids, and who, above all, in accordance with the canons, dispense suitable provisioning to widows, orphans, and paupers. And likewise, let those stewards show service appropriate for an orthodox ruler from the resources which are left over, so that in first place should come what pertains to the divine, and in second place what pertains to human service. For, if with prudent skill stewardship should be shown towards soldiers of the flesh so that they are paid all necessary salaries and if those who labor more in war's tumults and become ever more devoted, steadfast and useful to the success of the state receive more of reward and honor, how much more ought provision to be made for Christ's spiritual soldiers by whose sacred labors and prayers the state itself is preserved whole and unimpaired; enemies, too, both visible and invisible are overcome; an abundance of temporal benefits is increased by the event of prosperity; blessed angels are summoned to the people's assistance; the serenity of peace is restored; the dominion expanded; and finally, royal dignity and honor are extended long and happily with the Lord's protection and the sons of sons are rendered famous upon the summit of sovereignty.

> That ruler stands out orthodox and happy who,
> blessed with fear of God and fervent in love,
> always puts those matters ahead of the concerns of
> the court, by which the sweet glory of Christ everywhere grows;
> who preserves every privilege of the Church conscientiously,
> that the glittering white bride of Christ the King may rejoice;
> and who wards off rapacious wolves with royal justice,
> lest the Christian folds be oppressed by the wicked.
> That zealous ruler looms fiery like a thunderbolt and
> flashing like an avenging sword in pursuit of the wicked.[45]   10
> He scorns pretentious speeches with modest ears,
> lest honey from an advisor's mouth yield deadly poisons.
> For in his mouth the cunning flatterer bears honey-sweet words,
> while in the bosom of his heart he conceals poisonous stratagems.
> Let the Christian judge, the legal statutes, the custom and
> the order and the rules of the land resist such little men,
> and let him cherish God's ministers, shining in holiness,
> who have learned to please God in words, in heart, and in morals.

By the prayers of these blessed men, a blessed state
overflows with every good like the fruitful fields,   20
the prince's honor rules, and victories sound on the trumpet.
Everywhere there reigns a happy tranquility and peaceful joy.

Chapter XX.
How much ignominy follows insolent princes and what kind and how much glory attends orthodox princes both here and in the world to come.

Scanning divine and human histories, I have selected from many, O lord king, these few chapters of instruction for your Highness. I have been prompted to this little work by your love, knowing that I am a debtor in your Highness' service. I also thought it would be useful if I could briefly condense into one short work what are here and there found in divine and human discourses about certain good and wicked rulers or princes, whence your genius might be delighted and a favorable service of our devotion towards the clarity of your understanding might be shown. In this manner, the bees gather flowing honey from various flowers to be transformed for their masters' benefit and construct the most delightful honeycombs with skillful arrangement. Hence, let the sagacity of your genius quite often peruse and read through this epistle like a handbook, so that it might more easily reckon how many punishments supernal and divine justice weighs out to evil rulers and how many blessings to just ones. On the one hand, to false rulers it returns sudden misfortunes, calamities, captivities, bereavements of children, slaughter of friends, barrenness of the earth's fruits, unbearable plagues, short and unhappy days, long illnesses, most miserable deaths, and, above all, eternal torments. On the other hand, however, to just and holy rulers it grants many immediate consolations, abundance of riches, glory of triumphs, tranquility of peace, splendid offspring, many and happy years, and a perpetual kingdom in the world to come. For, just as all things either prosperous or adverse come to pernicious ends for impious princes, so, on the contrary, all occurrences of adversity or felicity work together for the good of the chosen of God. As the apostle says, "All things, moreover, happen for the good to these who are called holy according to his decree" (Rom. 8:28)—as for example, those troubled for a time by adversity but then abundantly consoled by the Lord in prosperity, and those despised by the arrogance of the haughty but then victorious with heavenly aid. For by the merits and intercessions of their holy prayers enemies have been overcome, princes captured, and the most fortified cities broken down like the web of a spider; the seas have been made passable; all that are strong have been made weak, while things deemed weak have suddenly become strong; the weather, too, has often fought against the rebels with winds, storm-clouds, and hail; Heaven has resounded above the enemy hosts with avenging fires and thunderings; the seas have unleashed the most violent commotions; the attendant companies of angels have raged;[46] the sun, the moon, and the other heavenly bodies have ceased to maintain their course; and the earth has swallowed the living and, likewise, spewed forth the dead from its bowels. Truly, all creatures had been made subject to them, because they remained subject to the Creator in heart, word, and deed. For their holy endeavor was to both to fear and to love God and to examine sacred discourses, recognizing that the glory of kings arises from their searching into the Word and gaining knowledge of God's wisdom, just as it is written: "Get wisdom, get perception, the beginning of wisdom; hold her close and she will exalt you; cherish her and you will be glorified by her; she will set a crown of grace on your head and will protect you with a glorious diadem" (Prov. 4:5, 7–9). And so, they studiously learned these arts pleasing to the Almighty, that is, to judge justly, to be humble and kind towards just men, but to be severe and reproachful towards the evil, to sustain the poor, to assist God's churches, and to fix no hope in the temporal and mutable kingdom, but rather always to invest prayer and longing in the felicity of the heavenly and everlasting kingdom.

It is fitting for you, O lord king, with utmost effort always to cherish, ponder, and imitate their examples and noteworthy deeds, as well as their prosperous life on earth and, above all, their glory of eternal reward. Then surely the Almighty Lord will be your guardian and defender against all your adversaries, whom with his magnificent might He will crush under your feet or subdue by the power of either war or peace. Moreover, He will adorn you with the crown of his grace in all things, extending your days with felicity and glory in this world, as well as fixing them with perpetual felicity in the fellowship of pious kings who have pleased God. Your sons will be around your table like a vine of olives, and after you they will sit on the throne of your kingdom. If they have walked in the ways of the Lord and preserved his commandments, the Lord will grant them long life and happiness in this world, and, above all, the kingdom of heaven, by the saving grace of our Lord and Saviour Jesus Christ, to whom there is perpetual glory and power along with the Father and the Holy Spirit for ever and ever, Amen.

The end of *On Christian Rulers* by Sedulius Scottus.

Notes

1. Triple world: air, earth, and water. The triple world (*trifido orbe*) may also refer to the three parts of the earth: Europe, Africa, and Asia. See the opening lines of the *Waltharius*, which refer to Europe as *"Tertia pars orbis* (one of the three parts of the earth); and a geographical poem by Theodofrid, Abbot of Corbie, which describes Asia similarly as *"in tertiaque parte orbis est."*

2. Lothar II, King of Lotharingia (855–869).

3. Emperor of Rome (d. 325 A.D.).

4. St. Augustine, *The City of God*, trans. Marcus Dods (New York: Random House, 1950), Bk. 5, Chap. 12.

5. *Porphyrio in Horatium*, Ep. 1. 62, ed. W. Meyer, 269.

6. *Dist. Catonis* in *Poetae Lat. Min.*, ed. A. Baehrens, 3:237.

7. Cassiodorus, *Historia Tripartita*, 9:31. Text refers to Theodosius I.

8. Esther: a Jewish girl who became a queen of Persia and saved her people from destruction. See the Book of Esther.

9. M. Antoninus in *Scriptores Historiae Augustae*, 22:4.

10. Antiochus: probably Antiochus IV, ruler of the Seleucid dynasty (175–163 B.C.). He persecuted the Jews, and his outrages embroiled him in the Maccabean war in which the Syrian armies were repeatedly defeated.

11. Nero, Roman Emperor (54–68 A.D.).

12. Egea? Unknown.

13. "Julian the Apostate," Roman Emperor (361–63 A.D.).

14. Theodoric, King of the Ostrogoths, (d. 526).

15. Pope John (d. 526); arrested and imprisoned by Theodoric.

16. Symmachus, father-in-law of Boethius; imprisoned by Theodoric in 524 and later put to death.

17. Compare these seven "beauties" with the *Proverbia Graecorum* of Sedulius Scottus in *Sedulius Scottus*, ed. S. Hellmann (Munich: C. H. Beck'sche Verlagsbuchhandlung, 1906), p. 130.

18. Aur. Victor, *Epitome*, chapter 24.

19. Valentinian I, Roman Emperor (364–375 A.D.); Cassiodorus, *Historia Tripartita*, 7:12.

20. Constantine the Great, Roman Emperor (d. 327 A.D.).

21. Jovian, Roman Emperor (363–64 A.D.).

22. Theodosius I, Roman Emperor (d. 395); Theodosius II, Roman Emperor (d. 450 A.D.).

23. Cassiodorus, *Historia Tripartita*, 9:30. Text refers to Theodosius I.

24. Antoninus Pius, Roman Emperor (137–161 A.D.).

25. 1 Sam. 22:17–23.

26. 1 Kings 2:12–25.

27. According to Pliny, the Silurus is a type of catfish (*Historia Naturalis* 9, 15, 17, #44). This catfish is most commonly found in the Danube, where it is known to reach a weight of 400 lbs. and a length of ten feet.

28. Exod. 17:8–16.

29. Hezekiah, King of Judah (724–695 B.C.). See 2 Kings 19:35–37.

30. Josephat, King of Judah (d. c. 850 B.C.). See 2 Chron. 20:1–30.

31. Orosius, *Seven Books Against the Pagans*, Bk. 7, p. 35.

32. Sapor II, King of the Sassanid Persians. The siege of Nisibis took place in 338 A.D.

33. St. James of Nisibis (early fourth century).

34. St. Effrem of Syria (c. 306–373 A.D.): Syrian biblical exegete and ecclesiastical writer.

35. St. Germanus, Bishop of Auxerre (d. 448 A.D.).

36. See *Proverbia Graecorum* in *Sedulius Scottus*, pp. 129–130.

37. Cassiodorus, *Historia Tripartita*, 1:19.

38. Publius Cornelius Scipio (185/4–129 B.C.).

39. Orosius, *Seven Books Against the Pagans*, Bk. 5, 8.

40. Amaziah, ninth king of Judah.

41. Jehoash, King of Israel (800–775 B.C.).

42. Cassiodorus, *Historia Tripartita*, 6:46, 47.

43. Ibid., 3:3.

44. 1 Sam. 2:12–17; 4:1–18.

45. The Latin text reads *Emicans et ultor ensis*, but it is possible that Sedulius wrote *Emicans ut ultor ensis*, which translates "flashing like an avenging sword" and matches the construction of the previous line, *ardens more fulminis* ("fiery like a thunderbolt").

46. The text has *deservierunt* ("zealously served"), but it makes better sense, given the context, to read *desaevierunt* ("raged").

The Poems

Poem 1.

Verses composed by Sedulius Scottus for Bishop Hartgar.

Glorious, swanlike Aegle, the muses' fair sister,
I implore you to sing your mellifluous songs.
O eloquent maiden and musical grace,
raise your golden head from the font of Pegasus;
so elegant in purple array and radiant hair,
grant a kiss to Sedulius with your rose-red lips.
Aegle, as you play upon the muses' lyre, compose a song
to delight the ears of noble Hartgar.
For pious Hartgar, Europe's star and fair renown,
deserves the praise of melodious songs.   10
Like a golden bough adorned by virtue's flowers,
he shines illustrious in morals and character.
The daughter of Zion rejoices in such a shepherd,
and the rich and poor exult with joy.
He builds a lofty tower, a hundred cubits high,
so that he may ascend above the stars.
Climbing the stairway rising towards heaven,
he instructs his flock with sage words and examples.
Hartgar, arranging all things with pastoral care,
wards off wolves and rescues his lambs.   20
His breast is fragrant with wisdom's golden must,
and from his mouth flow charming gifts of eloquence.
Youthful beauty illumines his visage,
but a more excellent beauty adorns his mind.
Babbling orators and chattering poets are struck
dumb when they hear the sound of Hartgar's voice.
Three languages ornament Hartgar's golden tongue,
like three witnesses uttering words of truth.
He exchanges worldly wealth for eternal rewards,
that he may someday obtain the riches of heaven.   30

Hartgar, blooming cedar of paradise, forever flourish,
as you bear on your head the ripe fruits of learning.
O shepherd of the Lord, you turn tears into joys,
and bring prosperity to your dear Franks.
Among bishops, your venerable authority and
respect reflect the highest episcopal dignity.
Dispensing all things with equal scales of justice,

you pursue the road to heaven with unwavering pace.
Gracious father, you give rest and comfort to the indigent
Irish and support them with cheerful kindness.   40
You watch over them, great shepherd, in tranquility,
and your words to them are always sincere and true.
Famed bishop, you clothe the Irish and nourish them;
you sustain them, too, with food and learning.
Never has the world seen such a father,
who possesses such treasures of piety.
Thus, your name, renown, and fame will forever
fly across the earth and be written down in heaven.

Poem 2.
Sedulius celebrates Hartgar's return to Liège.

I, Tityrus, mournful at heart, remain in the forests,
for the shepherd is away and there is no peace.
Shepherd, has anyone stolen you? Zephyrus or the horned Rhine?
Father, has some four-footed glory carried you off?
Perchance, has Aurora's brilliant team on reddish wings,
and flying Cupid, borne you far from home?
Aurora chose you, earth's most radiant star,
and for love of you spurned her Tithonus.
Or is it that God's gracious right hand and the angels
at the same time bear you away and return you?   10
May your splendid presence bless the Franks with grace,
and your sparkling glory illumine your churches,
even as Apollo wandering across shining Olympus lightens
the world with his glittering and wondrous lamp.
O golden light of the earth, you have come at last,
as the Lord brings hope and repose to your people.
Your words are more delightful than Hyblean nectar,
and you are more precious than a wealth of golden hair.
See, father, how the gleaming chorus and magnificent
ranks of Liège rejoice at your return!   20
Just as God entrusted his sheepfold to pious Lambert,
so Lambert commits his flock into your hands.
People of every age are filled with jubilation,
as they break into song to celebrate your arrival;
and my muse has not withdrawn with silent lips
but with clear voice chants harmonious melodies.
Light of the Franks, our golden hope, heir of
Lambert, and nobility worthy of the highest honors,
may you be with the Lord in the mountains of eternity,
where Jesus, our good shepherd, reigns forever. Amen.   30

Poem 3.
The arrival of Sedulius and his companions at Liège.

The rimy blasts of dread-visaged Boreas
terrify us with sudden clashes and threats;
the very land trembles, stricken with fear,
and the sea rumbles, and the hard rocks groan;
now the hostile north wind lays waste the fields
of air with dreadful screams and thundering crashes.
A milky fleece of thick clouds covers the sky,
and the pallid earth is decked in a snowy gown;
and suddenly the woodlands shed their hair,
and every oak trembles like a reed.　　　　　　　　　　10
Titan, once robed in radiant splendor,
withholds his rays and hides his face.
Wretched sight! Furious Boreas torments us,
learned grammarians and pious priests of God,
for that swift tempest spares no dignity,
as he mangles us with his sharp, cruel beak.

O Hartgar, flourishing prelate, support the weak;
receive the learned Irish with a gracious heart.
Hence, you will joyfully ascend to heavenly temples,
celestial Jerusalem and perpetual Zion!　　　　　　　20

The mercy and serene heart of that good bishop
triumphantly tamed the proud blasts of Boreas.
He kindly took in the weary and generously
snatched three scholars from the howling winds;
he clothed and enriched us with threefold honor,
so we became the flock of a most gentle shepherd.

Poem 4.
Sedulius complains about his gloomy dwelling to Hartgar.

Your halls are gleaming with serene light;
the ceilings glisten, adorned with art's latest style;
a multitude of colors smile upon your dome,
and many beauteous forms glitter throughout.
O garden of Hesperides, you who quickly wither in
sudden tempests, your flowers endure for but a day;
but here, however, your violets and beautiful roses
have clung to cupola and dome in perpetual bloom;
and purple-red or jacinth never fear the harsh

blasts from the scorching south wind.   10
Our halls, alas, are ever darkened with night,
and inside not a beam of light ever shines;
the charming beauty of painted decor is not here,
and neither bar nor key for our door protects us.
We have no arches adorned with gay-colored paintings,
but instead, soot sticks to our ceilings above us.
Ah, Neptune, when you send rain in dark showers,
you saturate our roof with a thick and heavy dew;
and when the east wind sounds its furious roar,
this ancient, battered hall begins to shake.   20
Cacus, Vulcan's son, had such a loathsome dwelling;
for our's resembles a labyrinth of darkness,
whose very image is blackness of night.
Our own abode—Ah, woe!—shudders in its
gloomy cloak of black:
when daylight finally comes, the shadow
of night permeates these sorry old walls.
These halls, believe me, are unfit for scholars
such as love the gifts of splendor and light;
our quarters would only suit a night owl,   30
and our dwelling is worthy of a band of moles.
O Lambert! Gather all who are lost in darkness
and lead them to our house;
may this gloomy house forever be
rightly called "Asylum for the Blind."
But now, great father, pastor of bounty
and might, help us in our miseries;
speak your gracious words so that this shadowy
house, deprived of daylight, may be embellished.
Adorn our ceilings with panels and lovely paintings,   40
and give us a new key and firm bar for our door;
then put in sparkling windows made of glass,
so that the streaming rays of gentle Phoebus
may illumine, noble bishop, with radiance,
your scholars who love the light.
O lord, may you one day dwell upon heaven's summit
in a dazzlng palace of charming beauty,
which has been decorated by God's hand in the
blessed abode of celestial Jerusalem.

Poem 5.
To Bishop Hartgar as he departs from Liège on a journey to Rome.

Are you leaving, good bishop, on a journey?
Yet, you remain fixed in our hearts;
and, though your face may depart from view,
your spirit and sweet love will always endure.
Our hearts will always honor and treasure you,
wherever God's divine right hand may lead you.
I swear by these fingers and my loquacious pen
that the Alps will never sever our ties.
O how delightful and clear the winter,
and how pleasing to me the ice and snow,   10
if you, noble bishop, our radiant father and sole
glory, would not leave your flock!
Monstrous Winter, shaggy with icy locks,
what catastrophe and crime are you preparing?
Will our tears and prayers not appease you,
a wild beast born from Scythian rocks?
Go, gracious father blessed by good fortune,
through the snowy fields and ice-glazed roads;
let your horses' pounding hooves trample Winter,
and let harsh blows lash its dire countenance.   20
Even as glorious Andrew once went to Peter's house,
may he now accompany you safely to his brother.
Golden Rome will rejoice at your arrival;
you will be the city's hope and tower of the Church.
As he buried icy storms beneath Scythian climes
with teachings of faith and evangelical light,
we pray that by Andrew's merits and prayers winter's
freezing storms will not cause you harm.
May the princes of paradise and heaven's holy bands
always be your comrades and faithful protectors.   30
Prosper in Christ, wherever you walk in the world—
O harmonious muses, make this your pleasing song!

Poem 6.
Sedulius to Bishop Hartgar at Rome.

O muse, entice our noble honor from the City,
and lead our flourishing prelate back to us.
Daughter of Zion, do not hinder our light,

nor force us, I pray, to dwell in darkness.
Dazzling Rome, return the gift desired by all,
and give back the hope of a mighty people.
You, lord Tiber, who swell with foamy crown,
send our father home to us, his flock;
accept the Rhine's charge upon your gleaming breast,
and take to yourself your horned brother's care.   10
The Rhine, shaggy with foaming waters, floods his cheeks;
he swells his jowls with thick grayish billows.
The Meuse awaits you, Hartgar, with streaming tears;
he laments his absent lord and cries out to you.
Every grove rustles, and the fields and hills sigh;
every grove rustles with the wood nymphs' grief.
For the fair shepherd of a glorious flock is gone,
and a watchful guardian has left his sheep alone.
Italian land, you who bear the fruitful olive,
send to us our bounteous father.   20
Sorek, joyously dispatch to his scholars a
flourishing vine laden with fruit.
Return his people their star of shining visage
and the sole consolation to us all.
I pray, father, that you may surmount sharp crags
with pious steps and conquer the highest mountains.
Ascend the Alps a triumphant victor, where even
Hannibal, that kingly hero, was vanquished.
For he lost an eye beneath his savage brow,
as he led his army across the lofty Alps.   30
Excellent father, may the flowery fields beyond the
Alps lie open to you and extend you their welcome.
May every rough place be made smooth for you,
and every good fortune attend your journey.
May sweet honey always flow to lord Hartgar,
and may he never lack the sweet gifts of Bacchus.
Gemini and Cancer, summon anew that blessed man;
golden constellations, call him once more.
Holy father, may charming Leo receive you,
like noble Daniel, in kindness.   40
O powerful, tawny Leo, bring back the shepherd
whom Aries lured to foreign lands.
May Leo be victorious and haughty Aries subdued;
may Leo, father, triumph by your return. Amen.

Lo, Spring approaches, bearing pious joys
and all the blossoming flowers!

A bright star drives away our gloom,
as our gentle solace draws near.
The olive tree glistens, the flowery vine bursts
into bloom, and the noble palm flourishes.   50
Let all rejoice and celebrate, for the cedar
of Lebanon, so rightly named, returns.
Hail, good shepherd! Reveal to us the sacred
labors of your long and difficult journey.
Your love for God lengthened your travels
and urged you to follow the harshest of roads;
but piety and strength, and wondrous faith,
overcame that most arduous passage.
Truly, Hartgar's love for the pope moved him
to visit Rome and to see that shepherd!   60
His merit of faith shines like jasper;
and, as toil increases, so does faith's reward.
Father, were you not a beryl of many facets?
Were you not a beryl in the temple of the Lord?
Now you glitter as topaz precious to all,
and you shine like the richest sapphire.
All cherish our pastor's glorious return,
and yearn for his arrival.
May that pastor abound in wealth and good fortune
and, rejoicing, overflow with manifold blessings.   70
Every Homer loves to praise him in verse
and exalt his fame in melodious songs;
but let the black raven desist throughout the
sun's cycles, and let the swan be merry.
May learned Virgil, the glory of his muse,
and the new Orpheus bring honor to the people.
The shepherd's pipe charmed our grace from the City,
and our muse led our noble pastor home to us.
Brothers, join the Irish in pious songs and
cry out with one voice: "Hail, good bishop!"   80

Poem 7.
Sedulius celebrates Hartgar's return from Rome.

I have hung my harp on the willow's branches,
for hoary Winter forbade me to sing my song.
A ragged beard stiffened on this scholar's chin,
and my face became more prickly than thorns;
my shepherd's pipe has sounded harsh,

since our noble pastor abandoned his flock.
Garrulous Camena grieved at that offence
and concealed from us her swanlike features;
that sacred maiden, robed in splendor,
submerged her head in the muses' font.   10
And I, the poet Orpheus, was sad and mournful,
since my wife, Eurydice, had forsaken me.
But when spring's lush season arrived,
Calliope sang such melodious airs;
this sonorous Greek, chanting Greek measures,
graced our halls with mellifluous songs.
Her sweet music comforted this sorrowful poet,
entranced by the mystic words of harmonious melodies:
"Be well, Sedulius, son of the river Meuse,
Virgil of Liège, and companion of the muses."   20
She sprinkled my heart and liver
with sacred drops of heavenly nectar;
she put to my lips an ambrosial draught,
wondrous to taste, from the regions of paradise.
As I sipped it, new joys surged in my heart;
I felt renewed love for art and fair Calliope.
Then, I shed my coarse, rough beard, and
my face was smooth and glistened anew.
As I saw myself adorned with the goddess' gifts,
I addressed these few words to her sacred ears: 30
"Whence do you come, O glory of the muses?
From the font of Pegasus or the Hesperides?
Alas, how this sad poet's heart has grieved,
because you, my lovely wife, have been away!"
Her charming voice gave a soothing response,
mixing words of music with gentle reproaches:
"Since sluggish Winter, hoar with icy crusts, kept
you from seeing Rome's magnificent summits,
I could no longer endure your inactive life;
instead, I followed my glittering pastor.   40
For, though you, garrulous Orpheus, were timid,
I willingly became my pastor's attendant.
It was right that I behold the Latin lands
in which my eloquent Virgil flourished in art;
it befit me to see sage Laurentian companies.
Perchance, will you alone be renowned Homer?
To you Liège is sweet like a loving mother,
but to me famed Mantua is no less dear.
Yet, if it pleases you to hear my secret reasons

for going to Rome, I will briefly relate them.　　　　50
By authority of Lothar, the Franks' supreme emperor,
and with prayers of peace and pious counsels,
and by the consent of our people and noble senate,
honorable Hartgar was chosen their ambassador.
Glorious Hartgar is graced by noble lineage,
and excels in mind and eloquence.
The country and synod decided to send
so lofty and distinguished a bishop
to visit Peter, the chief pastor of
heavenly Jerusalem and a mighty key-bearer;　　　　60
noble Rome, he comes to restore your magnificence!
For Rome is mother of kings and glory of Italians,
but is famed throughout the triple world by Franks,
faithful Christians and pious emperors.
We traveled winter's ice-glazed roads
through snow-covered fields and frozen paths;
but, by our pastor's faith, like mustard's heat,
the cold, snowy winter abated its chills,
and when dusky showers drew over us,
he mitigated the waters with streams of eloquence.　　　　70
Then he resembled blessed Bartholomew,
son of the Father who checks the clouds of rain.
One day Hartgar read your poems,
and then I reverently addressed that excellent man:
'I am Music, wife to your Sedulius;
gracious father, swanlike Calliope attends you.
Since your scholar cannot traverse the vast
lands of Europe with his small steps,
I come in place of your dark Orpheus,
who composes three prayers for you.　　　　80
At home, Sedulius scans the stars of heaven,
and changes to a Laurentian and learned Greek.
He assumes all forms with the sound of the wind,
driving his harmonious muses outside.'
As I spoke, the holy bishop smiled, gave
the kiss of peace, and said: 'Be our companion.
Receive this well deserved reward, Camena,
which I give to the poet Orpheus.'
He placed a brilliant diadem upon my head
and arrayed me in a marvelous robe of pearls.　　　　90
After so much time we caught sight of Laurentian
towns, dazzling cities, and a multitude of wonders;
the splendid peoples which Italy produces,

and fields full of flowers and riches.
Everywhere Lambert's noble heir issued
sacred streams of heavenly eloquence.
All citizens acknowledged that blessed bishop,
who seemed a radiant angel of heaven;
all men exulted, and mighty Rome rejoiced,
exclaiming, 'Lo, the father of peace.'   100
When serene Hartgar went to Simon Peter's court,
he glowed with splendor among angelic bands.
Approaching Hartgar, Peter said: 'Dear friend,
we welcome you, your Lambert's chief care.
All of heaven sings: "Hail, golden hope of
heaven, for you will always dwell among us." '
Peter and Hartgar's angelic voices uttered
mystical words in secret discourse.
O to have heard such voices,
surpassing the harmony of muses!   110
Our bishop showered his face and cheeks with tears,
and issued joyous streams of weeping;
his pure heart poured forth many prayers,
and, like a sacred dove, murmured in sorrow.
Hartgar invoked our Mighty Emperor and King of Kings,
and prayed on behalf of his people and king.
Then Peter, key-bearer of starry heaven,
said: 'The Heavenly Father hears your prayers;
and, though your earthly king loves you, Jesus,
our divine shepherd and eternal ruler, loves you more.   120
Refresh the city with timely rain,
thus begetting splendid gifts of peace.
Glory of Italy and splendor of Rome's senate, go forth!
Flourishing bishop, forever preserve your flock!'
When he finished speaking, Peter kissed our pastor,
and the pastor, in turn, pressed his mouth to Peter's.
At last, with affairs concluded, we left the city,
even as spring smiled, robed in purple flowers.
Flying through painted fields, brilliant Aries'
golden horns conveyed our pastor homeward;   130
but I, knowing your grief, Virgil, swiftly flew
to console you with happy news of Hartgar's return.
For mighty hymn-singing Pegasus and the muses' company
led your Calliope through clouds and storms.
I implore you, remove the frowns from your brow,
since your bishop and father is coming home.
Twice he has gone to Rome and twice come back to us,

for that prelate is a living jewel of many facets.
He visits Rome's summits out of love for God
and returns for the people's peace and prosperity.   140
Thus, he travels four times out of twofold love,
so that, lo, he flashes like the number six,
which is always the sign of noteworthy deeds.
O perfect pastor, rejoice in this mystic number!
Hartgar's glorious name of seven letters
suggests the sabbaths of celestial Jerusalem.
                    HARTGARIUS
These seven letters exalt him to the
heavens in excellent praises,
for ten times one hundred and two times seven
illumine this renowned pastor's name.   150
He will joy in the hundredfold fruits of God's law,
and in the double repose of the body and soul.
The Greek muses attest this name to be Pelasgian,
and so they call our noble father Ἀρτγαριον.
Because in his wisdom he glows with virtue,
Hartgar's name is worthy of merits.
He loves your muse, though she is dark—
let your shepherd's pipe greet this pious father!
Extend palm branches to our flourishing palm,
and let your harps sound from the willows!"   160

Poem 8.
To Bishop Hartgar on his victory over the Norsemen.

Just as a beloved and pious father
comes to his sons and noble land
so, bountiful father, you bear glad
          tidings for all.

As you return after illustrious conquests,
triumphant over enemies, with piety's arms,
accept the palm of victory with your
          worthy hands.

O shining glory of valiant deeds,
you rightly earned such a trophy.   10
Noble bishop, you brandish arms famed
          in heaven.

You ward off your enemies with the shield of

faith, a sacred lorica, and Christ's helmet;
and, flashing with salvation's golden sword,
    you destroy them.

Your gleaming host, so stout of heart,
dashes courageously through the enemy;
charging on the fields, it devastates the ranks,
    with arms of Hercules.   20

O youthful band, slaying fierce enemies,
receive this glittering crown of merit.
Lo, the rebel Norsemen have perished in
    bloody plunder.

The arrogant Goliath, too, has fallen,
who had been a mighty pillar of battle;
the rest, like the Cyclops, rivalled in stature
    the highest cedars.

The twin-horned Rhine bears witness,
and the field drenched with gore;   30
the reddish shore, white with bones,
    declares the victory.

Thus, the people join in celebration,
and extoll your name above all others;
they glorify your name and praise your
    noble warriors.

Good bishop, the divine powers acknowledge
your triumphs, and the verdant palm of victory
awaits you in heaven, where you will be crowned
    with Christ's abundant grace.   40

Poem 9.
Sedulius asks Bishop Hartgar for relief.

The twin beast of thirst and hunger torments us,
and wounds us with its tearing beaks.
No rich abundance of goods delights us;
rather, dreadful poverty oppresses our spirits.
We cannot revel in the sweet gifts of Bacchus,
and even honeyed mead shuns our halls.
The parched Meuse does not gladden us with wine,

and we lack the sweet grace of golden Ceres.
Thin beer, that cruel monster, vexes us scholars—
O Blessed Christ and Lord, help us in our need!   10
Such undrinkable beer is bitter to taste,
for it is not Ceres' sweet child,
nor the daughter of the Jordan or the Meuse,
but instead, that wild brook Kedron begat it.
It numbs all the skills of the scholar's mind,
as it drives away merriment and brings on gloom;
and though it has golden hair, it is not Ceres.
You gods, remove this beast from our lands;
drown this fiend in the Lethean stream or
plunge him beneath the Stygian waters,   20
so that there the beast that plagues us
may suffer tortures and endure his just deserts.
Why do I linger and buffet the wind with plaints?
O father, I beseech you, subdue these twin beasts;
dispense a healer, good bishop, for our little wounds,
and give a poultice to your servant Sedulius.

That pious bishop laughed at these little verses
and granted his scholar's request.

Poem 10.
To Bishop Hartgar about three sheep.

Our glory, grace, and serene light returns—
let all rejoice, our true glory draws near.
Darkness depart, and let your gloomy face be gone,
for now our great splendor is with us again.
Fair Daphnis, our just and holy shepherd, is here—
Tityrus, applaud, as beautiful Daphnis approaches.
Let our shepherd's pipe play, and from its three
holes let three sheep rise and appear.
O sheep, ascend the openings with proud nose and horn;
show yourselves, bearing your manifold pleasures.   10
Truly, your fleece may banish the chills of the air—
good fleece, I beg you, protect us with your warmth!
Your hide may yield a small vellum and eternal fame,
so arise, and spread your name beyond the heavens!
Despise your miserable life and choose a better one;
reject, O sheep, your short and sorry existence.
You may glitter among the stars as a new

constellation, or even, perhaps, like Aries himself.
Rise, you sheep, so massive in size;
raise for us your six mighty horns.   20
Celestial Throne, exalt our Daphnis on high,
and elevate him by your abundant power.
I can no longer write nor tolerate the muses;
without you, O sheep, I weep and do nothing.

Poem 11.
Sedulius describes a Christmas celebration.

It is the time of snow, gleaming with perfect light;
now is the season in which Lord Jesus was born.
O brothers, shine like the purest snow,
and glisten with unblemished souls.
The Blessed Virgin gave birth to Jesus,
Ruler of the World and son of the Almighty.
Thus, in our pageant the Church's chorus plays the role
of that radiant virgin bearing God's son.
Joseph, pious and holy, was Mary's sacred spouse
and the husband to the mother of God.   10
Our fair pastor, betrothed to us in joy, is here;
he appears to us in Joseph's noble likeness.
That holy man leads us from Egypt's darkness
and guides us safely to the land of light;
then the Messiah, the Bread of Life,
is born in the town of Bethlehem.
But here is the Lord's house, and bread too,
and the nourishing drink of indigent Bethlehem.
As the angelic chorus chanted harmonious praises
and sang melodious hymns to God on high,   20
so our excellent choir, with one voice,
celebrates, O Zion, your glorious triumphs.
The Angel of the Lord sounds the sabbath and
dispatches myriad prayers to heaven.
The Lord was our shepherd, and the shepherds his witnesses;
and the Shepherd was the child who was born in Bethlehem.
Lo, our just and noble shepherd breaks out in song
and glorifies our Great Shepherd in divine adoration.
Out of the east came the Magi bearing gifts,
hastening in their journey to the Christ child;   30
but now Irish scholars arrive from western lands,
bringing their precious gifts of learning.

The Virgin Mother and Joseph receive their gifts;
nor does she reject the gifts offered to her.
The chorus of the church, like her spouse,
accepts our muse's small and humble presents.

When the joyous day arrives, let all rejoice as one,
and let gladness and love rule every man's heart.
Divine radiance attests to Christ's birth,
and heaven's splendor adores our True Light.   40
Let us walk happily in the light of Christ,
and go directly to his sacred land. Amen.
Our pastor will be our guiding light to heaven,
even as Joseph, Mary's spouse, shone so brightly.

Poem 12.
To King Charles the Bald.

Hail, famed ruler, praise of the world and glory of the age;
scion and light of your grandfather Charlemagne;
powerful heir of Louis, our great emperor;
glittering star among the heavens;
triumphant glory of battle and warlike hero;
and golden bough and imperial splendor,
shining radiantly among your gleaming Franks,
just as Venus' beauty illumines the skies.
Behold, O peoples, a verdant flower and Christ's fruitful vine!
Strew fresh flowers in his majestic path,   10
and joyously proclaim: "King Charles draws near,
bearing his father's sceptre, like serene Solomon!"
The world reveres Solomon for only one temple,
yet Charles is famed for a thousand new temples.
Solomon was Jerusalem's glorious and celebrated king,
but Charles from his throne rules a thousand Jerusalems.
Mount Zion and the Mount of Olives rejoiced in Solomon,
while the snowy Alps do homage to our King Charles.
The Jordan's sparkling waters praised Solomon,
but the horned Rhine honors regal Charles.   20
Ancient wisdom enlightened Solomon,
yet Charles drinks waters fresh and ancient.
Gentle piety and abundant power adorn King Charles;
Christ loves him, and God exalts his name.
The Gallic land gleams and exults in such a ruler,

a leader whom Italy's blessed land awaits.
Around Solomon the people assembled together;
yield now, you kingdoms, in subjection to our
king and acknowledge Charlemagne's flourishing heir,
our heavenly gift and glory of all Christians!   30
Praise this valiant lord whose pious merits have
raised his name to the heavens on a lofty pillar.
O Franks, record his brilliant deeds and admire
the wondrous trophies of a magnificent leader.

O wise and gracious king, O splendid warrior,
may Christ dispense his threefold grace to you,
the Franks' great hope and arrow of victory,
and the Church's pillar and our stout shield.
The Irish sound your worthy name with love,
while trembling Norsemen fear your splendid camps.   40
You love lilies of peace mixed with roses of war,
and shine forth our leader in white and purple array.
You are the glorious son of supreme emperor Louis,
and, thus, you glisten like Isaac's blessed son.
Charlemagne, like Abraham, shone forth mighty,
and then Louis, like Isaac, succeeded him;
you, O king, come third, like Isaac's son Jacob,
for you are your father Louis' sacred heir.
Your honored name of seven letters suggests
the holy sabbaths of heavenly Jerusalem;   50
so, too, the number of those seven letters
exalts a ruler to heaven with noble praises.

KAROLUS

Lo, the number eight hundred twenty one
illumines the name of our lofty ruler!
For one hundred designates life everlasting,
and eight signifies heaven's blessed ages.
What prudent man, wise and learned, doubts
that three times seven is our triple repose?
Thus, your name is fragrant of divine mysteries;
it is famed on earth and will be written down in heaven.   60
Every Homer loves to extoll this name in verse,
praising the man and his arms with lofty songs;
but let it be Caesar's new Virgil, skilled in verse—
may Charles always love him, and God glorify him!

Poem 13.
On sacred vestments.

The Girdle

I gird myself around chaste loins,
a rule I receive from God's authority.
I, a dazzling ornament, adorn men as pure as the snow;
those I bind on earth, I lead through the stars to heaven.
But, alas, I confess that the harsh fates oppose me,
so I can never ascend to the blessed kingdoms.

The Maniple

I am bounteous in merits and rich in honor,
and I signify the joys of the blessed.
For whoever wears me gladly on his wrists
will reap in heaven what he sows on earth.   10

The Stole

I offer eternal renown to just men,
for without me no man sees God's face.
I lead fair companies, exalting those in stoles,
and station them among bands of angels.
Through me God's sacred multitude lays aside
the tunics of skin our first parents wore.

Poem 14.
To King Charles the Bald, King of the Western Franks (843–77).

Proclaim, O peoples, the heir to Charlemagne's
wondrous power. Is he not Charles reborn?
Charlemagne was an emperor, feared in war,
and a flashing thunderbolt against the Church's enemies;
this Charles, like Charlemagne, with zeal and pious
will strives to conquer arrogant tyrants.
Our noble Charles, ruler of Europe and imperial glory,
descends from a noble line of kings;
in this exalted king shines the threefold nobility
of Louis, Judith, and Charlemagne.   10
Charlemagne was wise and acted sagely in everything,
thus sacred wisdom illumines our new Charles.
Charlemagne, surpassing the riches of Croesus or Darius,
was merciful and gently loved each man;

yet our Charles dispenses lavish gifts,
both new and old, to all Christians.
Charlemagne extended his fame to India,
but our prince's fame reaches even to Thule.
Truly, the imperial fame and lofty grandeur of these
rulers fills all the regions of the earth.   20
Now a new star of shining visage glitters
among the people of all the western lands.
Your valiant king draws near—O France, rejoice;
hearken to the name my muse celebrates!
Here beams Charlemagne's image and splendor—
acknowledge the scion of mighty Charlemagne!
Neither lilies nor roses can excel such beauty,
as this star rivals the radiance of angels.

Poem 15.
On the arrival of two kings, Louis and Charles.

Behold two brothers who glow from Mount Lebanon!
Along with splendid Charles, Louis approaches.
Their arms of justice flash right and left,
the Church's avengers against savage foes.
Blessed Louis, elder king, you repel all
the fierce barbarians from northern lands;
and Christ's divine right hand exalts Charles,
who returns from the south with gleaming trophies.
These rulers are twin thunderbolts of war;
they are twin stars and the Church's glory.   10
Through them Almighty God and Christ the King
defend the Church's radiant horns,
Europe glitters, Zion's daughter rejoices,
and Christian peoples are everywhere invincible.
For Louis, our pious emperor, blessed them,
and bequeathed such leaders to the world.
Though some earthly kings illumined the world,
none have begotten such glorious roses;
for Louis alone under starry heaven
deserved to raise such sons as these.   20
Let victory, pomp, trophies, peace, virtue,
and prosperity attend Charles and Louis. Amen.
Let the babbling peoples, right and left, above all fear them;
for love and reverence comes from fear.
In turn, let these rulers initiate golden ages

and create prosperous kingdoms for the Franks;
let them govern their myriad subjects with
perpetual rule by God's will and favor.
Inasmuch as they love only harmonious peace,
O-Christ, protect these august leaders!   30

Poem 16.
Sedulius requests a dalmatic from Vulfengus.

Twelvefold hail, Vulfengus, for the sacred
band of apostles delights in this number.
I am Sedulius, a name of eight letters,
and I gladly utter the noble name Vulfengus.
However unequal our glory and merit,
I celebrate the end of both our names.
For "us" make up their last two letters,
since Lord Jesus loves us who worship him.
Vulfengus has three noble syllables,
since God loves that just man threefold;   10
and Sedulius contains four syllables, signifying
the sacred streams of the evangelical font.
Though neither of us is adorned with radiant hair,
yet we hope for hair as white as the snow.
For, as Scythian gems darken in the sun,
so its brilliance drives away night's gloom.
Embellish the dark poet of a glorious emperor,
and grant a dalmatic to this man of verse.
The swans with seven voices will not surpass me,
and my melodious tropes will increase your praises.   20
And, in return for little, you acquire the greatest
of treasures, immortal glory and perpetual wealth.

Poem 17.
A Sapphic ode on the death of Bishop Hartgar (855 A.D.).

Our spirits grieve with exceeding sorrow,
a violent storm strikes death in our hearts,
and a steady shower of tears pours down
        our cheeks.

All the Franks cry out in lament,
and the Irish land, and Rome in Italy,
sigh and mourn the death of our
        Bishop Hartgar.

ou rich and poor, high and humble,
dained ministers of the Lord of Hosts,   10
d fair nobles of every age and sex,
      shed your tears!

Since you have fallen, good bishop,
star and radiant light, the stars
flicker and grow dim, and the sun hides
      its gleaming face.

Lo, the streaming rains that fall from
the sky have joined in our weeping!
Even the elements mourn and tremble at
      your passing.   20

Resplendent lily, visage of the rose,
flourishing palm, and stout cedar,
see how sudden ruin has withered you—
      alas, good father!

Woe to me, your wretched poet,
for my words can barely express,
O Christ, the anguish that has seized
      my miserable heart.

O blessed saints rejoicing in heaven,
receive this glittering star of piety;   30
let Zion of heavenly Jerusalem praise his
      abundant trophies.

The earth is sombre, but heaven celebrates.
Angels, chant anew your melodious songs,
and let a precious crown forever adorn our
      holy bishop.

You saints, admire that sparkling topaz,
and venerate our celestial star;
greet our blessed father, and let the holy
      cities salute him.   40

Gracious Hartgar, may Christ, and the Father,
and the Holy Spirit of the Father and Son,
be your mighty support and joyous repose
      throughout eternity.

Pious bishop arrayed in bounteous light,
shield us from danger, and be our flashing
beacon of virtue upon Zion's high and
      lofty summit.

Poem 18.
On Bishop Franco's arrival in Liège (855).

O shepherd's pipe, delight the muses,
and sound melodious songs of joy;
play sweet songs, and lead the solemn feasts,
for our dearest pastor has arrived.
See the Lord's anointed, gleaming with chrism;
Christians applaud, for God's anointed draws near!
O daughter of Zion, chanting hymns of praise,
come and acknowledge your blessed spouse.
A man of the Lord approaches, Lambert's noble heir—
hasten and greet this distinguished prelate!   10
All the people shout joyous alleluias,
and resound in gladness a new hosanna.
This dazzling star, greatly beloved by Drogo,
is the shining glory of the Church.
Bear fragrant cinnamon to this splendid bishop,
and strew fresh flowers in his regal path;
delight him with balsam's rich perfumes,
and fill the air with sweet aromas.
Hail Franco, brilliant pastor, golden light of
the world, and your people's flourishing hope!   20
Once more the full moon shines in the sky
and betokens abundant joys for your city.

Poem 19.
Sedulius to a beloved brother.

Your songs, worthy brother, delight us,
for your prayers express your inner thoughts.
Paragon of virtue and manifold splendor,
you desire true peace and salvation for the just.
Friend, you rightly said: "Time, so fleeting, slips away,"
so let us ardently seek eternal treasures.

This life fails us, and man's wonders pass,
for what we are today, we will not be tomorrow;
but the blessed life remains forever stable,
since death and time cannot despoil it.   10
Truly, as your wish for me is from a pure heart,
so my will for you is from the depths of my soul.
Like a brother, I will gladly pray for you to God,
and so I ask you to intercede with him for me.
A friend's tears are beneficial, for they cleanse—
O how I long to wed your life to mine and mine to yours!
Your muse chants this prayer: "Eternal God and King,
defend us here and sustain us in heaven!"
Vouchsafe to your servants, O Christ, what is truly
pleasing, what is just, and what is upright.   20

Poem 20.
Sedulius to Irmingard, Queen of Lothar I (821–51).

O blessed Irmingard, praise of the earth and glory of Rome;
scion, splendor, and honor of your race;
and devout parent and golden light,
graciously accept your poet's humble verses.
Fair renown exalts you among all peoples,
and your fame and honor have even reached Thule.
The Hebrews cry out, and the Greeks and Irish praise you;
and they rejoice to have you as their queen.
All peoples, thanking God who turns the heavens,
offer prayers for you to the celestial throne;   10
they joyfully acknowledge that you justly merit
the temporal favors bestowed on you by God.
For your radiant beauty, character, fame, and
lineage are unsurpassed among the Franks.
Charming beauty adorns your face,
and perfect elegance illumines your gleaming visage.
Men despise the guitar's harmonious music whenever
they hear your angelic and golden voice.
Noble simplicity graces your heart,
and chastity's palm thrives in your mind.   20
Your face shines like ivory and blushes like a rose,
and excels the beauty of Venus and the nymphs.
A dazzling crown of golden hair adorns you,
and splendid topaz, as a glittering diadem.
A rare splendor, like a sparkling sapphire,

illuminates your lovely features,
and your milk-white neck glistens with beauty,
shining with the lustre of lilies or ivory.
Your soft white hands dispense myriad gifts,
whence they sow on earth to reap in heaven. 30
Irmingard, you love Christ with a pure heart,
and, in return, he has enriched you with blessings.
Lothar, our emperor and Solomon reborn, loves
and cherishes you, his most beloved empress.
Never, I dare say, have the Franks seen your equal,
and I believe none such as you exists on earth.
Splendid queen, let this oratory not displease you,
for all people attest to my muse's song.
Be well, noble daughter, your mother's
precious scion, and lovely flower of Eden. 40
As the emperor's wife, nurture your royal son
so he may exalt his name to heaven.
Be our mighty queen, amidst a golden age,
and always bring praise to the Franks.
After a long and joyous life, ascend to
heavenly Jerusalem, escorted by bands of angels!

Poem 21.
Verses on the virtues of the apostle Peter, composed for a silk pallium of Queen Irmingard (before 851 A.D.).

The Messiah summons Peter and Andrew from their boat.
By God's word, Peter catches great numbers of fish,
and immediately falls before Christ's gracious knees;
then Peter pays a stater for himself and his master.

God's right hand upholds Peter as he sinks below the waters,
so that Peter acknowledges Jesus to be God's son.
Peter becomes the gentle key-bearer of heavenly Jerusalem,
and God entrusts his flock to him after words of threefold love.

Jesus instructs Peter, so that Peter might follow him;
Peter fills the temple with the nectar of his words. 10
Aeneas receives the gifts of his longed-for healing,
and they show Peter the garments which kind Dorcas made.

Simon Peter raises Dorcas from the dead,
and she appears to the people, alive and rejoicing.

Peter, renowned shepherd and teacher of multitudes,
instructs Cornelius in Christ's sacred dogma.

Peter baptizes Cornelius in the holy font,
and mighty Antioch rejoices in Peter's splendor.
Peter and Paul bring fame to golden Rome;
Simon the magician flies against them with evil arts.   20

A lame man, jumping about, exults in Peter's mercy.
Impious Herod thrusts Peter into prison,
but an angel from heaven leads Simon
Peter out of his dark dungeon cell.

The angel leaves Peter and ascends to heaven;
then the Prince of the Church is received
with honor at the house of Mary, where he
tells of his torture and escape from prison.

Simon soars in the sky like a strange monster,
but that wretch falls, killed by a fractured skull.   30
A sacred cross crowns Peter, our shining star;
Paul, you lose your head for Christ, our Lord.

Blessed Queen Irmingard dedicated this ornament
and embroidered gift of love to Peter—
may she glitter in an eternal stole,
and bear an unfading trophy to heaven.

Poem 22.
A description of saints in a tableau or fresco.

First illustrious Martin glitters with light,
and Hilary gleams with joyous face and pleasing mouth.
St. Mark is robed in noble attire,
and learned Sulpicius utters golden words.
A brilliant halo adorns great Remigius,
and you, Severinus, glow with gentle visage.
Justus loves to array himself in glorious purple,
but you, Maximinus, wear a crown of golden hair.
The Prince of the Church has a radiant diadem,
and his mighty right hand guides Apollonaris.   10
Noble Ambrose rejoices at his master's left.

Poem 23.

On the birth of Charles, son of Lothar I and Irmingard.

Hail, noble scion, honor of the Frankish race
and hope of a mighty people!
Hail, fair nobility, blessed son of
Lothar and splendor of Irmingard!
Lo, a new Charles from the race of Charlemagne—
let all rejoice at his presence!
A new star appears, praise of the world, hope
of Rome, and light of Europe's peoples.
Louis, Charlemagne, and regal Lothar ennoble
this youth whose coming they have awaited.   10
Bring snow-white lilies, strew flowers before him,
for a radiant prince has come among us.
Here is supreme Lothar's invincible son,
and a worthy heir to his kingdom.
O Charles, may your fame transcend the Rhine
and Alps, and extend all the way to Rome.
Great prince, receive Christ's almighty grace,
along with the sacred anointing of the Father. Amen.

Poem 24.

Sedulius to Queen Irmingard (before 851 A.D.).

Let us chant songs of praise and acclaim
the honors of our excellent queen;
with melodious song, glorify our pious
empress and celebrate her lofty name.
It behooves us to exalt Irmingard,
whom the whole earth reveres,
God elevates with grandeur,
and heaven magnifies with grace.
For her honor, renown, and eminent
name are commended through the triple world.   10
Flourishing nobility begat this gentle flower,
and brought forth, as it were, this lovely rose.
This noble queen, our shining pearl,
is graced by illustrious lineage.
As a small girl and graceful beauty,
Irmingard was always prudent and gentle.
She was a spotless dove, simple, modest, and pure,

whose heart bore no bitterness.
Sweet hope of her mother and gracious father,
she excelled in every fine quality.   20
As she learned dogmas from divine books and
ardently studied the teachings of eternal life,
bounteous wisdom and a sincere love for Christ
illumined the radiant mirror of her mind.
A comely virgin, her angelic beauty
was unsurpassed upon the earth.
Neither lilies nor roses, nor lustrous
ivory, could match her dazzling elegance;
rather, virtue glowed in her heart,
and she flashed with divine splendor.   30
She was a wondrous beacon of virtues,
and rich in glorious wisdom.
Thus, her praise and glory, and great
nobility, were proclaimed through the lands.
And by God's divine will, Lothar wisely
chose her to become his wife;
he resolved to make her his fair
queen and majestic consort.
Never has the earth seen her peer,
nor has any emperor had such a queen;   40
though Queen Eudoxia resembles Irmingard,
she is in no regard her match or equal.
Irmingard is a lover of piety and saintly queen,
always pure, chaste, and celestial in mien.
She bore a splendid son, noble Louis,
the morning star of the world.
All the earth and all who worship
Christ rejoice in this blessed queen!

Poem 25A.
The arrival of Lothar at Xanten.

Raise the portals and open the gates!
I ask you, brothers, sing out to the king!
Lift up your voices that he may live long,
prosper, conquer, and be praised.
O Christ, preserve this youth for his people,
and make him worthy to rule his father's throne.
Let this flourishing vine abound in fruit
and yield in plenty the new fruits of justice.

I pray that Lothar, robed in purple, may always triumph,
and that neither sun nor moon may harm him. 10
Cast off all enchantments, glorious king,
heir to sceptre, chrism, lands, and cities!
You who come to Xanten, accept the fruits of your labor;
hereafter, good king, you will be holy with the holy.
Be a grandfather and great grandfather of kings,
and, in the fullness of time, ascend to paradise.
The ''Alpha'' has consecrated your peaceful kingdom;
peace shines within it, and the ''Omega of Peace.''

Poem 25B.
Sedulius praises Louis II, King of Italy.

Behold a warrior renowned for glorious deeds,
the hope of Rome and glory of the world!
Africa trembles before him, and the arrogant
Moorish host, which the raging south wind bears
from Libyan shores against Christians, shudders
before his invincible might.
Louis, our brilliant star, resolved to
end such abomination with ardent vigor;
Charlemagne's fervent power surged in his
winning heart, increasing beyond measure. 10
The swan host of valiant Franks stood
arrayed in arms against raven Moors.
Splendid camps resounded a chorus of alleluias,
raising hymns of praise to heaven's throne;
but the dark throngs of monstrous Saracens
could only screech their barbarous curses.
Lost in confusion, that black Moorish band was
struck down by the sword and cut to pieces.
Those Ishmaelites gnashed their teeth
as they fell lifeless upon their haughty faces; 20
that hostile, savage horde surrendered,
bending their necks in subjection to the Franks.
Truly, Christ's grace sustained the gleaming Franks
and the palm of victory glorified their host.

Hail, majestic king, Lothar's blessed
son and nobility of Irmingard!
With you as lord and leader, new joys
arise on the earth, and the people rejoice.

Mighty Rome applauds your great triumphs,
and proclaims your spectacular victories;   30
Italy, too, marvels and exults at the
remarkable deeds of its king.
Against the Moors you were our stout defence,
and the sword and shield of our deliverance.
Bold youth, seize your spoils of battle:
thieves, tyrants, and raven plunderers.
You alone will rule these Moors, descendants
of Hagar, never before subdued in battle;
I implore you now to pursue these wolves,
destroying them with your strong right hand.   40
For to vanquish arrogant tyrants with divine
zeal is a pleasing sacrifice to God;
Peter, witnessing your victories from
heaven, is filled with joy and wonder.
Your bold deeds delighted God and Peter,
and so I pray that you may always triumph.
Since the Lord's counsel raises the horns of the just,
may it exalt you, blessed king, above all other men.
We salute you, valiant king, our noble star,
and the praise, fame, and splendor of the earth!   50
Be every source of pride and honor to the Franks,
ruling prosperously throughout your days.
Never cease to defend Christ's church,
like an arrow of victory against the Moors.
In the fullness of time, ascend to celestial regions,
and there become an eternal citizen of heaven.

Poem 26.
Sedulius to Emperor Lothar I.

I bear a hundred thanks to our emperor:
may God's right hand exalt him!
But I have erred, for I will praise his myriad
victories not a hundred but a thousand times.
As many as the dew drops in paradise,
as much nectar as Sorek's vineyard yields,
as many olives as Mount Olivet bears,
so much, and more, I desire for my lord.
He adorned me, his poet, in splendid attire,
that the Franks might admire his gleaming sage.   10
He is a lover of piety and sacred peace—

O Zion, behold Solomon, your august king!
God's grace has sent us from heaven this
glittering star and illustrious leader,
more glorious than purple, more precious than topaz,
more pleasing than amber, and more delightful than mead!

Poem 27.
Sedulius prays for Dermot's safe arrival in Liège.

O Christ, we pray, protect Dermot with your shield
and lead him and his friends safely to our city.
Gracious Lord, skillfully pilot their ships,
for without you, Father, all hope is vain.

Poem 28.
Sedulius to King Charles the Bald (d. 877).

Charlemagne was the world's most glorious emperor,
as well as Europe's prince and imperial splendor;
now that famous son of lofty Pippin rules
new kingdoms in starry heaven.
Louis, Charlemagne's son and noble heir,
dazzled the earth as the Franks' bright glory.
Louis was kind to the kind and exceedingly mild;
a gentle dove to the just but fierce lion to the wicked;
a leader of Christians and a beacon of honor;
and our magnificent emperor, both wise and gracious.   10
When pious Louis died after a prosperous life,
the earth shook, and the dark sea trembled;
but now heaven's companies rejoice that blessed
Louis governs celestial kingdoms.

Applaud, Frankish peoples, applaud and be joyful;
with one voice raise hymns of praise and exaltation!
For Charles, our new star, glitters in the heavens
and illumines the earth with splendor.
Now the sea, earth, skies, and heavens celebrate;
now, indeed, unctions of joy fill pious hearts,   20
for Charles, our lord and august emperor,
rules the golden wheel of his majestic kingdom.
With his father's hand he turns that wheel,

justly oppressing the haughty and raising up the humble;
thus, the supreme right hand of Christ, our Lord,
exalts and glorifies our illustrious ruler.
Proclaim, you peoples, the heir to Charlemagne's
triumphant power! Is he not Charlemagne reborn?
Charlemagne was mighty in war, like another David,
and moved splendid camps against alien foes;   30
but this Charles, enthroned on high, like Solomon,
confers the joys of lasting peace to his people.
The world reveres Solomon for but one temple,
but Charles is famed for a thousand temples.
Solomon was Jerusalem's glorious king,
yet Charles rules a hundred Jerusalems.
Mount Zion and the Mount of Olives loved Solomon,
however the Alps wait upon Charles, our radiant king.
The Jordan's sparkling waters praised Solomon,
but the horned Rhine exalts and honors Charles.   40
Ancient wisdom enlightened Solomon's mind,
while Charles drinks waters fresh and ancient.
Yea, piety and power adorn our Charles;
Christ loves him, and God shows him favor.
The Gallic land, flashing, exults in its ruler,
a leader whom blessed Italy awaits.

O wise and pious king, and valiant warrior,
may Christ's peace and threefold grace always be with you,
the Franks' golden hope and our brilliant star,
the bane of the haughty but glory of the just,   50
and the splendid scion of Charlemagne's race,
bearing royal sceptres like peaceful Solomon.
O radiant heir to our great emperor Louis,
you glisten like Isaac's blessed son.
For Charlemagne, like Abraham, illumined the earth,
and then Louis, like Isaac, succeeded him;
now you, noble prince, like Jacob to Isaac,
are pious Louis' fair successor.
Three is the number of your royal line,
for the Creator of the earth loves that number.   60
Gracious king, enjoy complete prosperity,
and Charlemagne's strength and martial valor;
may every honor of Charlemagne's be yours,
and all peoples delight in your reign.
Bring grace and brilliant fame to the Franks,
and raise aloft the Church's glistening horns.

The Franks extoll your magnificent trophies,
and the Jews and Greeks praise your deeds in song;
the Irish from western lands love you, gracious king,
and their learned songs celebrate your name.   70
The Norsemen dread the sound of your name and
fear the splendid camps of an invincible leader.
Good Charles, be a radiant light to the Church
and Franks, brightly shining to a blessed old age.

Poem 29.
To a king.

   May piety, peace, power, fear of the Lord,
and a pious love for God be yours. Amen.
As you now abound in worldly fame and praise,
may your divine glory be increased forever;
though power and riches exalt you on earth,
may you possess the glory and riches of heaven.
O Christ, preserve this youth for his people,
and glorify him here and in the life to come;
grant him prosperity, and a long, happy life,
and lead him to the attainment of lasting treasures.   10

Poem 30.
To Louis the German, King of the Eastern Franks (843–76).

   Louis, paragon of kings and praise of the world,
glory of the earth and radiant star of heaven,
and princely nobility and glorious scion
of Charlemagne's royal line,
accept these splendid verses and poetic
measures with a serene spirit!
For you are the celebrated heir of
our most pious emperor Louis.
Never has the triple world seen a more
excellent or glorious ruler than Louis;   10
nor has any king or emperor ever matched
his holiness and wondrous compassion.
His fame spread beyond the heavens,
for he was ever exalted by worthy deeds.
After his death, the whole earth trembled,
and all men mourned his passing;

but now that blessed ruler dwells among
the saints and governs eternal kingdoms,
enjoying unending happiness and fame
upon heaven's summit and eternal mount.   20

O golden bough, Louis' radiant son
and Charlemagne's flourishing scion,
are you not a radiant light for your people,
glittering among men like a new star of heaven?
Libya rightly shines in the splendor of Canopus
and rejoices in its sparkling light;
but Europe draws its light from you,
her majestic ruler and brilliant star.
In you she perceives your father's virtue
and the divine authority of heaven's Lord.   30
Gracious king, what should I praise first,
your splendid trophies or perfect justice?
With kingly heart, you love the lilies of
peace mingled with the roses of war.
Valorous lord, your sublime father's glory
and dignity justly embellish you.
Your fame and renown have reached to
northern lands and to the ends of the earth.
Warlike Germans and barbarous Norsemen are
struck with terror at the sight of your power;   40
they gladly submit to your commands and
strive to carry out your every wish.
O how just to subdue men to God's will
and subject them to you before all others!
For now peoples once dark and blind without
the light of faith shine with radiance.
Great warrior, you snatch the spoils from the
dragon's jaws and liberate illustrious peoples.
God's sheepfold rejoices, for you unceasingly
increase it with a new and gleaming herd.   50
Lo, the happy gentiles wonder at their
transformation from ravens into doves.

Faithless ravens, accept God, if you wish to be white;
believe in the Lord, lest you perish in wretchedness.
For now people like you are clothed in the garment of Christ,
and no longer resemble what they once were.
Cast off, then, your old defiled appearance,
and shed your ancient Ethiopian attire;
become a glistening lamb, renewed by

Christ's grace among Catholic peoples.   60
Let the heathen tongue, resounding alleluias,
learn to sing and offer harmonious praises,
so that Louis' strong right hand and mighty
wrath will be forever appeased.
Now every rank and all the babbling people
hasten from their far northern lands;
pious Solomon, with prayers they long to honor
you and choose you for their lord and king.
You alone shall rule those whom the great
emperor Louis was unable to conquer.   70
Happy Germany delights in you, its royal star,
and shines brightly in your radiance;
the Franks and twin-horned Rhine proclaim
your victories and record them in their songs.
For the glory of your name, and your fame
and honor, are acclaimed in western lands.
The Irish lovingly extoll your name,
while the Norsemen can only tremble;
and even as the heathens mourn their fate,
splendid Gaul celebrates your thousand triumphs.   80
August prince, your kingly radiance illuminates
the earth, and the churches resound with joy;
your rule establishes a golden age,
bringing new prosperity to the Franks.

We salute you, noble ruler, fruitful
vine of Christ and vanquisher of warriors!
O royal scion, bounteous father of kings to come,
and puissant hero in war and battle,
be our increase of honor and warlike champion,
and the stalwart defence of the Church.   90
Nurture pride and gentle favor among the Franks,
that they may always abound in lofty esteem;
and rule your subjects with lasting authority,
that they may forever remain invincible.
May Almighty God grant you true happiness
and long life throughout the years to come;
may you ascend to the blessed kingdoms upon
wings of virtue and reign perpetually in heaven.

Poem 31.
Sedulius describes a hospital.

You who desire the joyous gifts of health,
run as swiftly as deer to this splendid house;
turn your steps to this font of healing,
where you may probe secrets unknown to learned Greece.
Gladly receive salubrious medicines, for, with
them in hand, you will depart victorious.

Lady Medicine

This mighty queen descends from shining Olympus,
dispensing gifts with healing visage to all men.
She conquers in battle the myriad pains of the sick,
and three lights illumine her lofty countenance.   10
Her breasts issue streams of healing nectar
to restore and cure great multitudes.
Accept the many treasures of Mother Medicine,
which she brings from the gardens of paradise.
First, ointments emit their sacred perfumes,
surpassing gifts of frankincense and balms;
second, fiery antidotes flash with light,
for they expel everything harmful to health
and Medicine, I believe, once brought them
from Hesperides' magnificent gardens;   20
and, third, are gifts from Mount Olivet,
mixed with potions, and golden like nectar.
Bless you, noble house, Medicine's chief care,
hope of all people, and treasury of sweet gifts!

Poem 32.
Sedulius describes a banquet at a splendid building.

Behold how dewy Iris, in a dazzling arc,
decorates the heavens with a rainbow and,
four-colored, leaves golden footprints as
she moves athwart the sun's bright rays.
Yet, if it is possible, another gay-colored
Iris gleams in your halls.
A golden hue, aglow with light, glitters above;
verdant green, springtime's own color, follows;

next shines royal purple, a wondrous sight;
and then sparkling sapphire exalts her fame.   10
Above and below, the shimmer of glass is seen,
gaily reflecting the silver sheen of the sea.
Here a design of glassy lines depicts the
manifold glory of Christ's noble cross.
The colors gold, green, purple and azure
befit the Lord God who rules the heavens.
Purple and green praise his human sufferings,
while gold and azure extoll God's kingdoms.
Phoebus, gazing from heaven, loves this hall,
consecrating it with his brilliant rays of light.   20
Truly, serene spring prevails even in winter,
and stormy winter yields to summer.

The words of a banquet

A noble assembly of brothers takes pious pleasures,
and you, renowned Lyaeus, dispense us fresh delights.
You offer kisses of peace with your draughts of cheer;
mighty Bacchus, you captivate all these learned men.
Here is liberty, for this Liber liberates all—
Father Liber, come that I may be liberated!
Blessed Vaast, let us not be confounded by strong Falernian,
but let sweet wine yield us glad refreshment.   30
Brothers, drink a modicum or measure of wine;
in all things keep the mean or measure of Bacchus.
That laudable measure excels in noble praises,
for God himself established such a quantity.
Let all the brothers consume a measure of wine,
since "modius" is a glorious six-letter word;
let each one drink two-sixths of a measure,
and every drinker sing iambic verses.
Indeed, let all six in a six-foot iambic
praise the six stages of the creation.   40
Perhaps God on his throne, as he sits upon
heaven's summit, will accept such solemn prayers;
excellent brothers, rejoice and make merry,
that our joys in the Lord God may be heard.

Poem 33.

To Bishop Franco of Liège (855–901).

May this fruitful vine arrive amidst rejoicing:
Franco, glory of the young and hope of the old!

Behold, Franco, how August sheds her copious tears,
and longs to look upon your gleaming visage;
see how September readies clusters of fruit
and nourishes dewy grapes for our new apostle.
In the seventh month, the sabbath will shine upon us,
as you bring the joys of the Feast of Tabernacles;
you, a propitious star glimmering in the heavens,
may not refuse to illuminate our lands.   10
Your Sedulius weeps, as my sage muse attests,
because now I cannot see my lord Franco;
and I pray that Christ may forgive you
for not quickly consoling your mournful poet.
Moselle, send to us soon this blessed man,
a glorious Carolingian, our hope and pious honor.
Then will I exult and break into song,
and my muse will surpass the seven swans.
Even as a deer longs for clear running waters,
so, beloved bishop, I yearn to see your face.   20

Poem 34.
Sedulius to his Irish companions.

Little poem, lovingly greet these illustrious
brothers, Fergus, Blandus, Marcus, and Beuchell,
whose noble images, preserved in my heart,
ever increase the affection I bear them.
I confess, brothers, I am not insensible,
nor do my feelings arise in a tiny heart of stone;
rather, my love for you burns bright within me,
for it is no fault to esteem such worthy men.
Even Codrus' heart is filled with envy,
whose insides, I pray, may burst asunder.   10
Fergus, always be my gracious arrow of victory,
and remember Sedulius in your divine petitions.
For from within you, brother, come plaintive tears,
sacred sighs, and prayers like heavenly nectar.
Never cease to reach the ears of the Lord,
that he may thoroughly cleanse me of my sins.
My muse, dark and bold, resounds from a learned heart,
and my Ethiopian maid, bearing her bow, will praise you.
Friend Marcus, I pray, ward off the Enemy's cruel attacks,
with the shield of faith and blessed deeds.   20

What will you do, Beuchell, valiant among warriors?
I beg you, crush the neck of the fierce viper.
Blandus, glory of war with flashing crest, and
gentle dove of God, raise thunder for Sedulius.
Four-span of the Lord, lights of the Irish race,
prosper throughout the passage of time;
in the end ascend to radiant temples of
heaven and join the fellowship of the saints.

Poem 35.
Sedulius to Fergus.

Fergus, prince of poets and glory of the splendid muse,
rejoice that you possess such sacred treasures of art!
Not in vain did fair Calliope from shining Olympus
inspire you with melodious rhythms.
For your song praises Charles' noble reign,
and your tropes exalt that golden ruler.
Your poem surpasses the art of Virgilian muses,
and even Ovid's pipe is silenced by your songs.
Truly, only eternal fame, not mere pompous praise,
can reward your verses, blessed herald—Adieu.   10

Poem 36.
Sedulius to Robert.

Good Robert, supreme glory, our muse's golden
hope, and splendor and fame of our solemn age,
show us your kindness in our time of need!
Lofty father, let your mercy grant us a ram,
that you may ascend to the heavens.
Let it frolic around our dwellings with its huge
body, buffeting the winds with its mighty horns!
Now, alas, a ferocious beast ravages our halls,
as cruel hunger tears us with his beak.
Destroy this plague with your gentle favor,   10
and expel this abomination and heinous monster.
Give us a ram, fearsome in battle and massive in
size, who butts with piercing horns and can
tear apart the menacing beak of ravenous hunger.
Great fame of victory will be yours,

and Christ's balsam will soothe your heart.
We Irish pray, send us a valorous ram,
since we alone can devour it in style.
And with clear voice, my sated muse, an Ethiopian
maid, will praise your bounty in mirthful songs.   20

Pious Robert even gave the flowing gifts of Bacchus,
presenting his poet with three hundred flasks of wine.

Poem 37.
Epitaph for the son of Count Eberhard of Friuli (d. 868–69).

O cruel, ravenous death, you spare no man,
and cut down the lilies and roses in bloom;
you devastate the earth even as the south wind
beats down the flowers with driving rains.
Eberhard's son, named for his father,
shone like a fair purple flower;
a new light illumined the earth, his parents'
hope, a golden bough, and a radiant lamp.
You, lad, like a crimson apple of purple beauty,
were beloved and dear to your father and mother.   10
Alas, fair youth, that death's savage jaws have
devoured such a lovely violet!
I pray, strew flowers upon his grave,
for a fresh blossom and flourishing scion has perished!
Renowned Gisla and gentle Eberhard, be not
mournful but joyous and filled with gladness,
for your precious son is with Christ in heaven
and stands glorious amidst angelic companies.
Do not despair, since you will bear another
splendid child by the bounteous grace of God!   20

Poem 38.
To Count Eberhard, Count of Friuli, on the birth of his son.

O Eberhard and Gisla, glorious parents,
we bear thanks to God, who renews all things;
for born to you is a new and excellent son,
the people's fair hope and jewel of the land!
Lo, the Lord has granted the petitions of noble parents
whose prayers have penetrated the precincts of heaven!
After your first-born son had ascended to

the citadel of everlasting Jerusalem,
everyone mourned the loss of your sweet hope,
and that a little flower of paradise had perished;　　　　10
but he reached the summit of starry heaven
and shines bright among the innocents.
Truly, you adorn heaven with your blessed child—
rejoice that you have begotten such a rose!
Splendid parents, join in celebration,
for God has blessed you with a new son,
our radiant star of hope, his father's image,
a precious gift, and a flourishing scion.
His grandfather Louis, a renowned emperor,
is reborn in this august child—what could be greater?　　　　20

　Prosper little prince, our joyous gift,
Gisla's bright flower, and Eberhard's dear love.
Nobly advance in illustrious virtues,
pouring forth alleluias with tender lips;
fill your soul with Christ's mellifluous teachings,
and let sacred wisdom gleam in the tablets of your heart.
Follow your father ever mighty with sword, who
in his youth drank wisdom's sacred waters.
Charming lad, enjoy a long, happy life;
be the Church's defender and our swift arrow.　　　　30
Attain the dazzling glory of the age,
worthy of your father's honor and dignity.
May the Franks exult in their mighty ruler,
and may the Church rejoice in your reign.
Be a light to the world and a star in heaven,
triumphantly raising your fame to the skies!

Poem 39.
Sapphic verses to Count Eberhard of Friuli.

Now we rejoice with joyous hearts,
for Eberhard returns, our glory and light,
immense victor, and glittering star
　　of piety!

Noble gem and pillar of the Church,
invincible enemy of the wicked, and
pious hero filled with goodness and
　　great in all things,

the arrogant Moor and proud Saracen,
tyrants you have learned to conquer   10
with pious arms in Christ's service,
    fear your mighty deeds!

Were you not then a stout hero, with
flashing helmet, glorious breastplate,
and blazing sword, and protected by a
    dazzling shield?

All the gleaming Frankish hosts joined
you in battle with valiant hearts;
rising in war, they flew across the fields
    against the Saracens.   20

All the sons of Ishmael and the dark Moors
shook with fear when they saw you;
in their black mouths, their frozen tongues
    stuck in their throats.

The enemy gathered in towering fortresses;
trusting in their fortifications, they cast
useless weapons and howled with a most
    horrible roar.

But the splendid Frankish army shot
swift arrows at their enemies;   30
they produced a rain of iron and inflicted
    wounds of death.

O how the Lord's zeal glowed in the heart
of Eberhard, a valorous leader!
Truly, Christ exalts the shining horns
    of the just.

Our hero, ever loyal to his duty, heaped up
ravenous flames around the Moors' defences;
the renowned chief, wondrous to behold, struck
    with lightning itself.   40

O fearless warrior, forever crushing tyrants,
your right hand delivered its response,
levying swift and terrible judgment
    against your foes.

Arms of piety have laid low the heathens,
and triumph exalts our radiant Frankish hosts;
Rome celebrates, and your people exult in your
      magnificent victories.

Fair Eberhard's fame reaches the heavens—
O blessed Peter, pray that God's sacred finger   50
will inscribe Eberhard's glorious name in the
      Book of Life!

Eberhard, you glitter among the Italians!
You defeat the Moorish hordes, subduing
fierce Saracen rebels with the mighty
      arms of Hercules!

Always you increase the universal esteem of the
Franks and extend their prestige across the earth.
Even the Irish and Greeks solemnly praise your
      feats in song!   60

Accept the victor's palm graced with merit;
adorn your head with a glittering diadem,
and be crowned in glory with wreaths
      of laurel.

Eberhard, we implore Christ, the Son of God,
that you may enjoy a long and happy life
and, in the fullness of time, ascend to heaven
      by your blessed deeds.

Graciously receive this poor, sage poet
of Christ, whose lips have chanted   70
and fingers written this new
      and melodious song.

Does not the cork, redolent of balsam,
endure the piercing of the iron corkscrew,
whence from the fissures flow such precious
      drops of liquid?

Poem 40A.
Epitaph to Hildebert (862 A.D.).

In this tomb rests Bishop Hildebert, who
shone with virtue and was taken up to heaven.

Poem 40B.
Epitaph to Adalwin.

O ancient and blessed Adalwin, a noble priest
of the highest merit, you rest in this coffin.

Poem 41.
A dog destroys a ram from Bishop Hartgar.

When Almighty God created the animals who
inhabit the sea, the land, and the heavens,
he endowed rams with lofty honor and
appointed them leaders among the sheep.
Our bountiful Creator arrayed them in fleecy coats
and covered their bodies with thick robes of flesh.
He armed their bent brows with curved horns
which won proud victories from horned foes;
he increased their haughty powers with double
nostrils and equipped the rams with menacing snorts.   10
Yet gentle simplicity was planted in their horns,
for no deadly poisons can afflict these pious creatures.
I confess, too, that I love them more each day;
their fleecy robe and plump body are my sole delight.
I swear in writing this eternal truth:
I desire, cherish, and always love such things.
Not even Lethe's waters can extinguish such love,
for the mouth speaks what the inner heart suggests.
Our little verses praise and salute your rams—
O bounteous father, you know I do not lie!   20
To us, your gloomy Irish, you have generously
granted swarthy rams and often white ones, too.
Alas, that the fairest and fattest has suddenly
perished, consumed by cruel death!
He was a glorious flock's noble defender,
and never have we seen his like or equal.
The enormous power of his stern horns surpassed

that of all the horned and gleaming flocks;
glittering with snowy fleece and little white eyes,
he was a valiant and mighty victor in battle.   30
Aries loved him with chaste affection
and longed for him to share his kingdom.
Admiring that ram's gleaming fleece,
Lucina sought to make him a star in heaven;
it is even said that Luna loved a woolly fleece,
and with a fleece Pan of Arcady deceived her.
I do not deny I loved him, for I am not insensible.
Who but a fool would not cherish that ram?
In your kindness, father, which refuses nothing,
you gave me a noble prize;   40
but Fortune, alas, ever hostile to good,
snatched Tityrus from this wretched poet.

There was a vile thief of Goliath's race,
like an Ethiopian and villainous Cacus;
ugly to see and with an evil black face;
and both savage in deeds and harsh in speech.
O pious ram, he stole and dragged you through
thorns with execrable hands—what horror and misery!
As you sped through the fields, piteous ram,
you were gentle and tranquil in spirit;   50
but then a fierce pack of dogs caught sight of
that thief and you, a horned and spirited chief.
Suddenly, that bold pack made swift leaps forward;
a great din arose, and loud crashings.
They pursued thief and loot with hungry mouths;
leafy wood roared, and every tree cried out.
Why say more? The gentle ram was captured, and
the thief, swifter than wind, fled in the dark.
The deserted ram stood and fought bravely,
butting with his horns and inflicting many wounds.   60
The outmatched dogs were amazed by that horned ram
and feared they had attacked a lion.
They barked at the ram with growling words,
but the noble ram spoke clearly and graciously.
"What madness seizes your hearts," he said,
"for am I not Bishop Hartgar's servant?
I am not a wicked robber, nor that petty thief,
but a pious ram, the flock's finest leader.
If it pleases you to vanquish a harsh tyrant,
let us assail that thief who lurks nearby;   70

yet if your fury and hoarse barking stir
bloody violence in my tranquil breast,
I swear by my head, horns, and noble brow,
to win fitting spoils of battle from you."
With these words he soothed the dogs' hearts;
peace came to pass as each side backed away.

Soon, alas, a howling Anubis approached,
whose grandfather was Cerberus, hound of hell.
Like skillful Cerberus, with three tearing mouths
he pursued swift deer and clumsy bears.   80
When he saw that fierce pack subdued,
he snarled, and puffed his hairy neck.
"Does this sheep," he said, "this fox with sly
tricks, deceive you in the false name of peace?
Yonder see that evil thief and here his foul partner,
and how together they crept through leafy coverts.
I hold this ram to be the cause of such evil,
who offers peaceful words, but threatens with his brow."
Then the ram, with strong, piercing horns,
attacked that liar's face and shattered two teeth;   90
his horns tore the dog's face, but he lost
sure victory by fleeing the battle.
The ram, as if victorious, flew swiftly from his enemy;
he ran recklessly about and openly took flight.
Soon he fell amidst thorns and cutting briars—
our proud ram became stuck among brambles!
Accursed Cerberus kept harassing the ram,
inflicting dire wounds with bloodthirsty jaws.
The ram, wondrous to see, fell lifeless to the ground,
splashing the briars with crimson blood.   100
The nymphs lamented, the trees burst into tears,
and the bleating flock bewailed that monstrous deed.

Radiant, twin-horned Luna, Aries of heaven,
you rightly mourn that snow-fleeced ram.
Wherein his guilt—so simple, just and true?
He refused the gifts of Bacchus and taste of liquor, too;
no drunkenness lured him from the righteous path,
nor feasts of kings, nor revels of princes.
His solemn feast was the grass in the fields,
and the clear Meuse gave him sweet drink.   110
He never eagerly sought clothes of brilliant purple,
but was content simply with his own skin;

not astride a proud horse did he gallop on fair greens,
but on his own legs justly made his way;
and he did not lie or speak idle words,
but uttered the mystic words "báá" and "béé."
As the lamb enthroned on high, God's son himself,
tasted sharp death for man's sins,
gentle ram, following death's road and mangled
by vicious dogs, you died for a sinful thief! 120
Even as a sacred ram was sacrificed instead of Isaac,
so you, good ram, are an offering for that thief.
O God, in your tender mercy and manifold power,
you do not wish men to endure an iniquitous death,
and so your supernal right hand saved the penitent thief,
when you promised him paradise as you hung on the cross.
Give thanks to God, O base, perfidious thief!
Proclaim these words along with the psalmist:
"Then the right hand of heaven's Lord exalted me.
I will not die, but will live to sing his praises. 130
His great power has corrected me with punishment
but has not left me to die or dragged me to slaughter!"

Epitaph

Adieu, splendid ram, noble chief of a gleaming herd!
Alas, my grassy green no longer feeds and fattens you.
Perhaps, friend, there might have been a hot bath for you
(but only to please my beloved guest, of course!);
I myself would have ministered with devout heart
to your horns, head, and hooves.
You I have loved, and your widow and mother, too;
forever will I love all your brothers—Adieu. 140

Poem 42.
About a church (before 855 A.D.).

Behold a radiant temple of heavenly form!
Renowned Bishop Hartgar, noble in deed and
glowing with a sacred love of celestial Jerusalem,
designed this church to shine with manifold splendor.

This house of the Lord has brilliant windows
through which Phoebus' rays stream with light.
Solemnly dedicated on the fifteenth day of May,
its myriad colors dazzle our eyes.

This splendid church honors Peter and Paul;
the Virgin Mary's sacred name also sanctifies   10
this glorious temple adorned with lovely flowers;
and the entire chorus of saints consecrates its precincts.

Poem 43.
To Berta.

Flower of Irmingard and glory of Lothar,
yours is the radiance of a silvery dove!
O shining amber, your mother's fair image,
Lothar's bright care, and Jesus' blessed spouse,
you flash with gems of virtue and ascend the heavens,
like a swift chariot upon wheels of justice.

Poem 44.
To King Charles the Bald.

Bear him cinnamon and precious gifts of myrrh,
and bring him sweet spices and Irish flowers!
For God, the All-Creating, has poured forth
oil from heaven and anointed him king.
O noble ruler, you are the third branch
and royal scion of two mighty emperors.
O peoples, spread Panchean flowers for your king;
strew lilies, I pray, in his most royal path!

Poem 45.
About a defeat of the Norsemen.

Let the heavens rejoice, the sea, and all the lands;
let Christ's happy peoples exult and marvel at
the mighty deeds of the Lord, the Father,
    thundering Godhead.

Behold the author of good, highest in praises;
see the Blessed Creator, wondrous in works,
whose universal power disposes all things in
    accord with his will.

Our holy Ruler, the hope and salvation of the world,
crushes the wicked but exalts the humble;   10

his lofty power even raises up the valleys and
    levels the mountains.

He causes Christ, the True Light, to shine in
faithful hearts and on the mirror of the mind;
a sustaining creator, abundant in love, he
    protects his people.

Let rich and poor, mighty and humble,
clerics in His tonsured order, and every
rank or sex, young or old, forever praise
    the Lord.   20

Give glory to God, for our Almighty Father's
strong arm has inflicted sudden ruin
upon rebellious Norsemen, the wicked
    foes of piety.

The battle is joined in open plain,
the splendor of arms glitters in the sun,
and myriad war cries seem to shake the
    frame of heaven.

Opposing hosts have cast their spears,
while the unhappy Dane counts up his losses;   30
an enormous army aims and unleashes its rain
    of iron.

Fierce tyrants drink the blood they have
thirsted for year after year;
it seems sweet to refresh themselves with
    the blood of men.

Those who dug pits have fallen into them;
a tower, once so haughty, has been toppled,
as Christ has annihilated that
    hostile race.   40

A stout and bold people is cast down,
a cursed mass crushed and crumbled,
and an evil issue consumed by death's jaws—
    praise to you, O Christ!

Thus they reckon the slaughter of men:
not counting unknowns, not counting menials,
three times ten thousand fell on that
        bloody field.

The judge is just, master of the world,
Christ the true glory of Christians,   50
prince of fame, and vanquisher of evil
        with highest authority.

A great tower is the Lord, and shield of salvation,
who destroys massive giants in battle,
and whose lofty name is blessed above
        all others.

His faithful people trust in their avenger,
who once drowned the Egyptians in the sea's
swollen torrents and pressed their swift chariots
        to the bottom.   60

Christ, in purple array, rules all
the Heavenly Father has created;
he is a blessed scion of the house of David
        and our true glory.

Offer votive incense to our God,
whom our pious prayers worship;
let the pipe of praise play a song for
        the King of Heaven.

Sing out with praise and shout hosannas
to the Father, Christ begotten, and the Holy Spirit: 70
you skies, waters, and lands, never cease to
        glorify him.

Poem 46.
Sedulius against a plague.

Set free your people, deliver your servants,
and allay your anger, most blessed Ruler;
look upon their tears and bitter weeping,
        merciful Christ.

You are our Father and divine Lord,
and we your servants, Kind Shepherd,
who bear the tokens of your crimson blood
    marked on our brows.

Deep in your black hell who will confess?
Will the dead sing your praises?   10
O dreaded Judge, we pray, spare us from
    your iron rod.

Set not before your people the cup of
your anger and of your just wrath;
rather, shine upon us your ancient compassion—
    hear our prayers!

Abolish our sins, we beseech you,
and keep us forever, holy prince.
Vanquish the shadowy gloom of our spirits,
    Light of the world.   20

Saint of saints and King of kings,
visit your people with your sacred right hand.
Look upon us, Lord, with your serene countenance,
    lest we perish.

Poem 47.
About an altar.

  The glory of the saints sanctifies this altar,
for it holds the sacred treasures of their relics.
Here reigns a holy piece of Christ's cross,
which harrowed hell and opened the heavens;
and the honor of the Virgin Mary, who bears
the sceptres of the throne of paradise, adorns it.
This altar forever preserves the apostles' fame,
among whom Peter and Paul shine victorious;
it holds, too, the martyrs' redolent ashes,
and foremost is Stephen's triumphant crown.   10
Rathbald, the Lord's bishop, erected this
divine altar during King Roric's reign.
He piously dedicated it to you, O Christ,
and devoted it to the honor of your saints.

Poem 48.
Verses written on a painted solarium.

An angel from heaven appears to Zacharia,
while the Archangel Gabriel addresses gentle Mary.
Elizabeth and Mary rejoice in their hearts;
then Jesus the Saviour is born in Bethlehem.

The angel announces the Messiah's birth to the shepherds;
Christ is presented at the temple amidst Simeon's rejoicings.
Lo, the magi give frankincense, myrrh, and gold to Jesus,
and an angel leads them homeward by a different route.

Joseph flees into Egypt with the child and Mary,
while cruel Herod savagely murders the innocents.   10
In the desert John preaches the way to salvation,
proclaiming the presence of Christ, the Lamb of God.

The Lord is baptized in the Jordan's gleaming waters.
When no wine is left, his gracious mother brings six
jars of water to Jesus, which he turns into wine.
The Messiah summons Peter and Andrew from their boat.

Poem 49.
Sedulius to Bishop Hartgar (840-55).

The crops are green, and fields all in flower;
the vines are full, for now is beauty's season.
Gay-painted birds fill the air with song,
and there's a smile on sea, earth, and starry sky.

But with it all, there's no mirthful drink for me,
no mead, no beer, no gifts of Bacchus.
Alas, how I lack the manifold substance
which the soft earth and dewy air produce!

I am a writer, a musician, Orpheus reborn,
and an ox treading corn, who seeks what is good;   10
and I am your champion bearing wisdom's arms.
O muse, tell my lord bishop of his servant's plight!

Poem 50.
Sedulius celebrates the arrival of a bishop to Liège.

An approaching angel illumines us with light,
like the herald Raphael bearing joyous gifts.
Alas, good father, we have dwelt in darkness,
and shadowy gloom has oppressed us;
but you, a bright and wondrous light,
give us new cause to celebrate.
The Moselle's gleaming waters have borne to
us a gentle herald and flourishing father.
Like John, who christened Jesus, you bring us
tidings of peace—peace be with you, Adieu.   10

Poem 51.
In a church.

Christ, the Master, controls these horses with piety's
reins and drives his four-horse team to heaven.

Poem 52.
In that same church.

The martyrs entreat the ears of the Lord of Hosts:
"O True Judge, avenge the cup we have drunk!"
When the Universal Judge comes, the sun will darken,
blood will stain the moon, and the stars will fall;
fearful peoples will seek to hide in gloomy
caverns before the tribunal of the Lamb of God.

Poem 53.
Hartgar gives a book on warfare to Eberhard of Friuli (d. 868-69).

In this book shine the precepts of valiant men
who gleamed with roses of war and by noble arts
and wise counsels conquered a vast multitude
of peoples throughout the triple world.
This brilliant, threefold array of warfare glitters
with mighty warriors and rouses hearts to martial deeds.
Here a terrible trumpet-blast resounds with clamor;

a rolling ballista hurls rocks through the air;
and a battering ram, sharp and menacing,
pounds and batters turret walls.   10
Men, too, with manifold skill, scornfully resist
sickle-armed chariots, judging them for naught;
even a fierce elephant, like a steep mountain,
is thrown to earth, subdued by their skill.
For war's victorious art conquers all adversities;
it defends, elevates, and gladdens the people.
Whoever esteems the art of war will find all
there is to know in this new treasury.

This worthy gift is yours, Eberhard,
a mighty leader, scion and glory of your forefathers,   20
defender of the Church, famed hero, ardent zeal,
and a strong right hand against the Moors.
Great warrior, the Slav and Saracen fear you,
as you vanquish the savage plagues of the Church.
May God praise and confirm your deeds;
may you forever triumph and eternally endure!

Poem 54.

Sedulius praises Emperor Lothar I of the Franks (840–55).

Hail, serene ruler, our glittering star under
heaven, the people's blessed leader, the Franks'
loving father, and our summit of honor!
Lothar, paragon of splendor and glory of Rome,
your fame flies across the earth,
and even Thule celebrates your name.
For you are David's image and worthy scion,
and Solomon reborn, redolent with gifts of peace;
and we pray that you, Zion's noble son and supreme
prince, may flourish throughout the ages.   10
Blessed emperor, ruling sceptres through Christ's favor,
reign forever in supernal kingdoms;
always be our brilliant star in the heavens,
eternally rejoicing in Jerusalem's light.

Poem 55.
Against liars.

A liar feigns ravens to be doves,
and calls the dove of God a raven.
By his head he swears that lies are truths,
and depicts truths as false inventions.
He reckons light for darkness, darkness for light,
and portrays bitter gall as sweetest honey.
Devouring gentle lambs with sharp fangs, he cries:
"Beware of these savage wolves!"
In his false heart turn two chambers;
one stores truth, and the other hides deceit.   10
For his gullet issues a black stream,
spewing lies and smoking masses;
in his gaping mouth prates a viper's tongue,
as if seven men were talking at once.
He shuns the light of truth,
and lies hidden in cavernous pits.
His Ethiopian garb cloaks truth with evil art,
and his reeking mouth spits thick clouds.
This Egyptian creeps in gloomy shadows,
as the night raven flees the sunshine.   20

Poem 56.
Prayer against false witnesses.

O God, eternal lamp and font of light and truth,
expose the deceitful with your clearest radiance!
In your justice, Lord, hear your people's plaints;
they implore and lovingly invoke your name.
Father of Truth and True God, ever true,
all of creation confirms the Lord of Truth.
Drive away, Infinite Light, the dense darkness,
and expose spurious masses with words of light.
O Son of David, wiser than Solomon and Prince of Peace,
do not confound your gentle servants;   10
rather, confound the lies of the faithless demon,
which that viper hisses at helpless sheep.
O Lion of Judah, O King and Christ our light,
banish dark deceptions with your splendor;
beam shining rays into falsehood's pit,

whence cunning speech spews flaming pitch.
Did you not once support chaste Susanna,
and unmask the false witnesses against her?
No artful duplicity, old age, or
evil poured from lying mouths availed them;   20
but by you, Lord of Truth and Perfect Judge,
black Hades swallowed those impious men.
For those conspiring frauds with sly deceivers
suffer just rewards among hyprocrites.
O God, supreme power is your gleaming conqueror
before whom falsehood's clouds must vanish.
We pray, O Christ, be our kind judge,
and grant us forgiveness from your throne.
We believe, too, Great Ruler, that you are God's son,
and hope that you will be a gentle master to the gentle.   30
As our lord and judge, do not weigh down
your servants with a harsh burden,
nor overthrow those who trust in you;
but destroy monstrous deceit with your sceptre.
Righteous Lord, weigh the scales of justice;
let truths fly heavenward, and lies descend to hell.
O Christ, be our shield and tower of deliverance;
be ever mindful of your humble followers.

Poem 57.
Sedulius complains to Bishop Hartgar(?) about a liar.

What did the little lying fox tell you, pastor?
Did he belch the lies that intoxicate him?
Perhaps his mouth vomited black coals,
or babbled deceitful arguments?
Perchance he feigned death with eyes closed,
as a trick to seize the birds of the air?
Did the red-bearded fox lurk in sheep's clothing,
lest he be suspected of his mother's tricks;
or did he approach you with devious steps,
leaving oblique circles in his winding tracks?   10
Has he informed you, too, that now the gleaming
Moselle is without fish or currents?

O Heavenly Father, Judge of justice and equity,
mark these deceptions with watchful eyes.
As the morning star dispels night's shadows,

illumine your people with the lamp of justice.
Great Judge, glow with righteous zeal,
and with brilliant judgment destroy this foul crime.
Confound those who have confused the tranquil,
and let not the rule of justice's cycle be silent.   20
Like Moses, shine radiant with your horned brow;
and like the judge Daniel, fiercely extinguish falsehoods.
Let those be slandered who spread,
speak, or cause any slander against us.
O sky, land, sun, and mighty sea,
hearken to my plaintive song!

Poem 58.
Some rhythmic verses.

"What a good man is Robert,
and Robert's praises ever flow.
O Christ, show favor to Robert,
and bless Robert with long life.

God keep you, Robert,
and may Christ be with Robert."
Robert, behold your illustrious
name in all six cases!

You shine in great deeds
like a stone of many facets.   10
Have I called you a stone?
Perhaps I used a hard word.

But lest I be stoned,
I beg you for clear waters;
and on account of hard speech,
let Bacchus fill my mouth.

If my words seem hard,
let Lyaeus attend me.
For the rich and poor
rejoice in your kindness.   20

Near the Meuse's clear waters
there is no one your equal;
the Moselle announces this,
and the Rhine proclaims it.

A thousand casks of purest
wine, and huge boars and
horned rams, forever
thunder it forth.

Many are the treasures which
Christ bestows upon you,   30
for, though you are eloquent,
you are even wiser in heart.

You are a father among fathers
and a sage among sages;
you issue showers of wit
from the Jordan river.

Glistening with heaven's dew,
you instruct men's minds;
you construct a lofty tower,
striving for the heavens.   40

You search the heavens
for propitious signs;
and from a sage you become
a bright, winged angel.

In the fullness of time,
may you rejoice with our
Blessed Father upon Zion's
celestial summit.

You who joy in consoling
the dejected with Falernian gifts,   50
may you drink from the font of life
in fellowship with the saints.

Such pleasing liquids do not flow
from Siloam's pool.
I've tasted your nectar, I do not deny;
I'll taste it again—beer, away!

Poem 59.

Sedulius celebrates the arrival at Liège of Emperor Lothar I of the Franks (840–55).

Hail, Lothar, glorious emperor, praise of the
world, and Charlemagne's fair scion!
We celebrate the arrival of a pious
emperor's imperial son and majestic heir!
Liège, see your king, of Charlemagne's blessed race;
rejoice, O Zion, as he approaches.
Greet this verdant flower and Christ's fruitful vine;
strew fresh flowers in his gleaming path.
O May, receive a ruler foremost in honor,
the Franks' serene and noble leader.   10
All rejoice, as the morning star,
hidden on Easter, glitters among us.
Though the rose does not yet bloom, in
Easter's festive season our emperor delights us.
For St. Lambert, who shone like a rose,
joyfully acknowledges this purple rose;
and Bishop Hartgar, St. Lambert's gracious heir,
lovingly welcomes this august lord.
O Meuse, join the Rhine and celebrate
your glory with melodious songs;   20
for Eridanus, lord of rivers,
pays homage to the emperor's fame.
Among us is a valiant warrior, mightier
than Hercules, who exalts his name to heaven.
Rejoice, happy Franks, for your Solomon is here,
a prince who always loves peace.
Radiant with piety, he glitters in
the garland of divine justice.
This splendid ruler loves the lilies
of peace and the roses of war!   30

Poem 60.

Sedulius praises the victory of Lothar I of the Franks (840–55) over the Norsemen.

Let us joyously exult with glad hearts,
for our pious and serene emperor returns,
bearing in his goodness the joys of
        lasting peace.

All the happy people, and every rank
and sex, are joined in celebration;
they give joyous praise to Christ for
        the emperor's arrival.

Behold the morning star, the Franks' bright
light, famed beyond the heavens;   10
and our pious emperor, the sole
        ruler of the earth!

This noble palm of victory is the Church's champion,
a valiant hero in gleaming arms,
Rome's golden glory, and the grandeur
        of the age.

O gracious daughter of Zion, receive your king,
a gentle, wise, and glorious prince,
and a peaceful ruler, wise
        like Solomon.   20

Greet this flourishing scion bright with flowers,
this sacred vine from Sorek's ancient vineyard,
this cedar of fair renown, and this
        regal star.

He is our mighty wall and stout shield,
a faithful ally and sword of deliverance,
and a blessed king of a lofty nation and
        powerful people.

O Lothar, did not the Norsemen fear you?
For, when they saw your gleaming hosts,   30
that hostile horde rushed to their ships
        in headlong flight.

The splendor of arms and the sole appearance of
a valorous leader vanquished the enemy,
as fear gave wings to their soles and
        naked feet.

No hope was left them but a single ship,
so they sought out cavernous pits.
They quake with terror at the arms of
        a bounteous prince!   40

Your ardent zeal, noble ruler, aroused
you against Belial's servants.
Supreme emperor, never have we seen
    your like or equal.

By such bold feats, you exalt the Frankish
name and spread its fame across the earth;
and in heaven you preserve abundant merit
    in the Book of Life.

Poem 61.

Sedulius praises Berta, daughter of Lothar I and Queen Irmingard.

    Hail, honor and glory of royal parents,
bounteous beauty, and spotless dove of God!
O blessed scion of Emperor Lothar,
and flower and praise of Irmingard,
Lothar alone deserves such a daughter,
and merits to call you his own.
No other queen shone on the earth more
holy, wise, or noble than Irmingard.
Her bountiful power excelled in sacred morals,
as she illumined the heavens like a glittering star;   10
though dwelling in this world, she yearned
for and tasted the joys of heavenly Jerusalem.
Never has the earth seen her equal,
nor any emperor possessed such a queen.

Berta, her garlands of virtue are fragrant upon you,
and your mother's image glows in your noble heart.
Wisdom illuminates the mirror of your mind,
and your inner heart burns with Christ's love.
You are a model of modesty and a serene light,
and the perfect reflection of Lothar and Irmingard.   20
How blessed are your parents, our emperor and queen,
who bore such a glistening pearl!

Poem 62.

Sedulius prays for an end to rain and floods.

We pray, Sacred King, with our words, minds, and hearts,
that your gentle mercy may grant us fair weather.

Lo, the stormy sky floods our lands with rain,
and raging torrents wash away the fertile fields.

We implore you, divine Master of all things,
to touch the earth's fruits with soft moderation.
Ruler of the Universe, thus we beseech you,
bless our vines with your fruitful serenity.

Poem 63.
Sedulius celebrates the feast of Easter.

This is the bountiful day, holiest of holy days,
and the glory and splendor of flowery spring.
For this is the day the Lord Jesus made,
on which the whole world exults with joy.
Lucifer, with gleaming hair and robed in
saffron by the rising sun, is filled with awe;
even bright Vesper glitters at sunset
and lovingly acknowledges the Lord's day.
The Great Bear illumines the heavens,
his seven lights honoring God's feast;   10
and radiant Canopus dispels Egypt's gloom,
emitting brilliant spheres from his mouth.
Golden Luna crosses the star-filled sky,
bearing a new royal diadem;
she marvels at the lofty horns of
Christ, her prince and ruler.
Titan, all aflame with his fiery wheels,
ascends the summit of glimmering heaven;
his flashing disk praises Christ's victory,
driving away the night with his sunshine.   20
Tellus swells with buds about to blossom
and glories in her embroidered robe of flowers.
A chorus of birds fills the air with song,
and with lilting voices proclaims God's triumphs.
The skies rejoice, the earth celebrates anew,
and alleluias resound in a hundred melodies.
Now the church's chorus, singing Zion's hymns,
raises hosannas to heaven's summit.

Poem 64.

Sedulius describes a problem in prose.

Truth is painted, and if truth is found, it will
not be equity. Again: if it is equity, truth
will not be found.

A poem on that same problem.

If truth is found, it will not be equity;
yet equity is the source of blessed truth.
If it is equity, then it will not be justice,
since truth may not be called by a false name.

It arises from equity, but now rejects equity;
and so we discern equity from what is not equity.
If it is true and equitable, remember this:
neither what is true nor equitable will be found.

Truth derives from truth, and equity from justice—
Alas how many good things are contrary to good things! 10
Whoever seeks the truth will not find it in equity;
but it is justice, if he has found truth itself.

Lords prefer it when equity is false,
and equity is greater, if truth is raised from equity.
The same remains true but appears false;
it is not called equity, yet holds equity's weight.

Poem 65.

To Bishop Liutbert of Münster (849–70).

Our hearts exult with joy and gladness,
for Liutbert, our precious glory, returns,
bearing for the people the sweet gifts
    of peace.

Darkness, depart, for our splendor approaches.
Lo, blessed Liutbert, a bishop filled with
holiness, glitters among his people in
    earthly glory!

Now the bishop's face glows with radiance,
befitting the holy scion of a sacred tree;   10
and blooming with flowers of goodness,
    he shines like a rose.

Do you not see our glimmering paschal star?
Both rich and poor celebrate his coming,
and his people overflow with jubilation—
    deck his path with flowers!

Christ has granted Liutbert his divine gifts:
a fillet glistening with holy merits,
and a tranquil heart adorned with love.
    O France, rejoice!   20

A triple palm of glory awaits him in heaven.
The first shines with honesty of heart,
and the second is graced by our bishop's
    eloquent voice.

Noble acts of goodness decorate the third,
adorning it with Liutbert's immense power
and the abundant piety of his generous
    right hand.

O God, preserve this patron for his people,
that he may guide your gleaming sheepfold;   30
deign that he may lead your flock to the pastures
    of life in heaven.

Poem 66.

Sedulius sings about the return of Bishop Franco (855–901) to Liège.

Lo, our good pastor returns,
our golden star of piety,
renowned prelate, precious lamp,
    and true glory!

Now shines a light of radiant beauty
and a flourishing scion of noble lineage,
who prospers like a redolent palm beside
    flowing waters.

Great bishop, we burst into happy songs,
sadness vanishes from the mirror of our minds,   10
and the full moon glorifies you with
      beaming light.

Behold St. Lambert's reverend heir!
All the people salute your arrival
and gladly witness that you fulfill
      their wishes.

Whence do you come, O glistening topaz?
Perhaps you dwelled in Eden's fair gardens,
for you bring to us the sweet fruits of the
      Tree of Life.   20

Or, noble bishop, has Phinehas' divine zeal
aroused your heart, in Christ's service,
against the fierce and haughty sons
      of Belial?

Were not the Norse hordes fearful?
Observing your gleaming hosts,
they flew swifter than wind to their ships
      and hid in the river.

They sought to fly with winged feet,
and regretted crossing Frankish borders   30
as they shuddered with terror at our
      mighty emperor's arms.

Your face, good bishop, is dear to us,
and we should give thanks to Christ that
a glorious garland reflects the fame of
      our pious father.

We beseech the Father, the Son of the
Father, and the Holy Spirit, that sweet balsam
may yield us its sevenfold gifts both now
      and forever.   40

Poem 67.
Sedulius greets Count Eberhard of Friuli (d. 868/69).

Our glorious count and serene light has returned!
Now our valiant lord Eberhard approaches,
whom the Alps and Lombardy have sent to us.
O Franks, joyously receive this excellent man,
our fruitful vine, splendid light, and Christian
glory, who arouses our hearts to jubilation.
This blessed son of Hunroc reflects our
victorious fame in war and martial spirit.
Africa trembles before him, the dark Moor fears him,
and you, Saracen, dread his feats of battle;   10
but Rome, admiring its leader's mighty deeds,
rejoices in Eberhard, Italy's pious shield.
More brilliant than gold and precious than
topaz, he shines in every noble virtue.
Christ arms him with the sword and shield of salvation,
and with the lorica of faith and helmet of hope;
not Hector nor mighty Achilles can rival Eberhard,
and none but Gideon, perhaps, can match him.
Eberhard is a lover of goodness and tranquil peace,
a valorous lord, and a glittering star on earth;   20
like Jacob, he ascends a ladder with wings of justice,
his strong right hand dispensing splendid gifts.
Abundant mercy rules his pious heart,
pleasing beauty adorns his face,
and glory illumines his wondrous deeds.
Thus I pray: "Kind Mary, Christ, cherish this man."
For in justice and virtue he has won a palm of
glory unsurpassed among the Franks.
He is gentle to the gentle, bounteous to the poor,
and in sacred morals a sheep among the fold;   30
but when zeal kindles the altar of his heart,
he suddenly becomes the fiercest of lions.
Neither din nor blare of trumpets scares him,
and the Norsemen cannot shake his courage.
Award him, I pray, triumphant palms of victory,
and adorn him with roses of war.
Eberhard loves Christ, and Christ loves Eberhard,
for through him Christ raises the Church's gleaming horns.
Applaud, O Franks, his remarkable deeds,
and cherish in your hearts his brilliant virtues.   40
I implore the Father, Son, and Holy Spirit,
exalt him on earth and glorify him in heaven.

Poem 68.

Sedulius to Gunthar, Bishop of Cologne (850–63).

> Your muse abides in crystal fountains,
> undefiled by the roaring Kedron;
> she even spurns the waters of Pegasus,
> drinking, instead, at Siloam's sacred spring.
> She disdains to visit Parnassus' peaks,
> but sings your praises atop Mount Zion.
> Your harp has played sweetly in our halls,
> and the pipe has sounded twenty tropes.
>
> May you hear the harmony of melodious voices
> which even Thracian Orpheus cannot match;   10
> and may they proclaim your generosity
> towards your scholar Sedulius.
> For my heart extends you twentyfold thanks—
> I yearn to increase them seven times more!
> Excellent bishop, surpass Eridanus in wealth,
> and receive the gifts which Pactolus bears.
> Enjoy Mount Olivet's dark green olives,
> and taste Sorek's clear wines.
> Pastor, let us hear the thunder of wine casks,
> and let abundance flourish amidst the needy.   20
> Prosper in Christ, and may your muse prosper, too,
> who needs not our muse nor another's food.
> For a glorious poet has composed pleasing odes,
> and a loving shepherd tended his gleaming sheep.

Poem 69.

Sedulius to Bishop Gunthar of Cologne (850–63) about a library.

> Behold this bible flowing from the font of life,
> and whose two breasts issue sacred waters.
> Here are the Gihon, Pishon, Euphrates, and Tigris rivers,
> refreshing pious Christians with sweetest nectar;
> an urn redolent with fresh liquids:
> divine honey, flowing oil, milk, and sweet wine;
> and the lush fruits of the Tree of Life,
> for mystic allegory prospers in figurative fields.
> Gunthar, a radiant light and Cologne's pontifical ruler,
> dedicated this excellent work and written   10
> gift to the key-bearer Peter—

O Peter, Christ, reward this pious man!
Blessed bishop, let us see you in September
after the Feast of Tabernacles. Amen.
May your glory, lord bishop, illumine us forever,
and evermore increase in splendor. Amen.

Poem 70.
Sedulius to Bishop Gunthar of Cologne (850–63).

Time flies on circular wings,
and the Great Bear fills the vault of heaven.
September flees, pursued by fleet October,
and Autumn finally reaches its end;
and hoary Winter, ragged with ice, hastens
glumly upon us with darkening clouds.
Noble bishop, you alone were our solace and
hope against the south wind's terrible blasts.
Alas! Lying like a locust in dark recesses,
will I not be able to see my beloved bishop?   10
These times prick me more than the sharpest thorns,
for the pastor so dear to me, his scholar, is away.
O woe! I reckon light for dark, day for night,
since I cannot see my brilliant lamp.
But when that kind prelate appears,
begone, you thorns, and vanish, wicked night!
Then gloomy clouds will flee pious hearts,
leaving peace, repose, and a pasch of the spirit.
Good bishop, may God's favor attend you
and forever dispense you his graces.   20
I am mindful of you, as my little muse attests;
be mindful of me, I pray, for I am mindful of you.

Poem 71.
Sedulius to Abbot Hatto of Fulda (842–56).

May God's right hand guide you, my brother,
as you cheerfully hasten towards home.
Safely cross the Rhine's swift waters,
escaping the snares of Scylla and Charybdis. Amen.
When you have duly forded the Jordan's waters,
mount horses for your onward journey,
till you joyously behold splendid Jerusalem
and a temple of the Lord richer than Solomon's.

The happy Franks, nay the whole of Europe,
rejoice in their Jerusalem!   10
In its glittering court rests the martyr Boniface,
whose praise, merit, and honor transcended the heavens;
for he is our apostle, with a diadem of roses,
and our brilliant star and glory of the earth.
After receiving Hatto's kiss of peace,
address these words to that pious father:
"Brother Sedulius, in greetings of fragrant cinnamon,
wishes you everlasting prosperity:
enjoy as many ambrosial draughts as there
are flowers on the Tree of Life, fruits that grow,   20
twigs of cinnamon in paradise,
and drops of water in Siloam's spring!
May God's mighty power multiply your days
and increase your reward on earth and in heaven.
Good pastor, prosper in Christ, and guide your flock,
whether roses of youth or lilies of old age.
O that I might gaze upon such stars,
that illumine the earth and are loved in heaven!
Father, show your favor to this earnest man,
that I might see Eden and joyfully repose there."   30

Poem 72.
Sedulius sends a greeting to Bishop Adventius of Metz (858–75).

May the angel of God accompany you,
brothers, and the path of your journey be smooth.
I pray that Grammar's elegant art, butting with
horns, and sacred Wisdom's shield may defend you;
that you may hear melodious songs of Music,
whose breasts you sucked with tender lips;
that the Messiah may everywhere support you,
along with flowery Spring and Aries of heaven;
and that Ethics, your adorner, may guide Christian
scholars to the Jordan's fertile banks.   10
May you joyfully behold your Jerusalem,
its splendor, wealth, and illustrious men.
There Bacchus reigns, and the muse resides—
happy the city where this god and goddess dwell!
But the greater glory of Stephen honors you,
for, like a mother, you exalt your sons on high.
Gracious mother, Adventius is your golden light,
radiant in morals and eloquent in speech.

God has anointed him with graces,
that this saintly bishop may guide his gleaming flock.   20
May his fragrant offering transcend the heavens,
and his burning incense surpass Panchean thyme!

I ask you, brothers, receive his kiss of peace,
and recite these words to that sage father:
"Sedulius, your scholar, prays: may your riches
in paradise outnumber the names and stately phrases
in illustrious poems, the sacred priests of the
muse, and their harmonious songs!
Bishop beloved by the muses, remember me:
remember me, I pray, with your winged prayers.   30
I am mindful of you, as my little muse attests;
be mindful of me, for I am mindful of you.
Be our blessed paragon throughout the ages,
and forever endure as the light of your people."

Poem 73 (Prose).
Sedulius offers a prayer for Bishop Adventius of Metz (858–75).

God has given to lord Adventius the
glory, honor, and throne of Stephen.
Adventius is our glorious pastor, wise, prudent,
and a patron of churches.
No man on earth exceeds his generosity;
for wondrous in deed and eloquent in speech,
he upholds piety and the palm of charity.

Saviour of the world, preserve this merciful man,
that he may remain our precious topaz,
Stephen's disciple, and the light of the Franks.   10
I beseech Christ, the Son of our Almighty Father:
"Guide him on earth and glorify him in heaven."
May we, too, be crowned in the reign of the
Lord of Glory and Christ, the Paschal Lamb!

Poem 74.
Apologia pro vita sua.

I read or write, and I teach or search for truth;
I call on heaven's throne by night and by day.
I eat, drink freely, and with rhymes invoke the muses;

and snoring I sleep, or keep vigil and pray to God.
My heart, full of shame, laments the sins of life—
O Christ and Mary, pity your wretched man!

Poem 75.
In praise of Bishop Gunthar of Cologne (850–63).

Poet

"Sacred muse, who has arrayed you in splendid attire,
and made your face beam with happiness?
Who, I pray, has wreathed your head in laurel,
whence you surpass the beauty of pale ivy?"

Muse

"I confess, Thyrsis, I have found great Homer;
I have found the muses and melodious song.
For the strong right hand of Bishop Gunthar
cheerfully adorned me in wondrous garments.
He taught me the muses' sweet songs;
more learned than Phoebus, he chants musical airs.   10
Good Christ, glorify this poet and father
with whom long-haired Apollo cannot compare."

Poet

"God bless you, gentle muse, for such praises;
may he who embellished you be forever preserved.
Yet may we not also seek such rewards?
May that prelate enjoy perpetual bliss!"

Poem 76.
Sedulius greets Hildwin.

Our hearts exult with jubilation,
for our peace and great renown draws near.
Lo, God's divine right hand has sent us Hildwin,
our glorious lord and glittering light.
Let our shepherd's pipe, surpassing music of
harp and bagpipes, resound its melodious songs.
Gleaming Meuse, receive this illustrious man
from the Rhine and Cologne, our sweet mother.

This flourishing man is a blooming tree of
virtues, glistening with showers of song;   10
the Church's glory and a fruitful tree of Eden,
never yielding to winds and fierce tempests;
and a tree unshaken by gales and swift torrents,
standing firmly upon its rock.
It bears roses of war and lilies of peace,
and always renews itself with verdant leaves.
Upon its branches are wisdom's sweet fruits,
surpassing the fragrance of balsam;
hoary Winter's raging winds cannot despoil it,
or ravage its fruit in howling storms,   20
for it abounds in flowers and plentiful fruit,
and, like a lofty cedar, reaches toward heaven.

O Rhine, behold the Church's honor, and
our golden lamp, thriving in your Jerusalem!
That wondrous city exalts your fame on earth,
yet does not Hildwin's light grace you even more?
Father Hildwin is a sage and dearly loves wisdom,
and his mind is rich in learning's treasures.
He has drunk deep draughts of celestial nectar,
and tasted sacred waters from the fount of life.   30
In famous deeds he sparkles like a jewel
and gleams a paragon of beauty among the Franks.
O Christ, God, protect Hildwin through time,
and prepare splendid fortresses for this gracious man!

Poem 77.
Sedulius praises a king.

Lo, beauty is here! Fields, display your flowers,
and let the trees release their blossoms.
The birds celebrate spring with melodious songs,
and their tiny voices announce the new season.
O sevenfold pipe of the muse, play your sweet
sounds surpassing the music of swans.
Our pious king approaches! Muses, compose a
regal song, and chant his praises.
Let whoever treats him harshly rant like
Codrus and overflow with bitter gall.   10
For this third palm descends from two
emperors and glitters like a royal star.
This glorious prince in purple array flashes

with valor and gleams with his lofty crest.
Yet he loves the unctions of peace: may this
majestic ruler enjoy a tranquil reign!

Poem 78.
Sedulius to Berta, Abbess of Avenay.

Dazzling Berta glitters among the Franks!
Behold our emperor's silver dove, a star of
beauty, Irmingard's radiant flower,
and our imperial glory.
Irmingard was an excellent mother and blessed queen,
noble in birth and in faith,
noble in saintly virtues,
and noble in mien and pious eloquence.
With holy zeal she loved the things of heaven,
fleeing every evil and pursuing every good;   10
she despised earthly riches to serve Christ,
thus attaining heaven's supreme rewards.
She joyously thirsted for the font of life,
and her thirst was fully satisfied by God.
Her gracious hand enriched more of the poor
than there are stars in heaven—who can count them?
Is there a learned clerk who can number her
gifts and the people on whom she bestowed them?
For herself she stored eternal treasures in heaven,
while on earth exulting to perform God's works;   20
sowing in plenty, she reaped a rich harvest,
as her generosity yielded copious blessings.
Your examples, splendid Berta, and saintly virtues,
truly reflect her fair nobility;
the people delight in you, our mirror of Irmingard,
and the rich and poor join in celebration.
Heaven's court has received your earthly husband;
but now God, your divine spouse, is ever with you.
O spotless heart, the cheeks of a dove glisten on your face,
and a chaste love of the Father glows within you.   30
Your spouse Jesus arrayed you in a snow-white gown,
and adorned your face with roses of chastity.
He graced your breast with gems of virtue,
and chose his bride with goodly hope.
Preserve, O Christ, the emperor's fair daughter,
and cherish, Blessed Mary, this lovely pearl.

Poem 79.
Sedulius to Berta, Abbess of Avenay.

Let us duly give thanks and praise to God,
who always honors his people on earth!
For, as he illumined the heavens with starlight
and decked the lands with verdant flowers,
so our bounteous Creator adorns his church
with virgins, widows, and pious wives.
Thus, the saints' threefold fruit prospers,
a glorious harvest which paradise reaps.
Marriage glitters first in sacred rank,
then come widowhood and fair virginity.   10

Blessed woman, yours is the highest honor,
whence you observed marriage's chaste laws.
You bore a flourishing son and noble light,
but that youthful heir of the Franks has perished.
Alas that cruel death struck your royal scion—
yet paradise now rejoices in his presence!
Hateful death seized your earthly husband,
but in his stead comes a heavenly spouse.
Your groom is richer than all the earth's kings,
and fairer even than violets and roses.   20
The sun and golden moon marvel at his beauty,
and the angelic chorus praises him on high.
His yoke is light and compassion sweet—
Bobila, too, exults in such a spouse!
He showers you with gems of virtue,
and prepares for you eternal treasures.
Whatever you cheerfully give to the poor,
will be forever inscribed in the Book of Life.
In heaven sumptuous riches await you,
which never pass away, but eternally endure.   30

Poem 80.
Sedulius composes a palindrome.

Mitis et Arcas ero, rore sacrate sitim—
arte mera modero, more domare metra.
I will be gentle Arcas; bless my thirst with dew—
with true skill and moderation, I will conquer meters with rule.

Our triumphant simplicity routs our trilingual brother—
joyous youth, award us the palm of victory!
Did not the digger of a pit fall into it with ruin,
and he who wished to conquer collapse in defeat?
A horned beast subdued his hornless enemy,
and a rhinoceros tore his opponent's brow.
Sage, contend not with the learned—
if he wants to fight, where are his horns?

Poem 81.

Contest of the rose and the lily.

The four seasons had completed their cycle,
and the earth, robed in splendor, burst into bloom.
Milk-white lilies contended with rose garlands,
when the rose's golden mouth spoke these words:
>   Rose:
"Purple bestows rule and reflects kingship's glory,
but whites, offensive in hue, are vile for kings.
Feeble whites grow pale with wretched guise,
yet the whole world venerates purple."
>   Lily:
"Fair Apollo deems me the earth's golden beauty
and has adorned my face with elegant grace.   10
Why do you prate, O rose stained with shameful red?
Are you conscious of guilt? Are you blushing?"
>   Rose:
"I am Aurora's sister, kindred to the gods,
and Phoebus loves me, his beloved herald.
The morning star illumines my visage with light,
but my virgin features blush with modesty."
>   Lily:
"Why do you utter such arrogant words
as will earn you pains of eternal damnation?
For your diadem is pierced with the sharpest spines—
alas, those thorns torture the miserable rose!"   20
>   Rose:
"Why do you babble so, harrowed hag?
What you reproach, the world esteems,
for our Almighty Creator armed me with thorns,
and with noble armor protects my beauty."
>   Lily:
"A golden crown adorns my lovely head,
but it is not a crown of thorns I wear.

From my snowy breasts flows the sweetest milk,
thus they call me the blessed queen of flowers."
                    Poet:
Youthful Spring alighted on a nearby flower.
His robe was painted with verdant green,   30
perfumes delighted his open nostrils,
and splendid garlands wreathed his head.
                    Spring:
"Dear children," he said, "why do you argue?
Are you not both sisters born of Mother Earth?
Is it right for sisters to stir up bitter quarrels?
Be still, lovely rose, your glory lights the world;
but regal lilies govern glittering sceptres.
Thus your radiant visage exalts you forever.
May the rose, modesty's emblem, decorate our gardens;
shining lilies, increase, reflecting the beauty of Phoebus!   40
O rose, crown the martyrs in wreaths of purple;
lilies, grace the virgin's retinue arrayed in stoles."
                    Poet:
Then Spring, the creator, with kisses of peace,
united the maidens in accord with ancient custom.
The lilies offered loving kisses to their sister;
but her thorns playfully nipped their mouths.
The lilies smiled at their sister's game
and refreshed her thirsty rosebed with ambrosial milk.
In return, the rose presented baskets of flowers
and enriched her gleaming sister with garlands of honor.   50

Poem 82.
Sedulius describes a series of paintings or frescoes.

This Cherub signifies the new mysteries of Christ's law;
another bears a vessel filled with purity's essence;
and another burns the sacred incense of prayer.

O lion, ox, man, and king of birds, attend heaven's throne,
with the Gihon, Pishon, Euphrates, and Tigris rivers.

Lo, a Cherub illumines the glory of the old law;
an angel bears the votive gifts of our pious fathers
and fills the air with incense, the fragrance of the soul.

Here six paths represent the six glorious disciples
through whom Christ's sweet perfume refreshes the earth.   10

Here a field of silver, issuing silvery streams,
designates the other six companions of the Lord.

Gunthar, bishop of Christ and esteemed by all,
ordered the creation of these gleaming frescoes.

Poem 83.
Sedulius prays for rain.

O God, eternal font, pity the poor Moselle;
replenish her cloud-borne waters with plentiful rain.
Who else, Lord, can rain clear waters with bounteous will,
for no one is, has been, or ever will be your equal?
For you rule the might of glittering heaven,
and the waters above the firmament praise you as God.
Look upon the lands, therefore, and bathe them with rain. . . .

Poem 84.
Easter Sunday.

Let us give thanks to the King of All and
to Christ, the Lord of heaven's hosts!
For all the elements glorify our King
    in harmonious prayers.

The citizens of celestial Jerusalem praise him,
for he rules the universe, seas, lands, and stars
and as our Lord Creator governs all creatures by
    his will.

He is our paschal lamb, the way and the life,
who descended into hell and rose from its depths;   10
by suffering death in the prison of the flesh, he
    saved us from damnation.

That provident guardian of the human race
conquered death and returned as our redeemer,
bearing back to life spoils snatched from the
    jaws of hell.

Now the moving planets gleam in the heavens;
the sun appears as a radiant mirror,

and Luna all aglow reflects the rays of
    her brother's light.   20

Now, too, heaven and earth rejoice as one,
and the nightingales so swift in winged
flight resound everlasting glory `
    to Christ.

Tado, our beloved father and gracious patron
from afar, may Christ's precious hand
forever exalt your dignity and show
    you his favor.

Poem 85.
To Tado, Archbishop of Milan (860–68).

  Tado, kindly hear your poet's pious prayers:
"prosper in God and witness the ages to come!"
Bravo! He instructs a bishop learned in Christ's law,
and whose mind contains the riches of art.
May the healing angel Raphael grant you
divine medicine and a long life,
so that you, our pastor and shepherd,
may forever preserve God's sheep.
Good bishop, may you ascend the summit of starry heaven,
escorted to paradise by bands of angels.   10

Lo, the bounteous day of Easter's triumphs is here,
and today the stars, lands, and seas rejoice.
Hail, blessed day, most sacred of feast days,
on which God vanquished hell and conquered heaven!
The earth displays her manifold fruits,
promising thereby to overcome the famine of our land.
Last night Christ, the True Son, rose from the dark,
and so, too, arose the mystic harvest of God's fields.
Now roving tribes of bees are happy at work,
collecting honey as they buzz over purple flowers;   20
gay-painted birds fill the air with songs,
and at night sounds the nightingale's sweet voice.
The chorus of the church sings praises to Zion
and chants alleluias with hundredfold harmony.
Tado, father of the land, forever taste the joys of
Easter and reach the threshold of light—Adieu.

Poem 86.
To Sofridus.

Sofridus, paragon amidst a splendid age,
receive glory among peoples and glory in heaven!
May the healing angel Raphael grant you
divine medicine and long years of life.
For Christ chastises those he loves with paternal care,
and, like a gentle lover, increases our eternal treasures.
In the fullness of time, ascend to the city of the sun;
become a citizen in the fortress of starry heaven,
where the reign of the saints, under Christ,
prevails over perpetual wealth and bounty.   10
Truly, what the world possesses and the orb of
the earth encompasses will pass away in its time.
May good fortune ever shine upon you
with heavenly rewards and every blessing!

Poem 87.
A poem in praise of Emperor Lothar I of the Franks (840–55).

O king, watchful in duty, pity our labors;
moved by poetical plaints, grant us your succor.
For in you rests a mother in repose,
and to you Wisdom imparts her pious laws.
Noble king, she fills you with understanding,
and abides in the summit of your heart.
She disclosed to you the law's hidden mysteries,
and the duties of the clerical order.
She even laid down what men seek in art's
instruction and what your majesty should uphold.   10
Your august mind divines the law of the stars,
reckoned in numbers and mystic signs.
You perceive, too, the spirit that turns the earth;
why sighing winds vex the seawaves;
why the sun rises in the eastern sky only
to fall again beneath the western ocean;
above all, the causes of things and why precious
man bears the image of our Almighty Creator.
In short, Wisdom adorned you with a magnificent
garland, and virtue increased your power.   20
For yours is the glory of ancient kings,
and your crown the authority of kingship.

Your pious sanctity conquers those whom
India has feared and utmost Thule served;
the perfidious necks of the arrogant will
bow to you, subdued by your humble spirit.

O king, duly reflect upon Wisdom's rules,
for her might treads upon the necks of the wicked.
Scripture relates that she erected seven lofty
columns and with them built her house.   30
Sovereign wisdom has overthrown harsh tyrants,
and powerfully trampled a multitude of necks.
Lord king, Wisdom's gifts exalt your name,
and her lasting supports uphold your fame.
Above all, she will render you the highest rule
and cause you evermore to delight in her dwelling.

Poem 88.
Sedulius to Emperor Lothar I of the Franks (840–55).

May our wise and gracious emperor,
to be ever glorified and praised,
open his ears to our song
    and lyre.

May our emperor's reign increase forever,
and his royal diadem eternally glitter;
may our song everywhere celebrate
    his fame.

Let every sex and age chant joyous
songs and greet our king's swift   10
approach to the verdant lands
    of our Latium.

Lo, a hideous cloud blocks the rays
of the glistening sun, yet driving
Boreas lashes that gloomy cloud-cover
    that the sun might shine!

Thus our august emperor, drawing
near Latium in his course, has
dispelled the darkness of our spirits
    with his brilliant visage.   20

O Judge who rules the eternal kingdom,
be a shield of protection to our king.
O Redeemer Christ, extend your right hand
    to your faithful servant!

Let him rule with his grandfather's sceptre,
rightly cherishing his subjects,
and let Rome rejoice to serve such
    a lord.

Trusting his rule, let him govern his
people freely amidst peaceful serenity,   30
while justly punishing rebels with
    severe laws.

Behold how power attends our king—
O Christ, by your will all we
could desire is fulfilled by our
    emperor's reign.

Supreme Majesty—Father and Son and Holy
Spirit—hearken to the prayers we
offer you, our True God, on behalf
    of our king!   40

Poem 89.

Verses inscribed on a chalice restored by Bishop Angilbert of Milan (824–60).

All may drink from this sacred cup of the lamb and kid,
who drink worthily and without stain of sin.
Glorious Bishop Angilbert restored this chalice,
adorning it with gold and sparkling jewels.

Poem 90.

Sedulius greets Tado, Archbishop of Milan (860–88).

Sorrow, leave our hearts, for joy is near;
our elder approaches and gladdens our hearts.
Let all rejoice that our glory, grace,
and serene light has returned!
Darkness, depart, and hide your gloomy face,
as our splendor arrives in our midst.

Shepherds come, and display your gifts,
for our gleaming shepherd appears in glory!

O Tado, father of your folk and honor of your people,
we thank God that you return from the City of the earth!   10
O radiant sun, light of our salvation,
behold your metropolis and all your lands.
Hearken, Tado, to the summons of Ambrose,
of the house of the Lord, and of your city.
By your return your people regain their
happiness, and choruses sing for joy;
by your rule God's people prevail in
Christ's light, and the just become strong.
Good shepherd, grant fleeces to your sheep;
extend your help to us in exile.   20
Thus may Almighty God show you his favor,
and confer upon you his gifts of life.
Above all, wise bishop, assemble your Irish scholars,
whom God placed in your charge.
If you receive what I have written, father,
know that I composed them to please you.
Father of peace, you traverse the earth
and visit cities, bearing gifts of peace.
It behooves us to thank the King of Heaven
and to dedicate new offerings to God.   30

Tado, abound in every blessing,
receive every honor, and attain divine rewards.
As the Church's patron, enjoy that peace and
bounty which blesses Italy's happy land.
May the Celestial Lord, who protects all
things by his will, forever preserve you. Amen.
Gentle shepherd, reveal to us the sacred
labors of your difficult journey.
For God's love urged you to visit
Simon Peter and to travel rough roads;   40
your piety and wondrous faith, bearing
treaties of peace, overcame all hardship.
Let the heavens, waters, and earth cry "Hail, noble shepherd";
let all the elements join in their celebration.

Poem 91.

To Liutfrid, uncle of King Lothar II of Lotharingia (855–69).

        Hail, supreme honor, born of noble race;
pursue the paths of life!
By God's favor, mighty Liutfrid,
every glory and virtue is yours.
O prince of Christ, the Prince of All, accept
these offerings of your priest of verse.
Peace and health be with you: may you
safely cross the salty seas of time.
After long, prosperous years in the pilgrimage
of life, enjoy perpetual blessings in paradise;   10
become a citizen of heaven, where the people
of God prevail, rejoicing in celestial light.
In the city of God and the land of light,
shine among the glittering powers.
Peter, porter of the court of heavenly
Jerusalem, will greet you with the city's key;
may St. Ambrose and the angelic chorus
escort you to the multitudes of Zion.
I beseech the right hand of God and Christ
to protect and guide you on your journeys.   20
Let the heavens, waters, and earth cry: "Hail, noble duke";
and let all the elements join their celebration!

Notes

Textual Notes

Poem 6
    21–22 Read *vitem*, not *vitae*.

Poem 8
    1 Read MS *piusque*, not *piisque*.

Poem 9
    7 *Biscocta* (twice-cooked) can also, as I have translated it, mean parched.

Poem 41
    10 Read *eos*, not *eas*.

Notes to the Poems

Poem 1
    1 Aegle: one of the Naiads or water nymphs.
    8 Hartgar: Bishop of Liège (840–55) and generous patron to Sedulius Scottus and his circle of scholars.
    15–17 Here Sedulius envisages the tower as a spiritual symbol rather than as an actual building. See Jth. 1:3 for a tower 100 cubits high and Gen. 28:12–13 for Jacob's ladder to heaven.
    27 Henri Pirenne, "Sedulius of Liège," *Mémoires couronnés de l'Académie Royale de Belgique* 33 (Brussels, 1882) 43: says that the three languages are probably "le latin, l'allemand et la roman."

Poem 2
    1 Tityrus: the name of a shepherd addressed by Virgil in his first eclogue.
    3 Zephyrus: the west wind.
    8 Tithonus: endowed with immortality and transformed into a cicada after reaching old age.
    9–10 See Dan. 14:32 f., where Habakkuk is carried off by the angel of the Lord to Daniel in Babylon and is then immediately returned to Judea.

21 Lambert (c. 636–700): saint and martyr; also Bishop of Maestricht from 670–700. St. Hubert, Lambert's successor, transferred his see to Liège, where Bishop Hartgar as Lambert's heir may have appointed Sedulius "scholasticus" at the Cathedral School of St. Lambert.

Poem 3

1 Boreas: the north wind.

11 Titan: the god of the sun.

Poem 4

21 Cacus: an immense giant who lived in a cave on Mt. Aventine and terrorized the countryside with robberies.

32 Lambert: See Poem 2, line 21; also, as Reinhard Düchting in *Sedulius Scottus* (Munich: Wilhelm Fink Verlag, 1968), p. 37, n. 43 points out, Lambert is the patron saint of the blind and those who suffer diseases of the eye.

Poem 5

21–22 John 1:40–42: Andrew goes to Peter to report the news of the Messiah; also, "Peter" may refer to Pope Leo IV (847–55); see Poem 6, line 40.

Poem 6

21 Sorek (vineyard): a valley near Jerusalem.

40 Sedulius plays on the biblical passage of Daniel in the lion's den. In regard to the invocation of Leo, Ludwig Traube (*O Roma Nobilis* (Munich: Verlag der k. Akademie, 1891), p. 46) asserts that Leo is not the pope but the sign of the Zodiac. Reinhard Düchting (p. 45) convincingly argues, however, that Sedulius refers here to Leo IV (847–55). The date of Hartgar's journey and the name of the pope are otherwise not known.

73–74 See Gen. 8:6–12 for the raven and dove sent by Noah to test the waters of the flood. Here the raven and swan are, perhaps, simply personifications of opposite emotions: raven, blackness and gloom; swan, brightness and joy.

Poem 7

1 Ps. 137:1–2.

7 Camena: the Muse.

14 Calliope: chief of the muses and goddess of epic poetry and sometimes all kinds of poetry.

45 Laurentian: a poetic word for Roman.

51 Lothar I, emperor of the Franks (840–55).

59 Pope Leo IV? See Poem 6, line 40.

63 triple world: earth, air and water. See *De rectoribus christianis*, n. 1.

71–72 See St. Jerome's *Liber Interpretationis Hebraicorum Nominum* in *Corpus Christianorum Series Latina*, vol. 72, Pt. 1, (Belgium: Typographi Brepols Editores Pontifici, 1959), p. 135, lines 20–21: "*Bartholomeus filius suspendentis aquas vel me.*"

141–44 The number four (four trips) and the number two (twofold love) equals the perfect number six. See the *Etymologiae* of Isidore of Seville 3, 4, 2: "*Senarius namque numerus qui partibus suis perfectus est . . .*"

147–50 Sedulius arrives at 1014 by computing the mystic numbers which correspond to each letter of the Greek alphabet in the Latin nominative form of Hartgar's name, (H)artgarius (transliterated into Greek Ἀρτγαριυς). He omits the H and counts each letter only once:

$$\alpha' \quad \gamma' \quad \iota' \quad \rho' \quad \sigma' \quad \tau' \quad \upsilon'$$
$$1 \quad +3 \quad +10 \quad +100 \quad +200 \quad +300 \quad +400 \quad = \quad 1014$$

Düchting (p. 49) suggests that 1014 has a theological meaning: 10 (*lex domini*, 10 command-ments) × 100 (hundred fold fruits — Mark 4:3 ff.) plus 2 × 7 (seven each for the *requies corporis* and *requies spiritus*).

153–4 Pelasgian (Grecian); the Greek accusative for Hartgar is written out in the Latin text in capitals: ΗΑΡΤΓΑΡΙΟΝ (Hartgarion).

Poem 8
5 The date of this battle is unknown.

Poem 9
8 Not only does Sedulius refer to the goddess of agriculture, Ceres, he also plays on her name's association with the Latin *cervisia* (beer).

Poem 10
5 Daphnis: Mercury's son, a young shepherd in Sicily and inventor of pastoral songs.
7–8 Sedulius wishes three sheep to rise from the holes in his pipe as a reward for his music.

Poem 11

15–19 See John 6:48–56, where Christ proclaims himself the bread of life that comes from heaven. Sedulius also calls Liège "a more illustrious Bethlehem," for the meaning of Bethlehem is appropriately "the house of bread."

Poem 12

1 Charles the Bald (king of the Western Franks, 843–77, and Emperor, 875–77). According to Pirenne (p. 52) "cette pièce fut probablement composée à l'occasion de l'arrivée de Charles le Chauve à Metz en août 869. Francon (Bishop of Liège and heir of Hartgar) fit en effet partie de l'assemblée des évêques que le roi convoqua dans cette ville pour se faire reconnaître héretier de Lothaire II." Consult the *Annales De Saint-Bertin* (eds. Félix Grat, et al., [Paris: C. Klincksieck, 1964], p. 159) for the year 869 (*videmus hunc regni huius heredem esse legitimum*), where Charles is crowned king of Lotharingia after the death of Lothar II (King of Lotharingia, 855–69).

53–58 α' κ' λ' o' ρ' σ' υ'
             1   +20   +30   +70   +100   +200   +400   = 821

See Poem 7, lines 147–50. According to the mystic numerology in medieval philosophy, the number 100 means a return to unity and the number 8 means the age of eternal life. For mystical numbers and their significance see Vincent Hopper, *Medieval Number Symbolism* (New York: Columbia University Press, 1938).

Poem 13
1 Luke 12:35, "Let your belts be fastened around your waists and your lamps be burning ready."
7 maniple: A eucharistic vestment consisting of an ornamental band or strip worn on the left arm near the wrist.
11 stole: an ecclesiastical vestment consisting of a narrow strip of silk or other material worn over the shoulders or, by deacons, over the left shoulder only.

Poem 14
10 Charles' father is Louis the Pious (Emperor of the West, 814–40); Judith, Empress,

second wife to Louis the Pious, (819–43); Charlemagne, King of the Franks (768–814), Emperor of the West (800–14).

18 Thule: an island in the extreme north of Europe; for some Iceland.

Poem 15

1 Charles the Bald (see Poem 12, line 1); Louis the German (King of the Eastern Franks, 843–76). Here Sedulius describes a meeting between these two sons of Louis the Pious; he does not name the date or location, however, in the poem. Düchting (p. 71) thinks that the meeting probably took place after the death of Lothar I in 855 but acknowledges that a date as late as 870 is possible. Pirenne and Traube also offer widely different interpretations of the location, date and reason for this conference. See Düchting (p. 71, n. 103) for a discussion of the debate about this poem.

15 Louis the Pious: King of Aquitane (781–814), Emperor of the West (814–40).

Poem 16

1 Little is known of the identity of Vulfengus. Ernest Dümmler, (*Sedulii Scotti Carmina Quadraginta* [Halle: n.p., 1869], 1) calls Vulfengus "*familiaris Hlotharii*"; he cites a reference in Flodoard's *Historia Remensis ecclesiae* to a "*Vulfingo cuidam ministeriale eiusdem imperatoris Lotharii*," to whom Hincmar of Rheims wrote two letters (*Histoire L'Eglise De Reims*, trans. M. Lejeune [Reims: L'Académie Impériale de Reims, 1954], 2:334).

3–12 Here again, as in Poems 7 and 12, Sedulius plays on numbers mystically related to the number of letters in a name. The name Sedulius, for instance, has eight letters. In line 12 the sacred streams are the four gospels. For a discussion of numerical composition in medieval literature, see pp. 501–8 of Ernst Curtius, *European Literature and the Latin Middle Ages*, trans. Willard Trask (New Jersey: Princeton University Press, 1973).

18 Dalmatic: a vestment worn over the alb by a deacon or bishop.

Poem 17

9–11 For such rhetorical formulas of praise, see Ernst Curtius' chapter on "Inexpressibility Topoi," *European Literature and the Latin Middle Ages*, trans. Willard Trask (New Jersey: Princeton University Press, 1973), pp. 15–62.

Poem 18

14 Drogo: Bishop of Metz (823–55, Archbishop from 844). Drogo was the illegitimate son of Charlemagne.

19 Franco: Bishop of Tongres and Liège (855–901); Bishop Hartgar's successor at Liège and the friend and pupil of Drogo of Metz (see line 14 above: "greatly beloved by Drogo").

21–22 These two lines in Traube's text (also in Dümmler's and Pirenne's before him) are the first two lines of Poem 19; however, they appear to belong to the last lines of Poem 18, as Düchting has rightly shown. The lines form an echoing distich (Poem 18 is in echoing distichs, but Poem 19 is not); and they make more sense in Poem 18 than in Poem 19 (surely Franco "light of the world" in line 20 is the "full moon" who shines prosperously over the Franks.)

Poem 19

1 The "venerable brother" is not known. Sedulius echoes the treatment of time and mutability in Venantius Fortunatus' "Ad Jovinum":

Time that is fallen is flying, we are fooled by the passing hours. . . .

Likeness is none between us, but we go to the selfsame end.

(*Medieval Latin Lyrics*, trans. Helen Waddell [Middlesex: Penguin Books, 1929], p. 77.)

Poem 20
  41 Probably Louis II, eldest son of Lothar and Irmingard.

Poem 21
  1–3 Matt. 4:18–20; Luke 5:1–8.
  4 Matt. 17:24–28; Peter pays the temple tax for Jesus and himself.
  5–9 Matt. 14:28–33; 16:16–19; and John 21:20–22.
  11–14 Acts 9:32–34 and 36–43.
  15–17 Acts 10:34–48. In stanzas 5 and 6 (lines 17–24) I have reversed the order in which
they appear in the Latin text of Ludwig Traube (*Poetae Latini Aevi Carolini*, [Berlin: Weidmann-
sche Verlagsbuchhandlung, 1896], vol. 3:187–88). Line 17 of stanza 5 belongs with lines
15–16 of stanza 4, since they both relate to the events of Peter's conversion of Cornelius; lines
21–24 of stanza 6, which describe Peter's imprisonment, must follow after stanza 5 and direct-
ly before lines 25–28 of stanza 7 to be meaningful and match the chronology of the life of Peter
in Acts.
  19 Acts 12:17; "He . . . left them to go off to another place." (It was conjectured that Peter
went to Rome at this time.)
  20 Acts 8:9–33; Peter and John, not Paul, have an altercation with Simon Magus.
  21–28 Acts 3:2–8; 12:1–17.
  29–32 See Bernard Pick's *The Apocryphal Acts of Paul, Peter, John, Andrew and Thomas*
(Chicago: The Open Court Publishing Company, 1909), pp. 111; 118–21; and 47.

Poem 22
  1–3 The beginning letters of the first three lines form the acrostic IHS (Jesus). Whether this is
intentional or not I do not know. Pirenne (p. 54, n. 1) considers this piece "la description d'un
tableau ou d'une fresque." The poem, however, mentions neither representation. The reason
for bringing together these eleven saints is unknown. The text seems to indicate that St. Peter
should stand in the center of the tableau with Apollonaris at his right and Ambrose at his left.
One possibility is that Sedulius, moving from left to right and then to center, is first describing
the four saints who appear beside Apollonaris, then the four saints beside Ambrose, and finally
the last three saints, with Peter in the middle and Apollonaris and Ambrose on either side of
him.
  1 St. Martin: Bishop of Tours (d. 397).
  2 Hilary of Poitiers?: Bishop of Poitiers, (c. 315–67).
  3 St. Mark the Evangelist.
  4 St. Sulpicius Pius: Bishop of Bourges (624–47) and titular saint of the church and seminary
of Saint-Sulpice at Paris.
  5 St. Remigius (c. 438–c. 533): "Apostle of the Franks."
  6 St. Severinus (d. 482): "Apostle of Austria."
  7 St. Justus: Bishop of Lyons in 350; died a hermit in Egypt in 390.
  8 St. Maximinus: Bishop of Trèves (d. c. 349).
  10 St. Apollonaris (date unknown): first bishop of Ravenna.
  11 St. Ambrose (c. 339–97): Bishop of Milan.

Poem 23
  1 This poem was probably composed on the occasion of the birth of Charles, the youngest
son of Emperor Lothar I (see line 3). The date of his birth is not known. Charles later became
the King of Provence (855–63).
  9 Grandfather is Louis the Pious; great-grandfather is Charlemagne; father is Lothar I.

Poem 24

19 Irmingard was the daughter of Hugo, Count of Tours.

41 Eudoxia is Athenais, daughter of a pagan philosopher at Athens, (d. 460/61). She took "Eudoxia" in baptism and in 421(?) married Theodosius II, Roman Emperor (408–50 A.D.).

46 Louis the II: King of Italy (844–75), Emperor (855–75).

Poem 25A

2 Lothar II, King of Lotharingia (855–69) and son of Lothar I.

13 Xanten: a city near Mainz.

18 At this point, according to Düchting (p. 95), the 74 lines of Traube's Latin text should be distinguished as two separate poems. At the end of line 18, the subject changes from Lothar II to Louis II, King of Italy (844–75) and Emperor (855–75); and line 19 of Traube's text differs from the first 18 lines in that it begins a series of echoing distichs. I have, therefore, designated lines 1–18 as Poem 25A and lines 19–74 as Poem 25B.

Poem 25B

11–18 Sedulius describes the Franks as fair and gleaming like a host of swans. He contrasts the swan host with the dark, raven-like Saracens. Traube (*O Roma Nobilis*, p. 63) states that Louis II fought against the Saracens in 848. Düchting's proposal of an earlier date for the poem, because Sedulius calls Louis, already 23 years old in 848, "puer" (line 35), is unconvincing. Louis at 23 would still have been quite young in his kingly responsibilities.

19 Ishmaelites: decendants of Ishmael, the son of Abraham and Hagar. See Gen. 16:12–21 and 21:14–21. Note Isidore of Seville's *Etymologiae* 9. 2. 6: "*Ismael filius Abraham, a quo Ismaelitae, qui nunc corrupto nomine Saraceni, quasi a Sarra, et Agareni ab Agar.*"

Poem 26

1 The king addressed in these verses is not named in the text. Evidence in the poem offers one possibility. In line 12 Sedulius cries: "behold Solomon, your lord." In his poems Sedulius most often addresses Emperor Lothar I as Solomon (see Poems 20:33; 54:8; 59:25; 60:18). Also the epithet *augustus* is found in lines 1, 2 and 8.

Poem 27

1 Dermot: an Irish companion of Sedulius. Dermot may have been a visitor rather than a permanent member of Sedulius' circle of Irishmen at Liège.

Poem 28

3 Pippin the Short (d. 768): the father of Charlemagne.

Poem 29

1–2 The person addressed in this poem is not named. Traube (*O Roma Nobilis*, p. 46) designated Louis II, King of Italy, as the subject of the verses. I agree, nevertheless, with Düchting (p. 108), who argues for Lothar II based on textual similarities between this poem and those in *De rectoribus christianis*, which Sedulius also composed for Lothar II.

Poem 30

25 Canopus: brightest star in the constellation Argo (visible in southern Europe).

51–60 N. Lukman in "The Raven Banner and the Changing Ravens," *Classica et Medievalia* 19 (1958): 135–36, has contended that these lines are the earliest proof for "the connection of the raven theme with the royal Danish family." For Lukman, lines 51–60 concern delegates for peace from the Danish King Roric I in 845, to whom the metamorphosis of the raven (Ovid, *Metamorphoses*, Book 2, lines 540–41) is applied. Ovid, however, depicts the metamorphosis of the raven from original white to black, while Sedulius wishes the return transformation from black to white, raven to dove, through the baptism and submission to Louis the German.

65 The raven Danes are "babbling" because it is the chattering tongue of the raven which originally changed him from white to black in Ovid's fable.

Poem 31

1–2 Sedulius describes a hospital which may have stood in Liège.

10 Why three lights? Note Isidore of Seville's *Etymologiae* 4 (De medicina), the three inventors of medicine: Apollo, Aesculapius, and Hippocrates.

Poem 32

1 Iris: goddess of the rainbow and messenger of the gods.

5–6 Pirenne (p. 22) suggests that here begins the description of a banquet to celebrate, perhaps, Hartgar's new palace. Pirenne's idea is supported by similarities in vocabulary between this poem and Poem 4, which also celebrates Hartgar's new palace.

7–15 The details in these lines are obscure, as is often the case in ancient or medieval descriptions of buildings or their interiors. Pirenne's guess (p. 22, n. 4) is that lines 14–15 "paraissent indiquer l'existence de vitraux ou tout au moins de peintures sur verre, dans l'édifice en question."

23 Here begins what Bernard Bischoff ("Caritas Lieder," *Mittelalterliche Studien*, 2 (Stuttgart: Anton Hiersemann, 1967), 166) calls a parody of the tradition of *caritas-lieder*, or songs of brotherly love, which accompanied the communal drink in monasteries on certain feast days.

24 Lyaeus: a surname of Bacchus, god of wine.

27–28 Sedulius plays on the Latin words *libertas* (liberty), *Liber* (a name associated with Bacchus), *liberat* (from *liberare*, to liberate), and *liber* (liberated).

29 St. Vaast (d. 539): Bishop of Arras.

31 Sedulius plays on the number six with the Latin word *modius* or measure which has six letters. See lines 35–40.

33–34 See 1 Tim. 5:23.

Poem 33

6 To call Franco "a new apostle" would indicate that these verses were composed soon after Hartgar's death in 855 and the start of Franco's succession in 855.

7–8 The seventh month: September, the seventh month of the Roman year reckoning from March. It seems Franco intended to be in Liège for the harvest festival (Feast of Tabernacles — an eight day feast from September 15, which commemorates the entrance of the Israelites into the Promised Land and marks the gathering of the crops and the foliage of the trees (Lev. 23:34)).

Poem 34

1–2 For a discussion of the identities and careers of these Irish scholars, see R. Derolez, *Runica Manuscripta* (Brugge: De Tempel, 1954), and Nora Chadwick et al., *Studies in the Early British Church* (Cambridge: Cambridge University Press, 1958), pp. 79–110.

9–10 Codrus: a wretched poet, hostile to Virgil (see Virgil's *Eclogues* 5. 11). Even Codrus will explode with envy when he hears Sedulius praise them.

Poem 35

1 Fergus: see Poem 34, lines 2 and 11–18.

5–8 We do not have Fergus' epic poem nor do we know which Charles he celebrated. Pirenne decided the poem was probably about Charles the Bald, not Charlemagne. He argued that "Charles le Chauve régnant à l'époque de Sedulius, c'est donc à Charles le Chauve que s'adressaient alors l'enthousiasme artificiel et les flatteries mythologiques, dont avant lui Charlemagne, puis Louis le Débonnaire avaient eu la primeur'' (p. 16). Fergus' poem, however, could just as easily have been dedicated to Charles (King of Provence, 855-63), the son of Lothar I, to whom Sedulius dedicated Poem 23.

Poem 36
1 Robert has been variously identified as an aristocrat (Traube, *Poetae Latini*, p. 200, n. Poem 36); a count (Dümmler, 1); a cleric (Manitius, *Geschichte der lateinischen Literatur des Mittelalters* [Munich: Beck, 1965], 2:322-23); and an abbot (Ebert, "Sedulius Scottus," *Allgemeine Geschichte der Literatur des Mittelalters im Abendlande* [Austria: Verlagsanstalt, 1971], 2:196). The evidence, however, is inconclusive for any of these alternatives.

Poem 37
15 Gisla: daughter of Louis the Pious and his second wife Judith.

Poem 38
7-14 See Poem 37.

Poem 39
17-20 The date and location of this battle are uncertain.
21-22 Ishmaelites: see Poem 25B, line 19.

Poem 40A
1-2 I have presented the four lines of Poem 40 in Traube's Latin text (*Poetae Latini*, 204) as two separate pieces, 40A and 40B. Lines 1-2 commemorate Hildebert, suffragan bishop of Cologne (834-62).

Poem 40B
1-2 These lines commemorate one Adalwin, who appears to have been an aged priest. Little is known of his identity. Since, however, his epitaph is placed with Hildebert's, he may also have been from Cologne.

Poem 41
17 River Lethe: in the infernal regions; the shades drank from it and obtained forgetfulness of their past.
34-36 Lucina: a goddess of childbirth (because she brings to the light); Luna: goddess of the moon, whose favor Pan obtained through the gift of a spotless white ram (see Virgil's *Georgics* 3. 391-94).
42 The ram is Sedulius' Tityrus or shepherd, because rams (line 4) are themselves "leaders among the sheep."
77-78 Anubis: an Egyptian deity which was represented with the head of a dog; Cerberus: the three- or hundred-headed monster of hell.
21-22 Gen. 22.
125-26 Luke 23:39-43.
129-32 Ps. 118:16-18.

Poem 42
1-4 These verses describe a church erected by Hartgar and dedicated on April 17th of a year (unknown to us) sometime before Hartgar's death in 855.
9-12 It seems the church is in honor of Peter, Paul, the Virgin Mary, and the entire body of saints. See Poem 47 for further comment.

Poem 43

1 Berta: daughter of Lothar I and Irmingard. After her husband's death (date?) Berta became abbess of Avenay, a monastery in the diocese of Rheims. For more on Berta's life, see Poems 61, 78 and 79.

6 According to Traube, this poem is a fragment (*non ad finem descriptum*). The verses, however, form a thematical unity. In praising Berta, the poet twice recalls the memory of her parents and closes with the thought that justice will bring the noble nun to heaven.

Poem 44

1–8 The heading of this poem bears the words "To King Charles." Internal evidence in the poem, however, indicates that it is addressed to Charles the Bald. It is clearly Charles the Bald who is the "third palm branch" in the imperial line. In Poems 12 and 28 Sedulius has already praised him as the grandson of Charlemagne and son of Louis the Pious, and compared his genealogy to that of the Old Testament patriarchs (Poem 12, lines 44–48; Poem 28, lines 51–60). The poem, moreover, contains obvious reference to the royal inauguration (the anointing of the king, royal sceptre, and celebration of flowers and gifts). Hence, the poem may belong to the anointing and crowning of Charles the Bald as King of Lotharingia in 869 (see Poem 12, line 1). Also, after line 8 the words "*et reliqua*" appear, and so I agree with Traube that the poem is probably incomplete as we now have it.

Poem 45

1 Sedulius praises a victory over the Norsemen, but neither victory or battle site are identified. Traube (*O Roma Nobilis*, p. 46) believed that Sedulius brought Poems 45–47 with him from Ireland and that Poems 45 and 46 are about a "siegreiche Schlacht der Iren gegen die Normannen." It seems more likely, however, that Poem 45 is related to Poem 8 which describes Hartgar's defeat of the Norsemen. Considering the number of Viking raids, it would be difficult to set the date and location of this battle.

37–38 Prov. 26:27; Gen. 11: tower of Babel.

57–60 Exod. 14:23–28.

Poem 46

1 Traube (*O Roma Nobilis*, p. 46) interprets the poem as a prayer against the Viking onslaught in Ireland. There is little support in the text, however, for this view (it has little in common with the themes and texts of other poems, 8, 39 and 45, on the Norsemen). Pirenne offers a more convincing explanation (p. 62, n. 1: "Peut-être est-ce après la terrible innondation de la Meuse en 858.") See *Annales Bertiniani* for 858: "*mense Maio in vico Leudico . . . tanta subito pluviarum inundatio effusa est, ut domos et minos lapideos seu quaecumque aedificia cum hominibus et omnibus quaecumque illic usque ad ipsam ecclesiam memoriae sancti Landberti violentae eruptionem Mosam fluvium praecipitaverit.*"

7–8 Exod. 12: recalls the avenging angel, passing over doors marked with blood.

9 Ps. 6:6.

11 Ps. 2:11.

Poem 47

11 The identity of Rathbald is unknown.

12 Traube (*O Roma Nobilis*, p. 46) identifies King Roric with King Rhodri the Great of Wales (d. 877). This seems unlikely, since Sedulius makes no reference to either the British or the English in any of his poems. "King Roric" may refer to the King Roric who was a leader of Viking pirates "*quem Hlotharius cum comprimere nequiret, in fidem recepit eique Dorestadum et alios comitatus largitur* (*Annales Bertiniani*, [850], p. 59). Another alternative is King Oric or Horic of the Danes.

Poem 48
1-6 Luke 1:10-21, 26-55; and 2:7-12, 25-35.
7-13 Matt. 2:1-12; and 3:1-6, 13-17.
14-16 John 2:1-11; Matt. 4:18-20.

Poem 49
1-5 Compare with Virgil's *Eclogues* 3. 56-58; 7. 55 and *Georgics* 2. 126. For a discussion of a possible Virgilian influence in these verses see Gerard Murphy, "Vergilian Influence Upon the Vernacular Literature of Medieval Ireland," *Studi medievali* n.s.5 (1932): 374-76. For translations of this poem see Helen Waddell, *Mediaeval Latin Lyrics* (Middlesex: Penguin Books, 1929), p. 133 and James Carney, "Sedulius Scottus," *Old Ireland*, ed. R. McNally (New York: Fordham University Press, 1965), pp. 228-50.

Poem 50
1 The verses do not identify the "angel" and "good father." Since Metz lies near the Moselle (lines 7-8), it could be Adventius; however, it could also be Bishop Franco, Hartgar's successor, for there are strong similarities in vocabulary and spirit between this poem and Poem 33, which is dedicated to Franco and in which Sedulius invokes the Moselle to bring his "father" to Liège.
2 See Tobit 11:9-18 in which the angel Raphael heals Tobit of his blindness.

Poem 51
1-2 The church and its location are not known. The lines, meanwhile, may be based upon the biblical passage concerning Elijah's journey to heaven in a flaming chariot in 2 Kings 2:11.

Poem 52
2-6 Mark 10:38; and Rev. 6:9-10, 12-17.

Poem 53
1 Sedulius composed these verses in the persona of Bishop Hartgar, who is represented as giving a copy of the *Epitoma rei militaris* of Flavius Vegetius Renatus (c. 400) to Eberhard, Count of Friuli.
23 See Poem 39.

Poem 54
7-8 Lothar I is most often addressed as "Solomon" by Sedulius. See Poem 26, line 1.

13-14 In the Latin text these two lines appear also as lines 15-16 except in reverse word order and are followed by "*sicut et alii.*" Traube (*Poetae Latini*, p. 213) interpreted lines 15-16 as alternative readings for lines 13-14; by the words "*sicut et alii*" he concluded the poem was a fragment. W. Meyer (*Ges. Abhandlungen z. mittellat. Rythmik* 2 (1905):352) has shown, however, that the lines belong to the "kunstuck der drehbaren Verse" and "man kann jeden Vers von hinten wie von vorn lesen." The phrase "*sicut et alii*" in this case would indicate that lines 15-16 are examples of such reversal for all the other lines.

Poem 56
17-22 Dan. 13.

Poem 57
5-10 See Isidore's *Etymologiae* 12. 2. 29.
21-22 Exod. 34:29-36; and Dan. 13.

Poem 58

1–6 Robert: see Poem 36, line 1. Robert's name appears in all the six Latin cases: nominative, genitive, dative, accusative, vocative and ablative.

50 Falernian gifts: wines from the Falernian territory, famed for its wine, in Campania.

54 The pool of Siloam: a reservoir in Jerusalem.

Poem 59

11–12 Traube (*O Roma Nobilis*, p. 47) says that the poem "kann sich nur auf Lothar's aufenthalt in Lüttich (854) beziehen . . . Lothar's aufenthalt ist erwiesen nur für den Februar; Sedul schreibt im April–Mai. Lothar hat offenbar Ostern (25. April) in Lüttich verbracht." Sedulius, however, calls on May to greet the King and implies that the King was not in Liège on Easter as Traube seems to think.

15 St. Lambert: see Poem 2, line 21.

21 Eridanus: the mythical and poetical name of the river Po.

Poem 60

33–40 The date and location of this battle with the Vikings are not known.

Poem 62

1 This is a prayer against the rains, or perhaps, the flood which inundated Liège in 858 (see Poem 46, line 1). It also contains an unusual number of plays on words: line 4 (uber and uber); lines 2, 5 and 6 (tempora, temperator, temperatio, and t(e) imperator).

Poem 63

1 The model for this poem, as Düchting (p. 175) has noted, is the "De Resurrectione Domini" of Venantius Fortunatus, in which are found such elements as the arrival of spring, the abundance of the earth, the singing birds, the honey bees, and the praise of the stars.

5 Lucifer: the morning star.

7 Vesper: the evening star.

21 Tellus: goddess of the earth.

Poem 64

Problem. I agree with Traube (*Poetae Latini*, p. 219, Poem 64) that the solution of the prose enigma "Truth is painted . . ." seems to be *iniquitas* meaning unfairness or injustice. Both this problem and the following poem are similar to the operations of a syllogism (see Dieter Schaller, "Lateinische Dichtung in St. Galler Handschrift," *Zeitschrift für deutsches Altertum* 93 (1964):281–99 for a discussion and some examples of such medieval syllogisms). The basis for the problem lies in that the word *iniquitas* belongs to the root "*aequ-*" ("*nascitur ex aequo*," line 5). Note Isidore's *Etymologiae* 10. 132: "*Iniquus proprie dictus quia non est aequus, sed inaequalis est.*" Isidore also brings together *fucata veritas* or "painted truth" (19. 16): "*pictura autem dicta quasi fictura; est enim imago ficta, non veritas. Hinc et fucata, id est ficto quodam colore inlita, nihil fidei et veritatis habentia.*"

1–16 The solution to these verses appears to be *iniquus*, meaning what is unfair or unjust.

Poem 66

22 Phinehas: see Num. 25.

32 Lothar I? If the emperor is Lothar I, the poem could be dated sometime in 855. Franco succeeded Hartgar in 855 and Lothar died in September 855. It is also not clear whether Lothar loaned Franco arms for battle or whether Franco himself served in the ranks under Lothar's command.

Poem 67

1-3 According to Dümmler ("Fünf Gedichte des Sedulius Scottus an den Markgrafen Eberhard von Friaul," *Jahrbücher für vaterländische Geschichte* 1 (1861):171), Eberhard attended the peace conference at Coblenz in June, 860. At that conference peace was concluded between Louis of Germany (843–76) and Charles of France (843–77); they swore an oath of allegiance to each other and to their nephews, Louis of Italy (844–75) and Lothar of Lotharingia (855–69). Sedulius, therefore, probably composed this panegyric for Eberhard while the count was at Coblenz.

9-10 See Poem 39.

18 Gideon: famed warrior and leader who delivered the Israelites from the pagan Midianites (see Judg. 7).

21-22 See Gen. 28:11–15, where Jacob dreams of a stairway to heaven. Upon it God's messengers were going up and down; and the Lord stood beside it and addressed Jacob.

Poem 68

1 Gunthar's poetic talents are known only through Sedulius.

2 Kedron: a valley along the eastern side of Jerusalem, in which a brook or river flows with water only during the winter.

3 The waters of Pegasus: the fountain of the muses.

15-16 Eridanus: see Poem 59, line 21; Pactolus: a river in Lydia, which was said to bring down golden sands.

Poem 69

1 Traube (*O Roma Nobilis*, p. 47) rightly asserts that these verses represent "das Widmungsgedicht für eine Bibel, die Gunthar in Rom dem Papst überreichen will. Sedulius schickt es nach; Gunthar bleibt den ganzen Winter über fort."

3 The four rivers in Eden (Gen. 2:8–14).

11 The popes during Gunthar's episcopate were Leo IV (847–55), Benedict III (855–58), and Nicholas I (858–67).

Poem 70

21-22 Hans Walther discusses love expressions of this type in "Zur Geschichte eines mittelalterlichen Topos," *Liber Floridus* (St. Ottilien: Verlag der Erzabtei, 1950), pp. 153–64.

Poem 71

6 river Jordan: the Rhine.

7 Jerusalem: the monastery at Fulda.

11 Boniface: "Apostle of Germany," who became Archbishop of Mainz in 747 and played some part in the founding of Fulda. He was martyred in Frisia in 754.

Poem 72

10-11 river Jordan: Moselle river; Jerusalem: Metz.

22 Panchean thyme: from a fabulous island in the Erythraean Sea, east of Arabia, rich in precious stones, incense, etc.

31-32 See Poem 70, lines 21–22.

Number 73 (Prose)

1 This is a prose piece in praise of Adventius of Metz. Sedulius may have wished to versify it.

Poem 75

5 Thyrsis: the name of a shepherd in Virgil's *Eclogues* 7. 2.

Poem 76

3 There is much debate as to Hildwin's identity. Traube offers two possibilities: Hildwin, Bishop of Cambrai (862–63) (*Poetae Latini*, p. 226, Poem 76) and Hildwin of Cologne (842–49/50), the predecessor of Bishop Gunthar (*O Roma Nobilis*, p. 47). Léon Levillain, however, has proposed Hildwin of Saint-Bertin, who became bishop of Cologne in 869–70 ("Date et Interpretation D'un Poeme De Sedulius Scottus," *Le Moyen Age* 45 (1935):199–211). Nevertheless, the evidence for any of these choices is inconclusive.

9–14 Matt. 7:24–27.

24 Jerusalem: Cologne.

Poem 77

8 Traube (*O Roma Nobilis*, p. 47) identifies this king as Charles, the third son of Lothar I and King of Provence (855–63). He is descended from two emperors: Louis the Pious, his grand-father, and Lothar I, his father. Louis the German (King of the Eastern Franks, 843–76), however, is also a viable choice. His grandfather, Charlemagne, and his father, Louis the Pious, were both emperors (see Poem 30). For Codrus (line 9) see Poem 34, lines 9–10.

Poem 78

1 Berta: See Poem 43, line 1.

2 Emperor Lothar I of the Franks (840–55).

4 Irmingard, wife of Lothar I, (821–55).

27–28 After her husband's death, Berta became abbess of Avenay, a monastery in the diocese of Rheims.

Poem 79

3–10 These lines are based on the parable of the four seeds (see Mark 4). The man who hears God's message and takes it in will bear a yield of 30- or 60- or 100-fold. Medieval exegetes deduced that these numbers (30, 60 and 100) referred to the three degrees of sanctity or chastity within the Church: to the conjugal was allocated the 30; to widows, the 60; to virgins, the 100.

24 Bobila: probably Berta's daughter.

Poem 80

1–10 These verses refer to the Latin palindrome above, in which each line reads the same backward as forward. It appears that Sedulius has been challenged to wordplay and that the palindrome is intended to vanquish his "trilingual brother." Traube's Latin text of the poem includes the following four lines:

> Our golden Apollo came forth after Luna, his sister,
> who is more lovely even than Hyblean violets.
> An illustrious apple, within which the wondrous power
> of life is hidden, flourishes now upon a tree.

These lines do not fit the context of lines 1–8 nor do they seem to belong to the poem at all. They would be more appropriate in Poem 81 about the contest of the rose and the lily. Düchting (p. 207, n. 286) has suggested inserting lines 11–12 above into the first speech of the rose in Poem 81, who boasts of her red color and lines 9–10 into the first speech of the lily, who claims the golden color of Apollo. That, however, as Düchting admits, would destroy the symmetry of the verses in which the dialogue of the rose and lily is divided into three four-line speeches by each.

Poem 82

1 These seem to be legends for a series of paintings or frescoes executed by order of Bishop Gunthar of Cologne (850–63). See Wolfgang Braunfels and Hermann Schnitzler, *Karolingische Kunst* (Düsseldorf: Verlag L. Schwann, 1965), p. 385.

4–5 See Ezek. 1. The lion, ox, and king of birds (eagle) are also the beasts associated with the evangelists. Here we have the lion of Mark, ox of Luke, and eagle of John. For note on the rivers, see Poem 69, line 3.

Poem 83

1–7 This poem is a fragment, since the text breaks with the hexameter.

Poem 84

25 Tado: Archbishop of Milan (860–68).

Poem 87

11–18 See Boethius' *Consolation of Philosophy*, Book 1, Poem 2, lines 10 ff.

29–30 Prov. 9:1.

Poem 88

25 Lothar's grandfather: Charlemagne.

Poem 90

13 St. Ambrose (d. 397).

Bibliography

Alcuin. *Carmina.* ed. Ernest Dümmler. *Poetae Latini Aevi Carolini.* 1.

————. *Epistolae Carolini Aevi,* in *Monumenta Germaniae Historica.* 2. Berlin: Weidmannsche Verlagsbuchhandlung, 1895.

Anton, Hans. *Fürstenspiegel und Herrscherethos in der Karolingerzeit.* Bonn: Ludwig Röhrscheid Verlag, 1968.

Archpoet. *Gedichte des Archipoeta.* ed. M. Manitius. 1913.

Bieler, Ludwig. "The Island of Scholars." *Revue Du Moyen Age Latin* 8 (1952): 227-34.

Bischoff, Bernard. "Caritas Lieder." *Mittelalterliche Studien* 2(1967):165–86.

————. "Das griechische Element in der abendländischen Bildung des Mittelalters." *Byzantinische Zeitschrift* 44 (1951):27–55.

Boyle, P. "Sedulius Scottus of Liège." *The Irish Ecclesiastical Record* Vol. 5 (ser. 7) (1916):548–55.

Braunfels, Wolfgang and Schnitzler, Hermann. *Karolingische Kunst.* Düsseldorf: Verlag L. Schwann, 1965.

Brunhölzl, Franz. *Geschichte der lateinischen Literatur des Mittelalters* Vol. 1. Munich: Wilhelm Fink Verlag München, 1975.

Byrne, Francis. *Irish Kings and High Kings.* London: B. T. Batsford Ltd., 1973.

Carlyle, A. J. *A History of Mediaeval Political Theory in the West* Vol. 1. Edinburgh: William Blackwood and Sons Ltd., 1927.

Carney, James. "Sedulius Scottus." *Old Ireland.* Ed. by R. McNally, pp. 228-50. New York: Fordham University Press, 1965.

Cathvulf. *Epistolae,* in *Monumenta Germaniae Historica.* 4.

Chadwick, Nora and Dillon, Myles. *The Celtic Realms.* London: Weidenfeld and Nicolson, 1967.

Chadwick, Nora, et al. *The Early British Church.* Cambridge: Cambridge University Press, 1958.

Contreni, John. *The Cathedral School of Laon from 850 to 930: Its Manuscripts and Masters*. Munich: Arbeo-Gesellschaft, 1978.

Curtius, Ernst. *European Literature and the Latin Middle Ages*. Trans. by Willard Trask. Princeton, New Jersey: Princeton University Press, 1973.

Derolez, R. *Runica Manuscripta*. Brugge: De Tempel, 1954.

Düchting, Reinhard. *Sedulius Scottus*. Munich: Wilhelm Fink Verlag, 1968.

Dümmler, Ernest. "Die handschriftliche Ueberlieferung der lateinischen Dichtungen aus der Zeit der Karolinger. II." *Neues Archiv der Gesellschaft für ältere deutsche Geschichtskunde* 4 (1879):239–322.

———. "Fünf Gedichte des Sedulius Scottus an den Markgrafen Eberhard von Friaul." *Jahrbücher für vaterlandische Geschichte* 1 (1861):169–88.

———. ed. *Sedulii Scotti Carmina Quadraginta* Vol. 1. Halle: n.p., 1869.

Ebert, A. "Sedulius Scottus." *Allgemeine Geschichte der Literatur des Mittelalters im Abendlande* Vol. 2. Austria: Verlagsanstalt, 1971, pp. 191–202.

Grat, Félix, et al., eds. *Annales De Saint-Bertin*. Paris: C. Klincksieck, 1964.

Green, Alice Stopford. "Sedulius of Liège." *Journal of the Ivernian Society* 6 (1914):231–34.

Hellmann, S. *Sedulius Scottus*. Munich: C. H. Beck'sche Verlagsbuchhandlung, 1906.

Hincmar of Rheims. *De regis persona et regio ministerio*. Ed. by Migne, in *Patrologia Latina* Vol. 125:833–56.

———. *Hincmari Rhemensis Epistolae*. Moguntiae: Typis Joannis Albini, 1602.

———. *Histoire L'Eglise De Reims*. Trans. by M. Lejeune. Reims: L'Académie Impériale de Reims, 1854.

Hopper, Vincent. *Medieval Number Symbolism*. New York: Columbia University Press, 1938.

Hughes, Kathleen. *The Church in Early Irish Society*. Ithaca: Cornell University Press, 1966.

Jarcho, Boris. "Die Vorläufer des Golias." *Speculum* 3 (1928):523–79.

Jonas of Orleans. *De institutione regia.* Ed. by J. Reviron, in *Les idées politico-religieuses d'un évêque du IXe siecle; Jonas d'Orléans et son "De institutione regia."* Paris: J. Vrin, 1930.

Kenney, J. F. *The Sources for the Early History of Ireland: Ecclesiastical.* New York: Octagon Books, 1966.

Laistner, M. L. W. *Thought and Letters in Western Europe.* London: Methuen and Co., Ltd., 1931.

Levillain, Léon. "Date et Interpretation D'un Poeme De Sedulius Scottus." *Le Moyen Age* 45 (1935):199–211.

Lowe, E.A., ed. *Codices Latini Antiquiores.* Pt. 4. Oxford: Clarendon Press, 1947.

Lukman, N. "The Raven Banner and the Changing Ravens." *Classica et Medievalia* 19 (1958):133–51.

Lupus of Ferrières. *The Letters of Lupus of Ferrières.* Trans. by Graydon Regenos. The Hague: Martinus Nijhoff, 1966.

Manitius, M. *Geschichte der lateinischen Literatur des Mittelalters* Vol. 3. Munich: Beck, 1965.

Meyer, W. *Ges. Abhandlungen z. mittellat. Rythmik* Vol. 2. Berlin: Weidmannsche Buchhandlung, 1905.

Murphy, Gerard. "Vergilian Influence upon the Vernacular Literature of Medieval Ireland." *Studi medievali,* NS 5. (1932):372–81.

New American Bible. New York: Benziger, Inc., 1970.

O'Connor, Frank. *A Short History of Irish Literature.* New York: Capricorn Books, 1968.

Pick, Bernard. *The Apocryphal Acts of Paul, Peter, John, Andrew and Thomas.* Chicago: The Open Court Publishing Company, 1909.

Pirenne, Henri. "Sedulius of Liège." *Mémoires couronnés de l'Académie Royale de Belgique* 33 (1882):3–73.

Pseudo-Cyprianus. *De duodecim abusivis saeculi.* Ed. by S. Hellmann, in *Texte und Untersuchungen zur Geschichte der altchristlichen Literatur* 34 (1909).

Raby, F. J. E. *A History of Secular Latin Poetry.* London: Oxford University Press, 1957.

———. *A History of Christian Latin Poetry*. London: Clarendon Press, 1927.

Saint Augustine. *The City of God*. Trans. by Marcus Dods. New York: Random House, 1950.

Saint Jerome. *Liber Interpretationis Hebraicorum Nominum*. In *Corpus Christianorum Series Latina*, vol. 72., Pt. 1, 1. Belgium: Typographi Brepols Editores Pontifici, 1959.

Schaller, Dieter. "Lateinischer Dichtung in St. Galler Handschrift." *Zeitschrift für deutsches Altertum* 93 (1964):281–99.

Smaragdus of St. Mihiel. *Via regia*. Ed. by Migne, in *Patrologia Latina* Vol. 102:935–70.

Stokes, Whitley and Strachan, John. eds. *Thesaurus Palaeohibernicus* Vol. 2. Cambridge: Cambridge University Press, 1903.

Theodulfus. *Poetae Latini Aevi Carolini*. Vol. 1. Ed. by Ernest Dümmler, in *Monumenta Germaniae Historica*.

Traube, Ludwig. *O Roma Nobilis*. Munich: Verlag der k. Akademie, 1891.

———. ed. *Poetae Latini Aevi Carolini* Vol. 3. Berlin: Weidmannsche Verlagsbuchhandlung, 1896.

Ullmann, Walter. *Carolingian Renaissance*. London: Methuen and Company Ltd., 1969.

Venantius Fortunatus. *Opera*. Cameraci: A. F. Hurez, 1822.

Waddell, Helen, trans. *Medieval Latin Lyrics*. Middlesex: Penguin Books, 1929.

———. *The Wandering Scholars*. Boston: Houghton Mifflin Company, 1927.

Walther, Hans. "Zur Geschichte eines mittelalterlichen Topos." *Liber Floridus*. St. Ottilien: Verlag der Erzabtei, 1950:153–64.

Whicher, George. *The Goliard Poets*. Cambridge, MA: n.p., 1949.

Sedulius Scottus is the first English translation from the Latin of two important works of this ninth-century Irish poet and scholar. These faithful and lively translations of *De rectoribus christianis* and of the Poems (translated line by line) now offer medievalists access in English to the works of this man who was both one of the founders of political writing in the Middle Ages, and was recognized as a distinguished Carolingian poet. Celticists will find these texts useful in determining the level of Latin learning and scholarship attained by this eminent Irish scholar.

The Introduction offers a comprehensive overview of Sedulius Scottus: his life, career, achievements, and the cultural, political and intellectual milieu in which he lived and worked at Liege. Dr. Doyle surveys existing scholarship and places *On Christian Rulers* within the genre of "mirrors for princes." The Introduction further discusses the poetic tradition and genres to which the poems belong.

Edward Gerard Doyle received his M.A. and Ph.D in Celtic Languages and Literatures from Harvard University, and a Master's degree in Medieval Studies from the Medieval Institute at the University of Notre Dame. He held teaching fellowships at Harvard before joining the staff of the Boston Publishing Company.

mRts

medieval & Renaissance texts & studies
is the publishing program of the
Center for Medieval & Early Renaissance Studies
at the State University of New York at Binghamton.

mRts emphasizes books that are needed —
texts, translations, and major research tools.

mRts aims to publish the highest quality scholarship
in attractive and durable format at modest cost.